Atlantic Hearth
Early Homes and Families of Nova Scotia

Nova Scotia boasts nearly four centuries of European settlement. Its early history is rich in conflict between French and English and within families split by the American Revolution. Its people included colonists from France, Planters from New England, Loyalists (black as well as white), explorers and rogues, sailors and shipbuilders, merchants and innkeepers, politicians and preachers, magnates and mothers.

Mary Byers and Margaret McBurney tell the stories of these people in a lively text illustrated by pictures from the past and present. During several years of research, they have scoured provincial and municipal archives; sifted through newspaper files; and interviewed archivists, scholars, and local historians.

We learn about people such as Cape Breton's wily Peter Smyth, whose name lives on in a Gaelic curse; of Enos Collins, whose privateering ventures made him the richest man in British North America; of Liverpool's Simeon Perkins, whose daughter, Mary, somehow survived daily plunges into icy well water as a cure for 'Rickety Complaint'; of Lunenburg's John Creighton, who defended the town during a privateer raid; and of a 'monster' who strayed into the crystal clear waters of Halifax harbour.

Chris Reardon has photographed a hundred historic buildings mentioned in the text, illuminating the architectural development of the province. He shows us Cape Cod cottages, Halifax and Lunenburg town houses, sturdy Scottish stone dwellings, and graceful frame churches.

The authors previously have traced the links among home, culture, and history in four popular books, combining outstanding photographs of early buildings with carefully researched texts about the people who built and lived in them. In doing so they have brought to life the social history of our country.

This book is the first to extend their work beyond Ontario. In it, they take us through periods of settlement, slavery, war, scandal, and prosperity, yet never lose sight of home and hearth. The result will delight anyone who knows Nova Scotia, or plans to visit there.

MARY BYERS and MARGARET MCBURNEY are the authors of *Rural Roots: Pre-Confederation Buildings of the York Region of Ontario*; *The Governor's Road: Early Buildings from Mississauga to London*; *Homesteads: Early Buildings and Families from Kingston to Toronto*; and *Tavern in the Town: Early Inns and Taverns of Ontario*.

MARY BYERS & MARGARET McBURNEY

Atlantic Hearth

EARLY HOMES
AND FAMILIES OF
NOVA SCOTIA

UNIVERSITY OF TORONTO PRESS

TORONTO BUFFALO LONDON

© University of Toronto Press Incorporated 1994
Toronto Buffalo London
Printed in Canada

ISBN 0-8020-2935-3 (cloth)
ISBN 0-8020-7762-5 (paper)

Printed on acid-free paper

Canadian Cataloguing in Publication Data

Byers, Mary, 1933–
  Atlantic hearth : early homes and families of Nova Scotia

  Includes bibliographical references and index.
  ISBN 0-8020-2935-3 (bound) ISBN 0-8020-7762-5 (pbk.)

  I. Historic buildings – Nova Scotia. 2. Pioneers – Nova
Scotia. 3. Nova Scotia – History.
  I. McBurney, Margaret, 1931–   . II. Title.

  FC2312.B94 1994   971.6   C94-931014-X
  F1037.8.B94 1994

University of Toronto Press acknowledges the financial
assistance to its publishing program of the Canada Council
and the Ontario Arts Council.

Contents

NORTHERN NOVA SCOTIA
AND THE EASTERN SHORE

CAPE BRETON ISLAND

Introduction

Nova Scotia is a mosaic. The variously inlaid pieces of its cultural history, each with its unique hue and shape, form a diversified whole. From Halifax's British core, along the south shore through distinctively German Lunenburg, the home of the *Bluenose*; past staunchly Loyalist Shelburne and the former black settlement of Birchtown; through Yarmouth, whose sea captains made the ocean their home; 'upshore,' past the homes of returned Acadians, to the verdant Annapolis Valley, home of so many New England Planters; and on to the homes of the Scots of Pictou; then across the causeway to Cape Breton – itself a mosaic, where Gaelic is still spoken and sung, and Scots, French, Irish, British, and Mi'kmaq mingle – the colourful pieces of the mosaic reflect one another.

Each piece of the mosaic represents a portion of history, part of the years of conflict and settlement that shaped Nova Scotia.

The province's variegated history can be sensed through the sound and music of place-names that recall the past or the atmosphere of the locale, while they entice investigation in the present: Musquodoboit, Creignish, Gaspereaux, Mistake River, Privateer Cove, Sissiboo, Wittenburg, Antigonish, Bras d'Or Lake, Ovens Point, Shubenacadie, Kejimkujik, Isle Madame, Tatamagouche, Puzzle Point, More-Rum Brook, Lobster Bay, Money Point, Creek Aux Navires, Grosses Coques, Whycocomagh, Gallows Hill, Paradise.

A great many of these names are those given by the province's original residents, the Mi'kmaq – among the many are Whycocomagh from the Mi'kmaq 'Wakogumaak,' meaning 'beside the sea,' and Shubenacadie from the Mi'kmaq 'Segunbunakadie,' meaning 'the place where the ground nut grows.' The sound of these names evokes the Mi'kmaq heritage, a very visible part of Nova Scotia today.

Another dominant piece of that mosaic is French. The colony of Acadia was founded in 1605. Its history was one of almost constant conflict as the French/English struggle for power in North America continued for more than a century. That power struggle did not officially end until 1763, when, at the end of the Seven Years War, the Treaty of Paris was signed. Then France ceded all her possessions and rights in North America to Great Britain, with the exception of the islands of Saint-Pierre and Miquelon and fishing rights on the coast of Newfoundland. (Louisiana was ceded to Spain.) The most victimized during the period of conflict were the Acadians.

Acadia included the southeast part of Quebec, eastern Maine, Nova Scotia (which, until 1784, encompassed what is now New Brunswick), and Île Saint-Jean (now Prince Edward Island). The first stage in its history was one in which businessmen came in search of fish, furs, and power – De Monts, Champlain, Poutrincourt, and others. They brought no women with them and so they left no progeniture of French extraction. By 1632 whole families were emigrating to Acadia. This group, mainly farmers, represented the real origin of settlement in the region. By 1671 most of the immigration had taken place and there were approximately 500 Acadians in Nova Scotia, 70 families farming the marshes near Port-Royal and the rest along the Atlantic coast. These settlers were extremely prolific. In fewer than eighty years, their numbers had reached 10,000. Acadian settlement had spread from Port-Royal up the Bay of Fundy to the Minas Basin and Cobequid Bay, and around Cape Chignecto to Beaubassin. Their agricultural economy was based on the cultivation of marshlands reclaimed through an extensive system of dikes.

In 1710 the British took Port-Royal, and in 1713 the Treaty of Utrecht confirmed British control of peninsular Nova Scotia. The French presence in the region was now located in Île Royale (Cape Breton Island) and Île Saint Jean (Prince Edward Island). For the next thirty years there was relative peace; then, in the 1740s, a decade of war between Britain and France began. In 1745 Louisbourg fell to forces mainly from New England. Three years later it was, to the New Englanders' disgust, handed back to France in the Treaty of Aix-la-Chapelle.

Both England and France sought to strengthen their

positions, the French around the Isthmus of Chignecto and territories in present-day New Brunswick, the British by founding Halifax in 1749. The British demanded that Acadians take an unqualified oath of allegiance to the Crown. The Acadians preferred to qualify the oath with guarantees of freedom of religion, neutrality in time of war, and the right to emigrate. These rights were unacceptable to the British, although freedom of religion 'as far as the laws of Great Britain may permit' had been granted them in the Treaty of Utrecht of 1713. The Acadians were viewed as a threat, an enemy in the back yard, loyal to France and friendly with France's friends, the Mi'kmaq.

Charles Lawrence was appointed governor of the colony in 1754. He proposed a drastic solution: the deportation of the Acadian population. In 1755, at the beginning of the Seven Years War, the deportation began. (Not by accident, it took place in early fall, after the Acadians had harvested their crops.) About 6,000 Acadians were put on ships destined for Georgia, North and South Carolina, Virginia, Connecticut, Massachusetts, Pennsylvania, and New York. Another 4,000 either escaped to New Brunswick, Île Royal, or Île Saint-Jean, or were deported back to France via England. Nine years later they were allowed to return to Nova Scotia, but their lands had been granted to other settlers. Among the scattered locations they were given was the area known today as the French Shore (near Yarmouth, along St Mary's Bay and at Pubnico), and land in Cape Breton at Cheticamp and at Isle Madame. French names and the French language predominate in those areas today.

Halifax, founded in 1749 to counterbalance the French presence at Louisbourg with a stalwart British presence, had a population made up initially of settlers sent out with Edward Cornwallis, the colony's first governor. They were from southern England, and were later joined by New Englanders and some Acadians hired to work on the fortifications. The population of about 4,000 that endured the winter of 1749 dwindled as many left for more settled conditions elsewhere. But Halifax was and remained a British garrison town. It was here that the powerful families – of the military, merchants, politicians, judiciary, and clergy – were located. Halifax, distinctively British, became a central piece in the mosaic.

Even before the Acadian deportation, after the founding of Halifax, the Board of Trade in England had been working to encourage immigration to Nova Scotia of settlers loyal to the Crown – immigration from Britain and some Protestant regions of the continent of Europe. Between 1750 and 1752 about 2,500 German and Swiss families, called 'foreign Protestants,' mainly from Friesland, Hamburg, and the Rhine Valley, swelled the population of Halifax. Free land was available for those who had the courage to start a new life in the wilderness of 'Neu Schottland.' By 1753 these families had been relocated on the South Shore, mainly in Lunenburg County, where their heritage added a predominantly German piece to the mosaic.

Other desirable settlers were close at hand. The New Englanders, descendants of Pilgrims and Puritans, were familiar with conditions in the New World, and loyal to the Crown. Nova Scotia wanted them and they were seeking new lands in a secure British colony. There was keen interest in the sites left vacant after the deportation of the Acadians, but conditions were not settled and there were periodic clashes between French and English. As well, there was as yet no assembly in the colony, and representative government was a necessity to those who were accustomed to voicing their opinion at the New England town meeting. They could not accept the governor and his appointed council as a legislative authority. The Seven Years War broke out in May 1756, and potential immigration was postponed again.

Then on 2 October 1758, a reluctant Governor Charles Lawrence called a meeting of the first representative assembly in what is now Canada. Ten days later he issued his proclamation, an offer of free cultivated and uncultivated lands with grants to a maximum of 1,000 acres. The New England Planters (an old English term for settlers) began to arrive in 1760. By 1768 they numbered approximately 8,000, at a time when the population of the whole of Nova Scotia was 13,000. Their arrival established a piece of the mosaic reflecting the British and New England influences along the Annapolis Valley and the Minas Basin; on the South Shore in the Liverpool, New Dublin, and Chester areas; and at Yarmouth and Barrington on the southwestern tip of the colony.

After the Treaty of Paris of 1763 ended the century of the French/English contest for North America, the British government stepped up its efforts to populate Nova Scotia with settlers loyal to the Crown in order to solidify her gains. The Board of Trade and Governor Wilmot placed no check on indiscriminant land grabbing. Officials in Halifax had an open-door policy, and many entered. From the point of view of those who wanted land, the settler and his family who wanted a farm, or the speculators who wanted thousands of acres, land acquisition was at a peak. Peace was considered imminent; in addition, many of those in the 'old colonies' anticipated the Stamp Act and were pressing for grants in order to avoid stamp duties.

The Philadelphia Company, made up of residents of Pennsylvania, New York, and New Jersey, included those prominent in colonial affairs – men such as Benjamin Franklin. A Northern Irishman from Philadelphia, Alexander McNutt, was granted 100,000 acres, including valuable shore land in Pictou and Colchester counties – some of which he kept for himself. The largest grant – 200,000 acres – went to the Crawley group from Philadelphia. Their land became known as the Philadelphia Grant. Their first small group of settlers came on the *Betsey* in 1767. Then, on 15 September 1773, another 200 exhausted and sick passengers arrived at Pictou to take up land in the Philadelphia Grant. They had endured a voyage on the *Hector* in which dark and crowded conditions, foul air, seasickness, dysentery, and smallpox prevailed. Eighteen had died and were buried at sea. But the settlers rallied their spirits and disembarked. They set foot on land in Nova Scotia to the sound of the bagpipes, following their piper, John MacKay. Another piece of the mosaic was in place. Over the years thousands of Scots followed them through the port of Pictou.

Between 1772 and 1774 many boatloads of settlers came from the north of England to settle in the Cumberland County area in northern Nova Scotia, and in nearby Westmorland County in New Brunswick. This wave of settlers became known as the Yorkshire immigration. These men and women were mainly literate and arrived with fair sums of money, enough to guarantee their independence and to allow them to buy land and set up a social community. Some settled on former Acadian farms, but their community included Acadians as well – some who had escaped the deportation. Mainly Dissenters, the Yorkshiremen became staunch Methodists, giving the English part of the region that distinctive characteristic. Their surnames remain today – English and French – in another part of the mosaic with a colour of its own, a part from which Father of Confederation Jonathan McCully was descended.

In 1775 the population of Nova Scotia was 20,000. The next stage in immigration in the colony would double that number. The Loyalists, some 40,000, came, starting in 1783. Some had been persecuted for siding with the British in the Revolution, some wanted free land, and some, the blacks, turned to the British side in order to gain freedom from slavery. (Other blacks, however, came as slaves when their owners emigrated, bringing them along with their other possessions.) Some 20,000 Loyalists settled in Nova Scotia, mainly in what is now Shelburne. According to historian Marion Robertson, 'the careful muster of Loyalists, disbanded soldiers, and Blacks made in the summer of 1784 under the direction of Colonel Robert Morse, chief of the Royal Engineers in North America, gives the total for Shelburne as 7,922.' The rest of the Loyalists moved on, with the largest group settling in what became New Brunswick when Nova Scotia was divided at the Chignecto Isthmus in 1784. A distinct Loyalist flavour was added to the mosaic throughout the colony.

More than 3,000 Loyalists settled in Cape Breton. In 1784 the island was separated from Nova Scotia, with Sydney (Spanish Bay) as the capital. But the Loyalists were not the first piece of the mosaic on the island. Before their arrival the Mi'kmaq and many returned Acadians were a permanent presence, as was an Irish population. Cape Breton had been a haven for some of the Irish who had settled in Newfoundland and, when the French settlements there were ceded to the British in 1763, had left with the French, with whom they shared a religion. Later more Irish arrived, coming for the economic opportunities to be found in Cape Breton and mainland Nova Scotia and New Brunswick.

During the first quarter of the nineteenth century, men and women in the Western Highlands and Islands of Scotland, depressed by a seemingly endless series of setbacks in the economy, began to think of ways to raise the money to transport their families across the Atlantic. In the mid eighteenth century the relationship of the Highland chieftain and his clan had changed. The battle of Culloden in 1746 had broken the hereditary power of the chieftains. Feuds between clans were now outlawed by a central authority, and the chieftain's bands of fighting men became his tenant farmers.

Tenant farmers who had been renting from the clan chieftain had formerly been able to eke out an existence by farming their plot of land and grazing cattle on a communal pasture. This system had represented a form of security, even though the tenant farmers did not own their land and were forced to augment their income by collecting and burning kelp and selling the alkali ash to glass and chemical factories. The tenant farmers in turn supported the cottars, who had no land at all and had to get by in any way they could – kelping, growing potatoes on a bit of waste land, scouring the beach, or begging. The system worked, however, at least in good years.

But the price of meat and wool rose around 1800, during the Napoleonic Wars, and clan chieftains saw huge profits in leasing their land to sheep farmers. The demand for kelp rose, and landlords saw profit there too. They turned tenant farms into kelping communities or, to discourage tenant farming, divided communal holdings into small crofts, so small that the land had to be heavily fertilized to produce a decent crop. Rents were raised until it was no longer possible to make enough money to support a family. But then the market for kelp collapsed. As well, too many people were trying to earn a living from too little land. Many crofters who had enough cattle left to sell and could put together the expensive passage money with some to spare decided it was time to cross the Atlantic. They came by the thousands, with Cape Breton the favoured destination in the 1820s and 1830s. As conditions worsened in Scotland, emigration increased. The destitute heard of the free land offered across the Atlantic and listened to the land agents with their tall tales of a life of ease and comfort. Finally, when the free-land policy was terminated in Cape Breton, those with little backing took the poorest sites on rocky land not suited for farming, or squatted on Mi'kmaq land.

By 1850, 40,000 Scots had found their way to Cape Breton. The sight of the ceilidh, with its vigorous step-dancing and the distinctive sounds of the bagpipes and of spoken Gaelic, represented another colourful piece of the mosaic.

This book offers a view of that mosaic and the history of the province through its first settlers: their triumphs, tragedies, foibles, and struggles. We believe that, through the lives of the men and women who settled here by the sea, the particular flavour of the development of Nova Scotia emerges – a flavour that lingers today – and that it is best illustrated in human terms.

Young Acadian Benoni d'Entremont was deported in 1755 and saw his home in Pubnico torched. The Eisenhauer brothers emigrated from Wilhelmsfeld, Germany, settled in Lunenburg, and built fine homes, one with three wells so their descendants would never be without clear water as they had been on the voyage over. The German farmers who came for land of their own had sons who were fishermen and shipbuilders. It was the men of Lunenburg who built great ships like *Bluenose I* and *II*.

New England Planter Simeon Perkins emigrated to Liverpool. He had lost his young wife, and was seeking a new home and a new life. But, like his fellow New Englanders, Perkins was about to have his loyalty tested by war. The American Revolution put severe strains on traditional loyalties and family ties with the colonies along the eastern seaboard. Many, like former Bostonian Jonathan Locke, initially offered assistance to captured privateers from the American colonies, assuming old allegiances were strong. Later Locke was a victim of plundering by privateer ships manned by former countrymen. Old bonds were quickly severed.

Halifax merchants prospered in wartime. John Black was well rewarded for running blockades to supply British troops in the Napoleonic Wars and built himself a fine mansion on Halifax's prestigious Hollis Street. During the War of 1812 vessels lawfully captured by Nova Scotian privateers operating with a royal letter of marque were sailed into Halifax harbour. The booty might include brandy, silks, spices, and gold and silver coins. Enos Collins's *Liverpool Packet* was the terror of the coast in those years and helped found the fortune that made him the richest man in British North America. During the American Civil War, most Nova Scotian merchants sided with the South. Benjamin Wier became a legend when he refitted a Confederate vessel that slipped by night out of the harbour, evading the watch of hovering Yankee ships.

To many, Nova Scotia seemed a haven. To a Loyalist like Captain Stephen Shakespear of Shelburne, it meant life under British rule, with advantages like good mill and town sites. For Nantucket Quakers it meant a haven in Dartmouth, a release from reprisals after they chose not to fight in their colony's war. Cape Breton was a special haven – for Loyalists like Ranna Cossit, preacher, activist politician, and educator; for the Acadians of Arichat; for Irish fishermen; and for an Irish boy who sold ribbons from a pack and became a merchant with a company store to which so many were indebted that he inspired a graphic Irish Gaelic curse. It was a haven to Scots like the settlers of Middle River who got good land and, after thirty years of hard work, built fine stone houses there.

The new land was harsh and many suffered. But they were tenacious. 'Red' John MacMaster and his wife, Mary MacIsaac, built their log home near the shore in Creignish. It was destroyed in a gale, and they and their children nearly lost their lives. They quickly built a second home, of stone, away from the ocean's force, and started again.

Then there were some for whom the promised haven never materialized. Under British rule, slavery was legal in British North America and there had been both free and slave blacks in Nova Scotia since European settlement began. Some slaves had come with New England Planters. Then, at the end of the American Revolution, Loyalists, looking for a home in a British colony, brought their possessions with them. Among these were their slaves. In Nova Scotia, in addition to the 3,000 free blacks and former slaves who had fought for the British in the American Revolution, some 1,200 slaves came with their owners. Most settled in Birchtown, outside the Loyalist settlement of Shelburne. Richard Preston, a determined black preacher, arrived after the War of 1812 and fought for an end to slavery and for land and opportunity for his people. When slavery was abolished in the British Empire in 1834, it had long since ceased to exist in the Maritimes. Men such as Chief Justices Andrew Strange and Salter Blowers of Nova Scotia and Ward Chipman of New Brunswick had joined the crusade.

But as late as 1801, Benjamin Belcher of Cornwallis was bequeathing slaves as his personal property:

I give and bequeath my Negro woman to my beloved wife during her lifetime and after her death at her disposal. I give and bequeath my Negro boy called Prince to my son Stephen Belcher during his life after that to his eldest surviving son. I give my Negro girl called Diana to my daughter Elisabeth Belcher Sheffield and after her death to her eldest Heir Male of her body I give my Negro man named Jack and my Negro

boy Samuel and Negro boy James and Negro girl called
Chloe to my son Benjamin and his Heirs forever charging
them my children unto whom I have entrusted these Negro
people with never to sell barter or exchange them or any of
them under any pretension except it is for bad and Heinous
offences as will render them not safe to be kept in the Family ... as soon as those young Negros shall become capable to
be taught to read they shall be learnt the word of God.

Across the stage of the province strode its nation
builders. While wars were waged and fortunes made,
the governments of the province and the country were
taking shape. Samuel Starr of Cornwallis and his fellow
Planters insisted on representative government as a condition of settlement and got their demand in 1758. Later
the irrepressible Joseph Howe spearheaded the move for
responsible government. His target was the tight-knit
group of men, mainly from Halifax, who formed the
Council of Twelve. They were appointed by the governor, from an oligarchy who controlled business, politics, and the church in the province. The battle for the
first responsible government in what became Canada
was an electoral battle only. Not a shot was fired. The
Reformers won the 1847 election. In 1848 the first responsible government in the overseas British Empire followed the first representative government by ninety
years.

Howe later fought Confederation to the bitter end.
He saw no good in ties to the west and the Canadas
when traditional strengths lay in links across the Atlantic
and down the easily accessible eastern seaboard. Most
agreed with him. In 1867, when nineteen members were
elected to the House of Commons from Nova Scotia,
eighteen were anti-Confederation. Charles Tupper, in
support, stood alone. Much of his hope for his province's growth was placed in the railway that his friend
and neighbour, the brilliant inventor and explorer Sandford Fleming, was building.

Other colourful and powerful men shaped Nova Scotia's history – men like shipping magnate Samuel Cunard and powerful and dominating men like Attorney
General Richard Uniacke; Richard Brown, mining engineer; and Samuel and Thomas Dickson Archibald,
shipbuilders. Nova Scotia had six Fathers of Confederation – Adams G. Archibald, R.B. Dickey, W.A. Henry,
Jonathan McCully, J.W. Ritchie, and Charles Tupper.
E.B. Chandler, born in Amherst, was a delegate from

New Brunswick. Tupper became a prime minister, as did John Sparrow Thompson and Robert Laird Borden.

Nova Scotian women made history as well. The efforts of most were never recorded, their achievements seemingly not worthy of mention. Some succeeded in business, often picking up an enterprise on the death of their husbands. In widowhood Marie Winniett took over her husband's faltering business and became a powerful factor in Annapolis and beyond. Innkeeper Rebecca Whitechurch made a success of her tavern and hostelry, a demanding business. Eliza Jost established a mercantile presence in Cape Breton. Some, as wives of wealthy Halifax merchants, exercised their artistic talents with considerable success. But for most it was a life of 'hurrying all morning' – and afternoon and evening. Rebecca Ells, for instance, was left at age forty-three, with an eighteen-year-old son and a farm to manage when her husband, Cyrus, headed out in 1898 to the Klondike Gold Rush and came home thirteen years later, penniless.

Most women were entirely dependent on their husbands and in a tenuous legal position. The house passed from man to man, even if left to a daughter, for on her marriage it became her husband's property. A woman could only hope that her husband had written a will and that he had been specific regarding her position after his death. Bequests to wives such as Elisha DeWolf's for 'the use of a good family horse chaise sleigh and harness ... the use of two good milch cows ... sufficient fire wood to be cut up at the door of her dwelling house,' or Benjamin Belcher's for 'the sole use of the East parlour and North bedroom ... the privilege of keeping her servant and doing her housework in the Kitchen of said dwelling house' were essential. If the widow's position was not spelled out, inheritance went to a son and she was dependent on his goodwill and the goodwill of the new head of the household, her daughter-in-law.

These men and women were nation builders, from royalty to the Halifax merchant or the young worker, like Samuel Sellon, who got a job on the docks in his teens and worked there all his life. Through their daily lives they wrote the history of their province.

Gaining a living or waging war at sea, there was hardly a family that had not lost lives there. Shipwrecks and the gales that caused them were legion. They brought the Hichens, Crowells, and Nickersons to Seal

Island to save lives. Perhaps the best-remembered hurricane was the 'Great August Gale' of 1873: in North Sydney twenty-six vessels were damaged or lost, one tied at Archibald's wharf. In the small town of Guysborough alone seven ships were destroyed, all lying at anchor in the harbour. The Jost barn was blown through the side of the Methodist church. Many ships and buildings were never replaced. Many families lost their men: it is said that more than a thousand men were lost to the sea that day.

For a taste of another life a royal visit or sojourn always made an impact in the province. Three princes were welcomed heartily in a variety of ways. The first to visit was twenty-one-year-old Prince William, third son of George III, later Duke of Clarence and King William IV. He came to Halifax in 1786 and 1787, and was stationed there for a few months in 1788. Known as a bluff, hearty seaman, he is said to have preferred 'a small snug party, with none of the great people.' One who was happy to provide such a snug party was Fanny Wentworth, wife of Governor John Wentworth. Fanny's liaison with Prince William even shocked Mme de St Laurent, mistress of the next royal visitor, Prince Edward, Duke of Kent. The prince, the future father of Queen Victoria, spent six years as commander of forces in Halifax, then commander of all forces in British North America. During this time he lived with Julie at the governor's villa on the Bedford Basin. The third prince, Albert Edward, then Prince of Wales and future King Edward VII, visited the music pavilion that his grandfather had built for Julie, and sent a piece of sweet briar from the site to his mother, Queen Victoria. On this 1860 visit Prince Edward made an unscheduled stop in Sydney and visited the home of Richard Brown. A loyal monarchist, Brown placed a gold spike in the floor to mark the spot where his illustrious visitor had stood.

Home is a special word in Nova Scotia. Love of home is an anchor expressed in such significant phrases as 'down home.' And so we have selected homes as the hook on which to hang our story. They too form a mosaic – Cape Cod cottages, Halifax town houses, sturdy Scottish stone dwellings, and places of worship, graceful frame churches. We have attempted to fill these buildings again with people, their builders and early owners, and bring their tales to life through our findings in original sources – wills, newspapers, and census records.

There is one other source impossible to ignore.

Legend is the unwritten side of history in Nova Scotia. It is in the atmosphere. When the sea is shrouded in fog or the 'wind so sharp it cuts the whiskers off your face' it is easy enough to be sure, as Helen Creighton was, that ghosts still guard buried treasure or make their presence known through eerie knocks, a forerunner predicting a death.

We have selected buildings that are still relatively unchanged since they were built, in order to illustrate the variety of architectural features prevalent in the eighteenth and nineteenth centuries. We have also selected them on the basis of the history of the first families who lived in them, in order to bring the period to life. There are drawbacks to this method. As we have tied the story to existing buildings, clearly some important figures are left out. And, since we are dealing with almost 300 years of built history, those homes that have survived are likely to be the well-built houses of prominent men and women – the homesteader's cottage may have succumbed to a gale long ago. Wherever possible we have included simple dwellings, even if they are not in prime condition today. Regrettably, there is no built legacy of the original residents of the province, the Mi'kmaq. We have, for similar reasons, told the story of black Nova Scotians through their churches. These significant buildings form a tangible link to their troubled past. For the most part we have followed the story of these houses only to the post-Confederation era and the end of the Golden Age of Sail.

In spite of these problems, we hope that the buildings are, once again, full of lively repartee, debate, and romance. We hope that the wit and terrible puns of a Thomas Haliburton, creator of Sam Slick; the excitement and pride of a W.D. Lawrence, builder of the country's largest square-rigged ship; the anxious tension of a Thankful Cossit, mother of thirteen children and wife of a poor minister; and the inviting laughter of a Fanny Wentworth, cigar-smoking wife of the colony's governor seem more present than past. Ours is a story of people. The architecture of their homes is a study illustrated by Chris Reardon's current photographs.

In our efforts to catch the flavour of the times in Nova Scotia, much of our research consisted of reading old newspapers. Some items stand out, not for their particular significance but because they catch the eye. It could be an article about the crystal clear waters of Halifax harbour where:

The Mackrel are so prodigious plenty ... that the like never was known before; 'tis supposed, that 1000 Barrels have been caught and cur'd within a Week past; and 'tis not doubted but that if proper Hands, Implements, etc were to be had, 10,000 Barrels might have been taken and cur'd in the same Space of Time. (*The Halifax Gazette*, 18 August 1753)

It could be a human-interest story:

A Canada farmer recently wanted his wife's funeral postponed on account of non-arrival of a professional gentleman who was to extract several teeth from her containing $12.00 worth of gold filling. (*The Halifax Evening Express*, 16 June 1864)

It could be a report of an interesting case for the courts:

A man was arrested Monday in Montreal, for trying to drown himself to spite his wife. The wife was the complainant. (*The Halifax Evening Express*, 4 July 1864)

Or the unexpected outcome of a kind gesture:

Last Tuesday an unhappy Accident happen'd off the Harbour of this Town, as two Fishing Schooners belonging to Ipswich met with and spoke to each other, the People on board one of them desired those on board the other to give them a Can of Beer, upon which the windwardmost steer'd down to the other, and one of the Hands endeavouring to step on board her with a Can in his Hand, unfortunately slipt between both Vessels, by which Means both his Legs were broke and he was otherwise much hurt; he was bro't here the same Day and put under the Care of an able Surgeon, but notwithstanding all Endeavours he died the next Day. (*The Halifax Gazette*, 21 April 1753)

Or the public appeal of an angry husband:

Whereas Mary the Wife of me the Subscriber has absented herself and Refused to acknowledge her Obedience to her Husband (supposed on Evil Advice) therefore I advise all Merchants, Traders and Others not to credit her on my Account, as I am determined not to pay any Debts she will contract till she returns to her duty, and whoever shall Lodge [or] Harbour ... the said Mary my Wife will be dealt with according to the Law. Nathaniel Pix. (*The Nova Scotia Gazette and the Weekly Chronicle*, 20 February 1781)

John Campbell Forrester ... makes use of this singular rem-edy for a cold. He walks into the sea up to his middle, with his clothes on, and immediately goes to bed in his wet clothes, and then laying the bed clothes over him, procures a sweat; which removed the distemper; and this ... is his only remedy for all manner of colds. (*The Colonial Patriot*, 16 April 1828)

We have chosen the buildings featured in *Atlantic Hearth* from the hundreds with a tale to tell. These are only a few shells from the beach. There is always another house down one of those inviting roads that lead to a cove, a beach, an ocean site.

There is always another house with history in its halls.

HALIFAX

CHAPTER ONE

Sea Monsters and Steeples

On Saturday last was taken within the Mouth of our Harbour, and Monday brought to Town, a Sea Monster, a Female of the Kind, whose Body was of about the Bigness of that of a very large Ox, and something resembling one, cover'd with short Hair of a brownish Colour; the Skin near an Inch and a half thick, very loose and rough; the Neck thick and short, resembling that of a Bull; the Head very small in Proportion to the Body, and considerably like an Aligators; in the upper Jaw were two Teeth, of about 9 or 10 Inches long and crooking downwards, of considerable Bigness and Strength, suppos'd to be pure Ivory; the Legs very short and thick, ending with Finns and Claws like those of a Sea Turtle; the Flesh and Inwards of this Creature upon being open'd appear to resemble those of an Ox or Horse; it has been shewn here for several Days past with satisfaction to the Spectators, and we hear the Fat of it is now trying up in order to make Oyl. (*The Halifax Gazette*, 30 May 1752)

No doubt the whole town turned out that May day in 1752 to admire the charms of the walrus that had strayed into the harbour. Halifax was then only three years old, and so the crowd would have numbered fewer than 3,000 hardy souls, including every man, woman, and child who lived 'within the Pickets of Halifax and in the north and south suburbs.' Perhaps Genchon Tuffs, Preserved Cunnable, John Tongue, and Ulrich Dilhoe turned out. Perhaps George Gerrish came with his eight children. These men and their families were hardy survivors – part of the group of 2,576 settlers who, with Nova Scotia's first governor, Edward Cornwallis, had arrived in the winter of 1749 to establish a new capital; or of those who joined them shortly thereafter. After only eight months, however, more than half of that original group had gone. Some had died; some had given up and fled to the American colonies.

Edward Cornwallis, Nova Scotia's first governor. The portrait was painted three years after he left Halifax.

The 'great long harbour' into which the curious 'Sea Monster' had wandered cuts through The Narrows to the deep waters of the Bedford Basin. The Mi'kmaq (Mimac) and French, who had known the area long before New England and Great Britain became interested, had occupied various sites there as recently as 1746. The original name of the bay area, 'Chebucto,' had come from the Mi'kmaq 'Chebookt,' meaning 'chief harbour.' The potential of the harbour, one of the world's largest, had recently been brought to the attention of the British government by Lord Halifax, president of the Board of Trade.

The political atmosphere in Nova Scotia was tense in 1749. The interminable rivalry between France and England for power in North America had begun when British troops destroyed Port Royal (later Annapolis Royal) in 1613, eight years after it had been founded by the French. For nearly 150 years the struggle continued, until France surrendered to Britain at the end of the Seven Years War, and the Treaty of Paris was signed in 1763. During that time the hostilities had an almost continuous impact on the colony of Nova Scotia.

The founding of Halifax in 1749 was part of the power struggle. Governor William Shirley of Massachusetts was adamant that the British government establish a strong military presence in the area as a protective buffer for the New England colonies. The fortified town of Louisbourg, founded by France on Île Royale (Cape Breton) in 1713 and taken by forces from New England in 1745, had recently been handed back to the French and seemed poised as a threat along the eastern seaboard. The decision to establish a British settlement was a strategic one. Of course, not incidentally, there was also a rich cod fishery waiting to be exploited.

It was Edward Cornwallis who selected the actual site of Halifax. Ignoring suggestions from experts a thousand miles away, he rejected the Bedford Basin, Point Pleasant, and the Dartmouth side, and chose instead a hill on the west side (now Citadel Hill) which commanded a complete view of the deep and sheltered harbour.

A steady influx of settlers, mainly British (from England or the New England colonies), gradually swelled the ranks of the Cornwallis group, replacing those who found that one winter in the colony was one too many. The settlers were, in Cornwallis's view, generally a pretty shabby lot. Britain had advertised free passage, free victualling for one year, and military protection. As well as the industrious few, the offer had attracted indigents and surplus disbanded military personnel.

Yet the first governor accomplished much. By 1750 there were 350 houses surrounded by palisades, in which were incorporated 5 blockhouses. Cornwallis, in his three years at Halifax, saw the original grid expand to the north and south. Never has the location he chose been questioned. And all this was done while looking over one shoulder for the French forces stationed near the Saint John River and the Mi'kmaq with whom they were allied, over the other shoulder at reviving French power at Louisbourg, while, at the same time, keeping an eye on the Wolfville area. There, the Acadians, not prepared to swear an unqualified oath of allegiance to the British Crown, were considered a potential problem. Through it all the British government complained that Nova Scotia was costing it too much money.

Among the group who arrived with Edward Cornwallis in 1749 was the Rev. William Tutty, who had been sent to Nova Scotia as an Anglican missionary at £70 per year. He arrived in June, but by the beginning of August he was already asking for permission to return to England – perhaps for business reasons but perhaps in despair at the 'profligate wretches' to whom he was supposed to be ministering, and about whom he had nothing good to say. He complained of their immorality and perverseness. To add to his problems his sole fellow missionary, the Rev. William Anwyl, a fellow appointee of the Society for the Propagation of the Gospel, was prone to drunkenness, as, it would seem, was most of

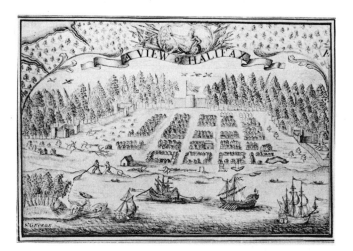

Halifax soon after its founding, defended with a wooden stockade: a pen and ink drawing by Moses-after Harris

the population. Tutty found that he was burying many more than he baptized, a circumstance he blamed on 'an inviolable attachment to New England rum.' The situation was summed up by one resident who reported in 1760: 'We have upwards of one hundred licensed houses and perhaps as many more which retail spirituous liquors without license; so that the business of one half of the town is to sell rum and the other half to drink it.'

In spite of these circumstances, Tutty stayed for three years. During that time he oversaw the construction of his church, now the oldest building in Halifax and the oldest Protestant church in Canada. St Paul's Church stood at the south end of the Grand Parade. Its architecture was based on drawings for London's Marylebone Chapel (later known as St Peter's, Vere Street) by James Gibbs, an apprentice of Christopher Wren. Marylebone Chapel was a brick church, St Paul's a replica in wood. Its pine and oak timbers were sawn in Boston, numbered, and shipped to Halifax, where – to Tutty's immense satisfaction – they were assembled in the spring and summer of 1750. At last he could write an enthusiastic letter to England, stating that the church was a 'great Happiness' and even the 'profligate wretches' had improved, mainly because 'intemperance [had] destroyed many of the worst.'

Tutty and Edward Cornwallis held similar views about the first settlers who accompanied them, concluding that they were 'old miserable wretches.' But one group sent to the colony by England proved an exception. The British government called it 'a mixture of foreign Protestants.' Cornwallis admitted that these Swiss

St Paul's Church and the Parade in 1764, captured by Richard Short

and German settlers were indeed industrious. Tutty, it is said, learned German in order to minister to them.

Most of these German settlers left Halifax for Lunenburg County in 1753. The few families remaining settled in the north section of Halifax, and by 1756 they were able to worship at their own church. They had acquired a small house, moved it to the northeast corner of Brunswick and Gerrish streets, and, with the help of a carpenter cum preacher and others of the congregation, had transformed it into a small architectural gem. Four years later the church was enlarged, and completed by a steeple topped with a weathercock.

Unfortunately for the small but growing congregation, there was a dearth of Lutheran ministers. In 1761 a conversion to Anglicanism occurred – a contentious adjustment to which some Lutherans strenuously objected. The tiny church was consecrated by Dr John Breynton, rector of St Paul's, whereupon it became –

St. Paul's Church today

with true British conviction – St George's. This conversion made it at once the oldest Lutheran church in Canada and the third-oldest Anglican church in Nova Scotia. In 1967, in the ecumenical spirit of the day, there was an interchurch service of reconciliation.

As the congregation adjusted to its Anglicanism and continued to grow, money was husbanded for a new church. Affluent English families like the Cunards joined the congregation. By the 1790s the parish had saved £200 for a new building. This was matched by £200 from King George III, and an astounding £700 from the citizens of Halifax. There was also sponsoring support from Prince Edward, Duke of Kent. The cornerstone was laid in 1800, and a round church arose at 2222 Brunswick Street, its circular exterior enclosing an interior reminiscent of an opera house with galleries, boxes, pit, and circle. The church members had moved from the graceful simplicity of what was called the Little Dutch [Deutsch] Church to the richness and refinement of St George's.

The new church, serving civilian and naval parishioners, had a seating arrangement accommodating both – civilians on the main floor, with military personnel and servants in the galleries. Adding to the building's distinction was a weathervane on the cupola, placed

The Little Dutch Church, corner of Brunswick and Gerrish streets

there in 1835 by the Rev. Robert Fitzgerald Uniacke, ninth child of Richard John and Martha Maria Uniacke, founders of one of Nova Scotia's influential families. The weathervane represented Halley's Comet, which had burst upon the scene that year. (In later years, St George's had a second rector from the Uniacke family, the Rev. James Boyle Uniacke, fifth child of James Boyle and Robina Black Uniacke.)

When St George's was opened, the rector of St Paul's, the Rev. Robert Stanser, claimed it as part of his parish. His attempt failed. As a result, the congregation in the new church was spared his lengthy and ponderous sermons. (Perhaps it was in anticipation of such a problem that they had installed a clock with a large, round face directly across from the pulpit.) At his own church, St Paul's, Stanser's parishioners had difficulty staying awake, even though the beadle with his long staff did what he could to ensure decorum and attention. None-the-less, Stanser was an eminent and successful priest, later becoming the second bishop of Nova Scotia. He died twenty years before a useful invention was announced in *The Novascotian* of 6 March 1848:

A curious invention to prevent sleeping in church has been brought out. It is a long squirt fixed on the deacon's seat, under the pulpit. It turns on a pivot, and being filled with cold water, can be aimed at an individual in any part of the house. One of the audience being discovered asleep, the deacon discharges a stream of cold water in his face, which has, thus far, never failed of waking up the sleeper. Much credit is due to the gentleman who planned this ingenious device for furthering the cause of virtue and religion.

St George's Church, 2222 Brunswick Street

CHAPTER TWO

The Prince and the Governor

HRH Prince Edward, Duke of Kent, and (opposite) his long-time mistress, Mme de Saint-Laurent

When the lieutenant-governor, Sir John Wentworth, laid the cornerstone for St George's church on 10 April 1800, Prince Edward Augustus, Duke of Kent, fourth son of George III and the future father of Queen Victoria, was living in Halifax. He may even have been on hand for the ceremony. Prince Edward, then thirty-two, had a great interest in the Germans of the congregation in the northern suburbs, at the time known as Dutchtown. (The area was settled by Deutsch, or German, immigrants in the 1750s and the name was incorrectly anglicized.) The Duke had encouraged the circular design of the church, a style to which he was partial and which was currently in vogue.

Wentworth, then sixty-three, and utterly loyal to the Crown, had shown his affection for the king's son ever since the prince's arrival in 1794. Wentworth offered him the use of his country house, called 'Friar Lawrence's Cell,' which, at his own expense, the prince enlarged into a comfortable, romantic retreat. It became known as The Prince's Lodge. Six miles from Halifax, on the shores of the Bedford Basin near Birch Cove, it became for the next few years home to the prince and his mistress.

Edward had incurred the displeasure of the king because of a scandalous liaison with a French actress and the birth of their illegitimate daughter in 1789. Sent a safe distance away, to Gibraltar, he was given his first charge as colonel of the 7th Foot. Within a year, however, he was joined by another young woman, Thérèse-Bernardine, Comtesse de Montgenet, known as Mme de Saint-Laurent, or Julie. Her arrival was in response to Edward's request for 'a young lady to be my companion and mistress of my house.' He was looking, said the prince, 'for a companion, not a whore.' Leaving her current lover behind, Mme Saint-Laurent joined the prince in what became an enduring relationship. She remained with him for twenty-seven years – in Gibraltar; in Quebec, where he led his regiment; in London; in Halifax; and, finally, in Brussels.

Edward and Julie lived in their Italianate villa until their departure from Nova Scotia in 1800. But while its setting offered the couple romantic seclusion, not everyone shared their joy – particularly the soldiers who, each winter, had to clear the six miles of rough road between the villa and Citadel Hill. The distance, however, appealed to Julie as it kept her well away from the sights of the parade ground and the sounds of prisoners undergoing brutal punishment. Customarily, the tallest drummer would lash the prisoner while drum rolls were sounded to drown out his screams.

At Bedford, all was idyllic. Legend has it that paths winding throughout the property spelled out 'Julie.' A heart-shaped pool was surrounded by classical gardens, with picturesque temples nestled here and there under the trees, inviting the dreamer. Nearby, in a wooded setting on a hill overlooking the Bedford Basin, the prince built Julie a small 'rotunda.' It was to be her music room and a setting for afternoon musical soirées.

The rotunda was a fanciful little building. Its perimeter was surrounded by sixteen Doric columns supporting a domed roof, on top of which a sizeable gilded ball gleamed in the sunlight. Inside, one looked up to see the night 'sky' with stars sparkling on a deep blue background.

The Music Room at the Prince's Lodge, Bedford Road, near Birch Cove

Today The Music Room is all that remains of the prince's romantic retreat. After he and Julie departed, the property fell into ruin. Now it is owned and maintained as a heritage building by the Province of Nova Scotia under the auspices of the Nova Scotia Museum.

Halifax was founded as a garrison centre. Throughout the eighteenth century its permanent population never exceeded 5,000, but there were times, especially during the Seven Years War with the French, when the rowdy, brawling town burst at the seams. In 1758, when preparations were afoot for the siege of Louisbourg, and again the following year, when James Wolfe and Jeffrey Amherst were mounting the campaign against Quebec, more than 20,000 military personnel were based there. Bringing up the rear were camp followers – wives, children, prostitutes – and attendant problems. Early Halifax papers told the tale:

Last Monday Thomas Jobbit, Richard Wheldon, and William Belcher, were executed here pursuant to their Sentence; they all behaved penitently; Belcher spake but little at the Gallows; Wheldon said he died in Charity with all Men, but declar'd himself innocent of the Fact for which he was to suffer; Jobbit acknowledg'd the Justice of his Fate, warn'd all People, especially his Fellow-Soldiers, to beware of those Sins which had bro't him to that untimely End, to have a greater Regard for the Sabbath, and to spend more of their Time at the Church, and less at the Gin-Shops ... (*The Halifax Gazette*, 28 November 1752)

Last Monday Night, a Soldier being pretty much in Liquor, as he was going along the Street, happened to run his Elbow thro' a Quarrel of Glass and broke it, upon which the Man of the House came out and stabb'd him in two Places in the Body with a Cutlass and cut off three of his Toes thro' a new Pair of ... Pumps, Sole and all. The man lays dangerously ill of his Wounds and the other is secur'd. (*The Halifax Gazette*, 6 April 1754)

Little had changed when Prince Edward arrived in 1794 as commander of the forces in Nova Scotia and New Brunswick. His arrival was, in some quarters, an occasion for rejoicing, and resulted in brilliant garrison balls and other festivities. But for other Haligonians life was unrelentingly harsh.

Edward was determined to introduce morality through the use of military discipline. The examples were there to follow. In the army, soldiers condemned to death were shot or hanged. The navy took a different tack. Its miscreants were keelhauled, lashed to death, or hanged from the yardarm. In 1809 six mutineers were hanged, their bodies tarred and displayed 'dancing in the wind' on gibbets at Mauger's Beach on McNab's Island – hence the name Hangman's Beach. This gruesome sight served as a warning to sailors entering Halifax harbour.

Some said that the prince was responding to a situation that demanded harsh reprisals. But George Ramsay, 9th Earl of Dalhousie, lieutenant-governor of Nova Scotia in 1816, later governor-in-chief of British North America, had his doubts. He noted in his journals that, while Prince Edward had many endearing qualities, '... his greatest fault was an overbearing and tyrannical system of military discipline, inconsistent with the nature and feelings of Englishmen.'

And yet, he said: 'a more plain and easy man in private life, a more honourable, upright and religious man, a more kind, sincere and faithful friend never lived upon earth. His recollection of Officers and men generally at 30 years now gone by always astonished me, and his letters which I receive by every packet to his old acquaintances in this Province confirm my assertion.'

The name of Edward, Duke of Kent, is still remembered in Halifax because, regardless of his disciplinary proclivities, his taste in architecture was exemplary. His legacy is seen in the city's landmarks. The Town Clock on Citadel Hill, for instance, now the symbol of Halifax, although not completed until after his return to England, was built on his instructions. The clock was made in England, arrived in Halifax in June 1803, and was installed later that year. As well, three other round buildings were erected as a result of his influence: St George's Church, The Music Room in Bedford, and the Prince of Wales Tower, the first martello tower in the British Empire. Completed in 1797, it was named after Edward's favourite brother, George. Whatever his failings, he was an influential figure in British North America. In 1799 the name of the Island of Saint John (Île St-Jean under French rule) was changed to Prince Edward Island.

In 1800 the prince and Julie left Halifax and lived together in London, then Brussels. But pressure was mounting that he 'get on with it.' His father, Parliament, the British people – all, it seemed, felt that he should marry and dutifully produce a male heir to the throne.

In 1818, after making generous financial arrangements for Julie, an unhappy Prince Edward left her. He acquiesced and married Victoria Mary Louisa, widow of the Prince of Leiningen, and a year later the future Queen Victoria was born. A few months after her birth Prince Edward died. Julie died, unmarried and childless, in Paris, ten years later.

Before Prince Edward and Julie left Halifax, a storm had begun to brew around the question of the lieutenant-governor's residence. John Wentworth and his wife, Frances (Fanny), were unhappy with the official residence, a two-storey frame building located on the Lower Parade. The building was 'in Danger of falling into the Cellar,' Wentworth complained. (It was, however, a step up from the bungalow that had housed the first governor, Edward Cornwallis.)

The Wentworths were accustomed to the best. They had lived in a fine mansion in New Hampshire when he was governor of that colony, and they had aristocratic relatives in England with whom they had lived during the American Revolution. (Because of his former position as governor in New Hampshire, Wentworth was often called 'governor,' in Nova Scotia as well, although that title had been replaced officially by 'lieutenant-governor' when Guy Carlton was appointed governor-in-chief of British North America in 1786.) John Wentworth, however, was not a mere socialite. Originally he had come to Halifax in 1783 to serve a seven-year appointment as Surveyor General of the King's Woods, seeking out the best timber for the British navy's masts and marking off timber reservations, some of which remained unchanged into the twentieth century. Virile, energetic, and conscientious, he travelled through the wilds in all seasons for months on end. He was often alone when no one else could take the strain. Wentworth had a genuine common touch and was well liked throughout Nova Scotia, particularly in Preston, a community of black settlers across the harbour, where he had an estate and where it is said that he left an illegitimate son.

While her husband was away in the woods, Fanny was making friends. In particular she developed a liaison with Prince William Henry, an older brother of Prince Edward, who had been shipped out of England by the king for dissolute behaviour and visited Halifax with the North Atlantic squadron in the 1780s. His association with Fanny Wentworth during his three stopovers

Sir John Wentworth, governor of Nova Scotia 1792–1808

in Halifax raised eyebrows but did little to curtail attendance at her lavish entertainments, called the most sumptuous ever given in the country. The liaison also merited the disapproval of Julie, who, while not totally accepted by the aristocracy of Halifax herself, may have felt Fanny's behaviour somewhat unseemly. The Wentworths, however, enjoyed a 'liberalized relationship' which, as biographer Judith Fingard remarked, 'included extramarital affairs for both in a style typical of the most civilized as well as the most debauched of Georgian aristocracy in England.'

Thomas H. Raddall, in *Halifax: Warden of the North*, had much to say about Fanny, her activities, and her considerable influence:

Halifax was full of naughty women, ranging all the way from the unwashed sluts of Barrack Street to the elegant wife of Mr John Wentworth, and Billy [Prince William, son of George III] knew them all. His favourite evening amusement was a tour of the town's bawdyhouses ... More than once William must have gone straight from these pretty scenes to the arms of pretty Mrs Wentworth, a fact of which she was doubtless aware, although it does not seem to have offended her in the least. Frances Wentworth at this time was forty-two, a little past her bloom but still slender, vivacious, adept, and experienced in the arts of the drawing room and the bedchamber ... while John strode the forest clearings levying fees upon the reluctant settlers his lady exerted her shapely self with no less purpose for the pleasure of their royal guest.

Lady Frances Wentworth

Wentworth was appointed lieutenant-governor of Nova Scotia in 1792. It took him five years to get

The first Governor's House and its neighbourhood in 1764, portrayed by Richard Short

approval for construction of a governor's mansion, then another two years to persuade the legislature to postpone plans for a new legislative building and start work on his residence; still, construction did not begin until the fall of 1800. By 1802 most of the money was spent, but the building had risen only as far as the first storey. Heated debate ensued in the legislature, with accusations of incompetence being hurled about. Finally, in late 1805, the building was close enough to completion that the governor and his lady could move in.

Fanny loved to entertain and had wanted the appropriate setting. Now she had it, but not without considerable drain on the public purse. The initial estimate was for approximately £10,000, but the final cost was twice that amount.

From the beginning Fanny filled the mansion with conviviality. It was the perfect setting for this vivacious and handsome woman whose conversation ranged from charming to bawdy, who enjoyed the occasional cigar, and who could now indulge her passion for entertaining. Here she had the space to work with – a large ballroom, drawing-room, dining-room, reception rooms, and a study on the main floor. Upstairs were bedrooms and the royal suite. As guests arrived they entered from Hollis Street, crossed a broad lawn, then climbed a double staircase to a welcoming door flanked by sidelights and topped by a delicate fanlight. The building, aesthetically pleasing and suffused with dignity, epitomized Palladian elegance and restraint.

Fanny never lost the ability to charm royalty of both sexes. Beamish Murdoch, in his *History of Nova-Scotia, or Acadie*, recorded that, in 1798,

Lady Wentworth, who had gone from Halifax to England in March, was presented at court to the king and queen by the

Government House in July 1819, a hand-coloured engraving by John Elliott Woolford

Countess Fitzwilliam, one of the Wentworth family, on the 5 July. It is said that she was admired by Queen Charlotte for her elegance and manners, and received the appointment of a lady in waiting, with permission to reside abroad and receive £500 a year salary.

Sir John Wentworth, created baronet in 1795, served as lieutenant-governor for sixteen years. He was well liked by the people and managed for a time to make Nova Scotia, so long burdened by debt and disputes, a solvent colony. Conflicts in the assembly marred the latter part of his term, and his political problems escalated until, in 1808, he was peremptorily removed from office. Two years later, plagued with financial difficulties, he and Fanny left for England. Hounded by creditors there, Wentworth returned to Halifax in 1812, where it is said he lived in lodgings on Hollis Street. Fanny, who had been ill for some time, died in England the following year. Wentworth himself died at age eighty-two, on 8 April 1820, a year that also saw the death of George III, the king he had served so loyally in America, and the death of his admired friend Edward, Duke of Kent. During his tenure as governor of Nova Scotia a devotion to home and sense of place emerged – a devotion which distinguishes its people today.

Government House, Hollis and Barrington streets, today

CHAPTER THREE

Thomas Akins and His Historic House

While royalty and its representatives entertained in the parlours and bedrooms of Government House, most of the men of Halifax laboured on the docks and on the ships that sailed from them. One of these, a shipwright, Samuel Sellon, began work at the dockyard around 1780, while still in his teens. Even at this early date, Sellon could boast roots in Halifax going back thirty years. His grandfather, also Samuel Sellon, had come out on the *Alderney* in 1750 with Lieutenant-Colonel Charles Lawrence, who later became governor of Nova Scotia. The first Sellon appeared to prosper, but two years later he was, for some reason, selling his considerable property. Perhaps he planned to settle elsewhere.

To Be Sold

By Samuel Sellon, in the South Suburbs, a new double House two Story high, 60 feet Front and 18 feet deep with a Garden thereto belonging, either together or in two Parts, at the Sign of the Spread Eagle: All said Sellon's Dwelling House, Store House and Wharfe, to be sold cheap for Cash, or one half Cash, the other half in such Goods as will suit. He also sells Iron and Brass Pots, Kettles and Skillets; Locks, Nails and Hinges; Carpenters and Shoemakers Tools; an assortment of Cutlery, Tin and Pewter Wares; Warming-Pans; Frying Pans; Gridirons, Copper Coffee-Pots, Iron shed Shovels, Axes, Billows, Files, Cotton and Wool Cards, Barber's Cards and Brushes, a Brass Hearth and an Iron Stove fit either for an Accompting-House or a Barber's Shop, Mahogany Tables, Desks and Chairs; also housed Hay by the Quantity or single Hundred. N.B. All Persons that have any Demands on said Sellon are desired to bring in their Accounts that they may be settled and receive their Due; and all Persons indebted to him

are desired to come and settle with him without further Notice. (*The Halifax Gazette*, 30 May 1752)

Samuel's son, Thomas, married Sarah Wickham in
1764 and their son, named for his grandfather, was born
later that year. In 1787, when young Samuel Sellon was
working on the docks, his grandmother's house on
Brunswick Street burned to the ground. She decided
to deed the property to him – half an acre in the north
suburbs. The area was well established, having been laid
out more than twenty years earlier as the first expansion
from the original town. (The north suburbs, Dutchtown, were bounded on the east by Upper Water Street
and the harbour, on the west by Gottingen Street, on
the north by North Street, and on the south by Cogswell
Street, but settlement was concentrated on Brunswick
Street.)

The house, perched at the top of a steep hill, had
been gambrel-roofed like most of the other cottages in
the north suburbs. From her door, Sellon's grandmother
would have had an unimpeded view of the crystal clear
waters of the harbour where the occasional whale sur-
faced and mackerel were found in 'prodigious plenty.'
Her lot sloped 250 feet towards the sea, and she assumed
that it was all hers. It was only when she tried to give
it away that she found she had never owned it.

The 1752 Crown grant had been to Ebenezer Fales
of Walpole, Massachusetts. Whether or not Fales built
the cottage in which the grandmother had been living
is uncertain, but, since she had been there for at least
fifteen years, the Crown did eventually deed the land

*Grandmother Sellon's
house would have been one
of those on the hill overlooking Halifax harbour in
this view by J.S. Meres,
painted in 1786. The next
year her house was de-
stroyed by fire.*

to Samuel, on the basis that Fales had been away from the province for seven years and had failed to develop the lot properly. In fact the Faleses were by then happily settled in the Annapolis Valley on 600 acres of land owned by Ebenezer and his son Benjamin. Seemingly all parties were satisfied. Sellon proceeded to build.

In 1792 Samuel and his wife, Charity, sold the southern half of the Brunswick Street property to Winckworth Norwood, a relative of Charity. Norwood either built the cottage that stands there today or enlarged a smaller structure put up by Samuel Sellon. This tiny architectural treasure stands at 2151 Brunswick Street, around the corner from the site where St George's Church rose a few years later.

Norwood and his wife, Catherine (who died at age forty-two), produced a large family. He too worked for a time as a shipwright but by 1805 he was a seaman and involved in pressing men into service, a rough life he described offhandedly in his journal:

1805 (to Bermuda)
23 May. Came on board the *Cambrian*.
25 May. Sailed from Halifax, boarded two American vessels. Pressed one man.
26 May ... saw a sail, gave chase and came up with her, proved to be a ship from Norfolk ... pressed one man ... stopped after chase a ship from New York bound to Holland, a ship from New York bound to Bourdeaux.
7 June ... hand-mate jumped overboard and was drowned. Got him on board.

Norwood died on 30 August 1821:

Sellon/Norwood/Akins house, 2151 Brunswick Street

Thursday morning, in the 56th year of his age, Mr. Winckworth Norwood, an old and faithful servant of Government,
having served 42 years in His Majesty's Naval Yard. He has
left a large family to lament his loss – His funeral will take
place tomorrow, Sunday, from his late residence in Dutch
town, near the round Church ... which the friends and
acquaintances of the family are requested to attend. (*The
Acadian Recorder*, 1 September 1821)

Norwood had conscientiously provided for his family, leaving his daughter Catherine Mary his 'best bed
and bedstead, with a sufficient covering of sheets, blan-
kets, and quilts and two Pillows and Pillow Cases and
the suit of Curtains belonging.' To his son Edward he
bequeathed his wearing apparel and Bible. Sons Christopher and William received his 'other books.' Norwood
instructed that the contents of the house were to be
sold, the house rented, and the income from all of this
used for the support of his daughters, Catherine Mary
and Elizabeth, until they were both married or the
younger came of age, at which time the estate was to
be divided equally among his six sons – Christopher,
William, Winckworth, Edward, John, and James – and
two daughters.

Nine years after Norwood's death the property (by
then substantially improved since its purchase from Sellon) was sold to John Murchison, who had been renting
it for some time. He in turn sold the cottage in 1832
to Sarah and Maria Ott Beamish. The man with whom
it is now most often associated is their nephew, Thomas
Beamish Akins. Akins, whose mother, Margaret Ott
Beamish, died ten days after his birth, had been raised
by her family in Halifax. He inherited the Brunswick
Street cottage from his aunts at age twenty-seven and
lived there until his death at eighty-two.

Akins's cousin, Beamish Murdoch, author of *A History of Nova-Scotia, or Acadie*, was also raised by the Ott-
Beamish family. Young Akins trained in Beamish Murdoch's law office, and, while there, assisted Thomas
Chandler Haliburton with research for his *An Historical
and Statistical Account of Nova-Scotia*, published in 1829.
His life-long interest in the history of his province was
sown and cultivated early. A shy and studious bachelor,
Akins retired early to devote his time to his growing
collection of historical documents and write and study
history. He became president of the Old Nova Scotia
Society, a select group made up of descendants of the

city's original settlers, and won a prize in 1839 for his history of Halifax. For the rest of his life he continued to add to that history.

Fortunately for the province and the country, Akins managed to convince the government leaders of the day that the public records of Nova Scotia should be located, catalogued, and preserved. His scholarship and quiet enthusiasm were recognized by both Joseph Howe and J.W. Johnston. Though political opponents, these two men sponsored a bill in the provincial legislature in 1857 that made Akins Commissioner of Public Records – in effect the first government archivist in the country. Just over a century after Cornwallis founded Halifax, and ten years before Confederation, Akins and Nova Scotia were preserving material which others considered of minimal interest. Today the collection is nothing short of priceless. In addition to his work with public records, he collected books and pamphlets which were the nucleus of the Legislative Library's collection, and gathered a private collection of some 4,000 volumes, including works from the fifteenth century. Eventually hundreds of his manuscripts, 2,000 of his 4,000 books, and other documents became part of the collection at the Provincial Archives of Nova Scotia. Other rare items are part of the Special Collection of King's College in Halifax.

Thomas B. Akins, probably in the 1870s

In 1865 Akins found himself the centre of public controversy after the publication of his *Selections from the Public Documents of the Province of Nova Scotia.* Included were documents relating to the expulsion of the Acadians. The gentle, scholarly Akins was accused of omitting compromising material, documents that would have thrown a favourable light on the Acadians' cause. The ensuing storm brought about international interest in the Acadian question and anguish for Akins, who defended his work. The charges were later disproved.

Years later, a contemporary, Dr Archibald MacMechan, described the legendary historian: 'He carried about him the atmosphere of the good old days, when the Halifax garrison was a major-general's command, a full brigade of infantry [and] when Royal governors had a petty court at Government House.' MacMechan recalled his first meeting with Akins:

On the first of May, 1890 [Akins was then eighty-two] I was taken to his home ... and introduced to the man who had done so much for the history of Nova Scotia ... A little old gentleman rose quickly from his chair by the window to greet us. He seemed shrivelled inside his clothes, which were worn and a trifle shabby. He was clean-shaven as was the custom in his youth; and he wore a high collar or stock which came up to his ears, and was wound about in the folds of a brown neck-cloth, after the fashion of the eighteen-thirties ... Though he was 'wrinkled deep in time' his eyes were bright and he did not wear glasses. When he laughed – and he laughed easily – there was a marvellous puckering and drawing together of all the face ... He referred to his chronic bronchitis, and added 'I am afraid to go out. I am talking and laughing but I am half dead.' He said it with a smile which was free from any moribundity or self-pity ... The last time I saw him was in the vestibule of Province House on a bitter February morning ... a quaint little figure in a short 'covert coat,' top-hat and muffled up in a woollen scarf wound round and round his neck with the ends tied in front. He might have stepped out of a Dickens illustration by Phiz. It was the only time I ever saw him outside his own house. He said with a cheery smile, 'I ought to be in my grave.' He died in May ... His memory was capious [*sic*] and precise in detail ... He was, I should say, a perfect raconteur.

MacMechin followed with an example of Akins's riveting stories: a personal experience on a steamer out from Charlottetown in a thick fog. Approaching the Gut of Canso,

Mr Crisp, who had been a sailor, and had surveyed the whole coast, was convinced that the vessel was off her course and was headed for the rocks below Cape George. He dared to remonstrate with the captain and was properly snubbed for his impertinence. When his arguments were exhausted, he went below and soon came back on deck, carrying his portmanteau and without his coat and boots, all ready to swim for it. The gesture was convincing. The helm was put hard aport; and only just in time. As the vessel swung round the excited passengers could hear the surf roaring in the caverns under Cape George. (*The Halifax Herald*, 31 December 1932)

After years of neglect Akins Cottage stood dilapidated and forlorn. Happily it was rescued by a firm of Halifax architects and given a new lease on life. The interior was partially gutted, and the exterior of the house and the main floor carefully restored. Six fireplaces and the wood trim were returned to their original Georgian simplicity. The top floor was renovated for use as additional office space.

Today this small building, so typical of the 18th century cottages that once surrounded it, stands in testimony to the benefits (both aesthetic and financial) of skilled architectural restoration. It is now, probably, the oldest dwelling in Halifax.

CHAPTER FOUR

Privateers and Politicians

The men who employed Samuel Sellon and Winckworth Norwood were a new breed of entrepreneur. For the most part they were native-born Maritimers who had replaced an earlier mercantile class from Britain or from New England. The new merchants were young, confident, and adventurous – men who sensed that prosperity was at hand, to be found in the oceans of the world.

There were several ways to net gold from the sea. One was through privateering, a hazardous but potentially lucrative venture that became the foundation of more than one fortune. Privateering was both legal and patriotic – highly profitable for the victors, disastrous for the enemy. Any partnership that could put together the money to buy or build a vessel could become privateers, provided they first obtained a letter of marque – in effect, a licence – from the governor. Without it, the venture was piracy and punishable by hanging. Privateering was legal only in time of war, but, in the late eighteenth and early nineteenth centuries, Britain, France, America, and Spain were at war with each other more often than not, so for most of that time vessels could be captured quite legally all along the Atlantic coast. Their cargoes, sold or auctioned through the Vice-Admiralty Court, provided 'prize money.'

A prime scourge along the eastern seaboard during the War of 1812 was the elusive *Liverpool Packet*, a sturdy, speedy schooner which captured prizes worth more than a quarter of a million dollars. One of her owners was Enos Collins. For him, privateering was only one of many lucrative ventures that, in time, made him a multi-millionaire. When he died, a venerable ninety-seven, in 1871, he left an estate of $6 million. He was, they claimed, the richest man in British North America.

Born in Liverpool in 1774, Enos Collins was the

second of twenty-six children of Hallet Collins and his three wives. Hallet Collins, when tending to business, was a merchant and trader out of Liverpool who, by the time he died in 1831, had amassed an impressive estate of £13,000. Enos took to the sea in his teens, and before he was twenty was named captain of the schooner *Adamant.* In 1799 he served as first lieutenant on a famed privateer, the *Charles Mary Wentworth*, a vessel named for the only son of John and Fanny Wentworth.

Collins amassed part of his fortune by running French blockades to supply British troops during the Napoleonic Wars. He received generous and tangible rewards for his efforts. Within a few years, after moving to Halifax, where prospects seemed limitless, he was buying part ownership in several ships. One was the *Liverpool Packet*, which, *The Boston Messenger* acknowledged in its issue of 1 January 1813, had captured 'eight or nine vessels of sail valued at from seventy to ninety thousand dollars. This same marauder,' it added, 'had but a few weeks before captured within ten miles of Cape Cod, vessels whose cargoes were worth at least fifty thousand dollars.'

Enos Collins as a young man

Collins built a warehouse to store the prizes from his enterprise. The booty and armaments from the captured U.S. frigate *Chesapeake* were kept there after she was brought under sail into Halifax harbour, the closest British port, by the victorious HMS *Shannon* on 6 June 1813, five days after a brief and bloody naval duel fought outside Boston harbour. The news of this brilliant victory spread quickly. As the defeated *Chesapeake* was entering the harbour, the service at St Paul's ended abruptly when the congregation rose as one and rushed to the scene. One spectator was seventeen-year-old Thomas Chandler Haliburton; in company with a friend, he rowed out to the *Chesapeake* and boarded her, but quickly retreated at the sight of the bodies and the blood-soaked deck.

At war's end, Collins branched into lumbering, whaling, West Indies trading, and other mercantile ventures, including the importing of manufactured goods. Everything he touched became profitable. He successfully speculated in currency, and was a founder of the Halifax Banking Company (an unchartered bank that was eventually absorbed by the Bank of Commerce), as part of a group that included Samuel Cunard. The bank was popularly known as Collins' Bank because it was housed in part of the ironstone warehouse that he built in 1823.

Along with great prosperity for Collins, all this had a beneficial ripple effect on the colony's economy.

In 1822 Collins, ever ambitious, decided to accept an appointment to the principal governing body of the colony, the Council of Twelve. This powerful merchant-official group, whose positions were filled by appointment, mainly those made by the lieutenant-governor, was a complex of interrelationships. J. Murray Beck, in *The Government of Nova Scotia*, pointed out that 'Brenton Halliburton [army officer, lawyer, and later chief justice of Nova Scotia] belonged to a Council in which his father, two uncles, two brothers-in-law, his father-in-law, son-in-law, aunt's brother-in-law, brother-in-law's father-in-law, and the latter's brother-in-law all held seats at one time or another, and five of whom were members at the same time.'

As a member of the Council, Collins, given to high-handed methods, created a furore during the celebrated Brandy Dispute of 1830. At issue were taxes on foreign brandy. The Council of Twelve, and Collins in particular, favoured little or no tax on the brandy, while the elected assembly demanded a full tax. An election was fought on the issue, and the full tax restored. Collins was seen as an opportunist. He stood against the rest of the Council when a charter was granted in 1832 to a second bank which, if successful, would represent competition. This was the Bank of Nova Scotia. It was indeed successful.

Not surprisingly, Enos Collins married well – although he waited until he was fifty-one to do so. His wife was Margaret Halliburton, the eldest daughter of

HMS Shannon *escorts the captured U.S. frigate* Chesapeake *into Halifax harbour during the War of 1812*

Collins' Bank and ware-house, Privateers' Wharf, Historic Properties, Upper Water Street

fellow Council member Sir Brenton Halliburton and Margaret Inglis, daughter of Bishop Charles Inglis. This marriage put him squarely in the upper echelon of Halifax society. Enos and Margaret Collins became the parents of nine children, only four of whom (a son and three daughters) grew to adulthood.

The family lived at Gorsebrook, a magnificent estate in south Halifax. In later years this house and a major portion of the grounds were purchased by St Mary's University. The subsequent demolition of the once gracious mansion led, in 1959, to the formation of the Heritage Trust of Nova Scotia, which protested its loss.

Collins's last political stand was one of vehement opposition to Confederation. While in his nineties, and still a fighter, he let it be known that were he twenty years younger he would 'take a rifle and resist it.'

A few weeks after his death on 18 November 1871, Haligonians were intrigued to read the provisions of his will, reported in *The Halifax Citizen*. Since Margaret Collins had predeceased him, their son, Brenton Halliburton Collins, inherited Gorsebrook, its contents, other property on Tower Road, and the buildings on the wharf. He was also the residual beneficiary. Daughters Eliza and Margaretta (the latter married to a future premier, Philip Carteret Hill) inherited his house at Fort Massey – Eliza the western half, Margaretta the eastern. Another daughter, Frances, and her husband, J. Winburn Laurie, inherited Retreat, the Collins house near

Gorsebrook, home of Enos Collins, in 1928

Windsor. Eliza and Frances also received $200,000 each, although Eliza was to receive hers only if the trustees deemed it prudent, 'having in consideration her state of mind and her conduct.' Margaretta inherited $160,000. Five hundred pounds were left to each of the Orphans' Home, St Paul's Church, the Protestant Episcopal Church of Liverpool, and the Halifax Home for the Aged, which institution Collins described as 'for the benefit of females who have seen better days.'

Today, on Upper Water Street, the bank and warehouses recall this eminently successful man – buildings which, like their original owner, seemed virtually indestructible. In recent years, however, it seemed that their end was in sight. Their survival has not been accidental, but attributable to the joint efforts of volunteers, architects, historians, and heritage groups who worked tirelessly to save them when their survival was threatened by plans for a new freeway. Parks Canada subsequently designated the seven buildings, now known as the Historic Properties, as a National Historic Site.

Like Enos Collins, John Black moved to Halifax to expand his trading opportunities and, like Collins, he succeeded. Black also built an imposing, well-located home. It stood as a symbol of his success. Unlike the Collins house, however, Black's house still stands to tell the tale.

When Black came to Halifax in 1806, he had already made his mark in Saint John, New Brunswick, where since 1786 he had successfully secured masts for the British navy. He had also used one of his fleet of nine ships to transport salted fish to the West Indies; on the return trip it carried rum and molasses, which was shipped to Britain along with the masts. He was one of those industrious Scots who buoyed up the commercial life of the city – at home in 'Scotch Row,' where commerce flourished in Saint John.

The Black fortunes grew with the British Empire as new trading areas were acquired. His own empire expanded from New Brunswick into Lower Canada (Quebec). He arrived in Halifax equipped with good connections among Scottish merchants there, a reputation as a quick-witted and honest businessman, a background in politics, and money. He was an immediate success. By promoting shipbuilding in Nova Scotia, New Brunswick, and Lower Canada, he was able to secure contracts to supply ships for Britain. He was a one-man trade ambassador for the Atlantic area. And, with privateering so prevalent, like Enos Collins and others he engaged in the speculative purchase of captured vessels with cargoes that had been condemned by the Vice-Admiralty Court.

Black's financial success was perfectly reflected in his home. He picked a prime location (1472 Hollis Street), next to Government House, and built a fine Georgian town house. It was commodious, comfortable, and impressive. Faced with granite (believed to have been imported as ballast in one of Black's ships on a return voyage from Scotland), it boasted the requisite symmetrical, well-proportioned façade. A central door, flanked with sidelights and a rectangular transom, led into a hall with spacious, high-ceilinged rooms on either side. Black was described as 'entertaining and convivial,' and this was a house meant for gracious living.

In 1819 Black, his second wife, Catherine Billopp, and their son and daughter moved into their grand new home. (Black also had a daughter from a previous marriage to Mary McGeorge, who had died in 1799.) But he had little time to enjoy his splendid house. His health was failing and, in hope of restoring it, he left for Britain, travelling there extensively until, in 1823, near his birthplace in Aberdeen, Scotland, he died. *The Acadian Recorder* mourned his death, recalling his 'reserved and quiet manners,' and 'the kindness of his heart.'

About nine years later, in 1832, Black's daughter, Rosina Jane (one of the two children born to John and Catherine), married James Boyle Uniacke. The couple took up residence in the bride's home. Uniacke was the eleventh child (and fifth son) of Richard John Uniacke

Black/Uniacke/Binney house, 1472 Hollis Street

and Martha Maria Delesdernier and thus, as he was a member of the provincial 'aristocracy,' his future seemed assured. The accomplishments of his father, Attorney General Richard John Uniacke, were legion. The senior Uniacke was unquestionably the most influential man in early nineteenth-century Nova Scotia. He was a power to be reckoned with and assumed that his sons would live up to, and even exceed, his expectations.

James Boyle Uniacke was expected to benefit from legal training at the Inns of Court in London, and to live his life in a dedicated, serious manner. But the young man had other interests as well, and they were well known around Halifax. He heartily enjoyed his pleasures – his horses, his fashionable clothes, and his drink – and he indulged himself liberally in all these entertainments, indulgences which did not escape notice and criticism. But Uniacke had considerable skills in the law, business, and politics. He became an incorporator and director of the Bank of Nova Scotia and president of the Halifax Gas Light and Water Company.

Of Richard John Uniacke's six sons, it was the charming and loquacious James Boyle Uniacke who achieved the most political success. He was a member of the Legislative Assembly from 1832 to 1854, and in 1838, according to biographer J. Murray Beck, became 'a member of the newly created Executive Council, although refusing to admit that it operated under any meaningful degree of responsibility.' In 1840 Uniacke had an abrupt change of heart and party, resigning from the Council and joining his former opponent, Joseph Howe, as a Reformer. In 1848 he became head of the first responsible government in British North America and attorney general. He was, however, no match for Howe's boundless energy in the reform cause, and his contributions in the new era of responsible government drew their sustenance from Howe.

Uniacke was a spell-binding orator – better even than Howe. 'Almost unequalled in his oratorical talents,' according to J. Murray Beck, 'he only occasionally disturbed a comfortable existence to display them to full advantage.' Some days he emerged the victor after volleys of rhetoric which, if nothing else, provided the assembly with lively entertainment:

I must now turn to the Address of the member for the County of Halifax [Howe], and he did give himself an unusual latitude on that occasion. He reminded me of a horse turned into a clover field, that knows not when to stop on being relieved from his bit and bridle ... He was like a modern preacher ... who tried various modes with his audience, – he first tickled, and then threatened, and then thumped them into his views ... He is like the Babylonian King, – and has set up a golden image, – and every man who refuses to worship it, must be cast into the fiery furnace of his wrath. He may heat the furnace seven times hotter, and cast me in, and I trust to come out as unscathed as Shadrach, Mesheck, and Abendnego. (*The Novascotian*, 21 February 1839)

Some days he no doubt wished that he had held his tongue. Once, after Uniacke had made disparaging remarks about the truck horses owned by a fellow member, John Young, comparing them unfavourably with his own winners, Young retorted that *he* selected *his* horses in the same way that '*some* gentlemen' select their wives – 'not for their beauty but for their *sterling worth*' – a clear reference to Rosina Black Uniacke, who, although rich, was not a beauty.

Uniacke and his wife both inherited sizeable fortunes, but he managed to go through these inheritances, losing capital in unsound investments. He died on 26 March 1858, intestate and virtually insolvent, having had to petition the House he had once led to provide him with a pension.

Some years before his death Uniacke had sold his house to the Rt Rev. Hibbert Binney, Bishop of Nova Scotia. The building, having passed through eras of business and politics, now entered its religious phase.

Binney had been born in Cape Breton, but left with his family for England when he was four. When he returned to Nova Scotia in 1851 he was already a bishop in the Anglican Church at age thirty-one, and unmarried. His appointment met with general approval for he was, as *The Novascotian* proclaimed, 'a Nova Scotian by birth, and connected with many of the most respected families in this country.' The young bishop held firm ideas on matters religious. The church should, he believed, be an all-powerful institution, with centralized authority under the bishop and absolute adherence to the Anglican Book of Common Prayer. For the next thirty-six years he dealt firmly but kindly with those who disagreed – and he usually got his own way. He ensured that the Anglican Church remained a powerful centralized institution in Nova Scotia.

Binney's lofty position in the church brought with

Rev. Hibbert Binney, Bishop of Nova Scotia, about 1880

it an equally elevated place in the social life of Halifax. He was the son and namesake of an Anglican rector, and the grandson of the Hon. H.N. Binney, Collector of Excise in Nova Scotia. His wife, Mary Bliss, was the daughter of Justice William Blowers Bliss. The house on Hollis Street once again became the venue for social gatherings, though undoubtedly of a more genteel order than during the Uniacke era.

When he died, Hibbert Binney left an estate of nearly $500,000. A mortgage on the Hollis Street house was to be retired, but after that came generous bequests to family and to the church: $2,000 to his successor for 'Diocesan purposes,' $2,000 to Synod for 'the education of children of two or more clergymen,' $2,000 to the Synod for the 'support of clergymen,' $2,000 for a 'refuge for fallen women.' To his wife, Mary, he left all the household furnishings except for those articles 'marked with the [Bishop's] mitre.' These were to be kept for 'one or both of my sons.'

In later years the house was gutted by fire, but was saved from demolition by Colonel Sidney Culverwell Oland, who purchased and restored it. The Black/Uniacke/Binney house is now dedicated to the service of veterans as local headquarters for the Canadian Corps of Commissioners. It received a Historic Sites and Monuments plaque in 1967 as part of Canada's Centennial celebrations.

Many years before James Boyle Uniacke married Rosina and moved into the Black house, his older brother, Crofton, built a dignified stone town house on Morris Street. Crofton, born in 1783, was the second of Richard Uniacke and Martha Maria Delesdernier's five sons, all of whom, tall and handsome, made their mark in the social, political, and religious life of Halifax.

Crofton, after study abroad, practised law in his father's prestigious Halifax law firm. While still a young man he married Dorothy Fawson and, in 1807, began the construction of their home. That fall, he wrote from Windsor with clear instructions to his wife as to how she should ready the house for his return. They were, by then, parents of two small children. The haughty mannerisms which were evident in many of his dealings were replaced in his letters home by a deep concern for his family:

Windsor, 17 September 1807
My Dear Dolly ... Do write me how you do for upon that

Entrance to Crofton Uniacke's home, 5248 Morris Street

will depend my journey I will not go to Annapolis if you expect to be sick before I return. Anything you want you can
get and keep the bills till I return. Do not neglect to have
everything ready at the house for our moving in on my return.
Get the fuele dry now I beg you to ask your father to see
about it for it will be impossible for us to go in without a
fuele ... your father will lay in the coals and I hope you will
get everything you want to make you comfortable – get any
beds or anything else and keep the bills – whatever you do I
shall be pleased with for I am indifferent about those things.
The grates I suppose are set before this for God's sake be
careful of fire for a little thing may ruin us in that
way ... God Bless. Your, Crofton.

Dolly replied:

... Your two little babes are well and I trust in God that they
will continue so ... Dick is sitting by me and tearing up one
of your letters and little Patty sends you a letter she held the
pen herself. Oh how I wish you were home once more don't
stay longer than necessary. Farewell. Yours, D. Uniacke.

Crofton Uniacke, thanks to his father's influence and
powerful family connections, became a judge of the
Vice-Admiralty Court. The appointment was not to his
liking, however, and he resigned two years later. In 1816,
then age thirty-three, he left for London, England,
where he practised as a barrister at Lincoln's Inn. That
same year he wrote to his children in Halifax. His words,
those of a loving father and a homesick man, were intended to be read in the event of his death:

To My Dear Little Children. In leaving you all in the bosom
of a beloved Mother, whose affection has been the source of
my greatest happiness, I go from you in the fullest confidence, that your infant years will not pass without that best of
all instruction, a good and virtuous example. Look to her for
those principles of religion and morality, which while they are
the only foundation of earthly happiness, are also the sure
path to a life of future bliss ...

After exhorting them to 'innocence, honour, moral
virtue, delicacy of feelings, the cherished memories of
departed friends, the sweet memories of an innocent
youth and the joy of an unsullied spirit,' he closed with:

Farewell – May you often read these few lines, flowing from

the warm and pure affection of your Father's heart, and watered by your Father's tears.

Farewell!

Crofton Uniacke

During his career in London, Crofton Uniacke served as defence counsel for Queen Caroline, wife of George IV, against charges of adultery. In a pamphlet called *Letters to the King by The Stranger*, published in 1820, Uniacke publicly disagreed with the king's actions. 'Instead of sending a search commission,' he argued, 'without the knowledge of Her Majesty, why did they not bring forward all who had any charge to offer and oblige them to declare it in the face of the Queen herself?' It was wrong, he declared, to condemn a woman for behaviour permissible for a man.

Crofton Uniacke died on 26 October 1852 at Mount Uniacke. He was sixty-nine. Dolly died fifteen years later. His home, the consummate Georgian town house, still stands at 5248 Morris Street. Except for the later addition of a mansard roof and decorative dormers, its exterior appearance has changed little. It is the only solid granite house in Halifax.

When Crofton Uniacke left for London in 1816, the Morris Street house was sold to a neighbour, Richard Harney, with the unusual provision that Crofton's younger brother, Richard John Uniacke, Jr (known as Dick), recently returned from three years in Cape Breton, could occupy the house; the full cost was to be paid only after five years had elapsed. When those five years had passed, Dick married Mary Ann Hill on 29 December 1821. Considered the most handsome man in Halifax, he was charming and outgoing.

Two years before his marriage, Richard John Uniacke, Jr, had fought the last fatal duel on record in Nova Scotia, a tragic event in which his opponent, William Bowie, was killed. *The Acadian Recorder* of 24 July 1819 described the duel:

On Wednesday morning between the hours of 4 and 5 o'clock, a meeting took place near the North Farm, about two miles from town, between Richard John Uniacke, Esq. the younger, and Mr. William Bowie, both of this place; after exchanging the second shot the latter fell mortally wounded. Assistance was immediately procured when Mr. Bowie was conveyed to the Farm House, and a messenger dispatched for a Surgeon, who, upon his arrival, found Mr. Bowie's friend by his side – On examining the wound, it was ascertained the ball which had entered a little above the right hip, had passed through to the left side, which was immediately extracted – but alas human skill was in vain, the approaching hour of dissolution became visible, and at 10 minutes before 6 o'clock, on the evening of the same day, we lament to state, Mr BOWIE breathed his last, in the 35th year of his age ...

A witness remembered the deceased saying to a gentleman, a few hours before he died, 'I forgive Mr. Uniacke, and I hope he will pray for me.'

At Bowie's funeral the next day the flags of all the vessels in the harbour were flown at half mast. Uniacke was to be tried for murder.

Young Uniacke testified that the deceased had made challenges to his character, honour, and respectability that he would not withdraw. To ignore them would have meant 'degradation, disgrace and infamy' to a member of a family whose character over the centuries was 'unsullied and untarnished.' These feelings of family honour, he continued, 'were nurtured at my mother's breast.' Had he not pursued the course he did he would have been 'branded as a coward, stigmatized and disgraced.'

He was found not guilty. His nephew later reported that Dick rarely smiled after that trial.

CHAPTER FIVE

The Trial That Launched a Folk Hero

Joseph Howe was the son of the revered John Howe, a Loyalist from Boston who had been apprenticed as a printer to the owners of America's oldest newspaper, the *Massachusetts Gazette*, and to the *Boston Weekly News-Letter*. In 1776 he left Boston and, after a brief stay in Rhode Island, he settled in Halifax with his young wife, Martha Minns. He lived there until his death fifty-five years later. John Howe published *The Halifax Journal* and a literary magazine. He became King's Printer and Deputy Post Master General of Nova Scotia. At one point in 1808 he acted as a spy for the British, making trips to the United States to assess the likelihood of war. Intelligent, energetic, astute, modest, and kind, he may well have been, according to biographer J. Murray Beck, 'the most respected person in the Halifax of his day.' He was mentor and best friend to his son Joseph, the youngest of his eight children.

Joseph was born in 1804, son of John's second wife, Mary Edes. He was virtually self-educated, his formal schooling consisting of only a few months in the Royal Acadian School, an unusual small establishment on Argyle Street, run by an army officer who was trying to provide an education to blacks, Mi'kmaqs, and the poor. After this brief period of formal education Howe relied on his father, the works of Shakespeare, and the Bible to train his mind.

In 1828 Howe persuaded Catherine Susan McNab to marry him. He was earning a living of sorts, having just taken over *The Novascotian*, but he also had an illegitimate child. The redoubtable Susan Howe raised this son as her own, and bore him ten more children, five of whom died in childhood. She was a remarkably capable woman. Left on her own for months while Howe travelled the province collecting debts, she too collected debts in Halifax and generally managed *The Novascotian*. She set type, designed page make-up, ran the presses, cared for her aging father-in-law, coped with their comparative poverty, fed unexpected guests even if all she had to serve was a mess of smelts, and patiently suffered the instructions Joseph Howe sent by letter. 'Do not neglect your dunning,' he advised, 'the more money you can collect the better ... Pray enjoy yourself as much as you can – indulge in every recreation you can, but stick to business at the same time.'

The Howe letters were published in *My Dear Susan Ann: Letters of Joseph Howe to His Wife, 1829–1836* (ed. M.G. Parks), and clearly illustrate his way with words. Describing a clergyman he had heard, Howe recalled that the man was 'on the whole ... fluent and sometimes gives a sentence a tolerable lift with his fist ... [he] got into the wide ocean of theology without compass or chronometer.' Howe's devotion to Nova Scotia could elicit flights of poetic fancy. The view on the ride from Mahone Bay to Lunenburg one day, he wrote, had him feeling 'so buoyant that I scarcely touched the saddle ... What a pity it is that some apparatus cannot be invented, for catching, without any physical effort, the thoughts and imaginations of the heart, as they rise, at certain times and seasons, with a sort of spring tide of exuberance.'

The Novascotian became the most popular and informative paper in the province. Howe covered all the sessions of the assembly, absorbing and reporting on the political scene that would be his future. He was gifted with intellectual energy and retained a respect for the people of his province whom he knew through nine years of travel on horseback, selling subscriptions and collecting debts. *Western Rambles and Eastern Rambles* described these travels. He also published Thomas Chandler Haliburton's two-volume history of Nova Scotia (a venture which lost money and nearly ruined him) and then serialized and printed Haliburton's famous *The Clockmaker*, the saga of Sam Slick.

It was *The Novascotian* that led him into politics. Howe had gradually come to distrust the group of powerful merchants who controlled the town, and in 1835 printed a letter from a reader accusing the magistrates of misusing public funds. As he would not reveal his sources, he was himself charged with criminal libel and tried before Chief Justice Brenton Halliburton.

The setting for the trial was impressive. The courts

then met in the Legislative Library of Province House on Hollis Street, a building that had been beset with problems from the beginning. The need for Province House was evident long before a shovel was put in the ground. Plans had been under discussion since 1787, but little progress had been made when, in 1799, Fanny Wentworth, the lieutenant-governor's wife, brought the whole operation to a halt. She demanded that the construction of a governor's residence take precedence. Thus the legislature continued to meet in rented quarters until, several committees later, the cornerstone was laid on 12 August 1811. Province House was opened in 1819 to suitable accolades. And, during an 1842 visit Charles Dickens called it 'a gem of Georgian architecture.'

Province House, like Government House, epitomized centuries of British experience. As with all Georgian architecture, balance and symmetry were essential elements, even when this meant glazing over blind windows. This was done in Province House, where the upper windows of the south wing are false but glazed to match those on the northern wing. Had they been true windows they would have ruined the interior design of one of the council chambers.

Province House was greatly admired by the populace. On the outside, the structural brick was faced with sandstone. In the interior, elaborate ornamentation in plaster decorated windows, ceilings, and walls with an aesthetically pleasing array of swags, roses, and shells, combining elements of exuberance and restraint. Province

Province House, Hollis Street. A trial here in 1835 made Joseph Howe a hero. His statue now stands out front, the arm held out, according to a descendant, to keep the women away

House is claimed to be the oldest, smallest, most historic, and most architecturally attractive legislative building in Canada. It was designed to confer dignity on the community and importance to the visitor. It does both.

It was here, in what is now the Legislative Library, that Joseph Howe rose to defend himself before the chief justice and the jury, certain that the former was not inclined to his cause and hopeful that the latter would listen to his arguments. He had borrowed law books and studied libel law for a full week. He spoke for six hours. Later he said that he knew he had won when he saw tears in the eyes of a juror. He was acquitted, and borne from Province House in triumph. The trial changed Howe's life. The newspaperman had become a politician who would shape the history of Nova Scotia and the future Dominion of Canada. One year later, in 1836, Howe entered Province House as a duly elected member of the Legislative Assembly, representing the County of Halifax. In March 1840, as a result of the trial, the judge's son, John Croke Halliburton, challenged Howe to a duel, alleging that Howe had made remarks prejudicial to his father at the trial. Halliburton missed his target, and Howe fired into the air, but the duel indicated that Howe's crusade for responsible government was making him enemies and therefore that it was succeeding. In 1841 he sold *The Novascotian* so that he could devote himself full-time to politics.

Joseph Howe in 1854, when he was provincial secretary

Howe had great popular appeal, this attraction not diminished by a strain of coarseness involving, at times, bawdy humour. It was his immense popularity that led to the election of a Reform government in August 1847. On 9 February 1848 a Reform administration took power, with Howe's former opponent, James Boyle Uniacke, as premier. Howe was provincial secretary. His flamboyance had kept him from the leadership initially, but nevertheless he steered the ship of the first responsible government in Canada. In 1860 he became premier of Nova Scotia.

Howe fought Confederation to the bitter end. At the Quebec Conference of 1864, which established terms for the union of Britain's North American colonies, eighty cents per citizen was proposed as an annual payment by the central government to help the provinces. Howe, outraged, railed: 'We are being sold for eighty cents each, the price of a sheepskin.' He argued that the disparity between the central provinces and the Maritimes would not be fully compensated for unless there was equal representation for each of the provinces in the Senate. As well, he claimed, tariff increases after Confederation would ruin Nova Scotia.

After 1867 Howe led the anti-Confederation faction, obtained better terms for Nova Scotia, and eventually joined Sir John A. Macdonald's first federal cabinet. The prime minister said of Howe, 'That man has more ideas in his head than any man I know.' In May 1873 Howe's life-long devotion to Nova Scotia was recognized with his appointment as lieutenant-governor. But it was an honour he savoured only briefly: he died three weeks later. Even *The Halifax Citizen*, always one of his most savage critics, called him 'the Noblest Nova Scotian of our day ... [a] stately figure that dwarfed into apparent mediocrity the many able and brilliant men by whom he was surrounded.' The paper lamented his loss:

Mr. Howe succeeded ... in carrying point after point in the face of resolute opposition, until at length the system of re-sponsible government as it now exists was established upon an immovable base ... The intellectual activity that marked his career from the time he entered Parliament down to the mo-ment when his physical constitution began to fail under the burden of his prodigious labours is absolutely wonderful.

Susan McNab Howe

In his will Howe remembered, as well as Susan and their five surviving children (Ellen Howe Thompson, Joseph, Frederic, Sydenham, and William), his natural son, Edward Howe.

Many years later, a granddaughter said that she re-membered Susan Howe as an old lady who kept pep-permints under her pillow, and slipped them to the little girl when no one was looking. Sadly, political correct-ness also crept into the granddaughter's remembrances. This same lady, a daughter of Sydenham and Fanny Wes-phal McNab Howe, later took history into her own hands when she learned that Howe had fathered an il-legitimate child before his marriage to Susan. Following the death of her own father, she spent 'three days in the back pasture' burning family papers – apparently to erase the memory of Howe. When asked about his statue that stands at the south end of Province House, she remarked grimly: 'Do you know why the hand on his statue is held up? It is to keep the women away.' Her illustrious grandfather, however, was the 'tribune of Nova Scotia,' the real folk hero of his province.

CHAPTER SIX

In the Shadow
of the Military

Although Halifax seemed to be controlled by its merchants, lawyers, politicians, and clergy, who made up the ruling élite, there was another major player in the life of the city. Halifax was still essentially a fortified colonial outpost. Authority, therefore, lay with the military. But the military was reluctant to share its power. Because of this continuing tension, Halifax was not incorporated until 1841. The legacy of the military presence endures.

One of the city's oldest buildings stands in Royal Artillery Park. Built to house the commanding officer of the Royal Artillery, it has been home throughout its long life to a succession of commanding officers, those of the Royal Artillery, Royal Engineers, and Royal Canadian Artillery. Today it is the official residence of the deputy commander, Maritime Command.

In February 1805, William Fenwick, Commanding Royal Engineer, reported to his superiors that the house was complete and that the first commanding officer to occupy the new residence, Lieutenant-Colonel Charlton, RA, had moved in. Fenwick had drawn up plans for the building more than three years earlier, but a host of delays had held up its completion.

The house was originally designed to serve as a residence for both the commanding officer and the adjutant, but Charlton had other ideas. Records suggest that only he (with perhaps a family) lived there. Fenwick's final report suggested that he had encountered difficulty in dealing with Charlton's demands. The commanding officer, it seemed, felt that he was 'fully entitled to have all his rooms papered,' while the prudent and efficient Fenwick refused to finish more than two rooms in this manner, since the cost of 'Paper Hangings and Borders were so extravagantly high [in Halifax].' In his enthusiasm, Charlton had selected wallpaper that cost more than £13 to cover the walls of the two rooms. The matter of the wallpaper had to be approved by the authorities in London.

The house seemed to have been designed for double occupancy even though Charlton elected to occupy the whole building himself. With requisite Georgian symmetry, each half of the building was a mirror image of the other. Both halves had entrances, located at opposite ends of the front façade. The mutual central entrance, where guests were welcomed, led into what was no doubt intended to be a reception area for the commanding officer. This main entrance had a staircase that led to the upper floor, as did the flanking entrances at each end of the house. At some stage the latter were removed, rendering the end rooms on the second floor accessible only through the adjacent rooms via doors that were about three feet high. Six-footers entered with more than a little difficulty. The resident ghost, which is said to frequent one of these small rooms, is little bothered, presumably, by the height of the doors. The basement level was also arranged symmetrically, with two entrances on the south side. On the ground floor, a spacious parlour, warmed by a fireplace, was flanked on either side by two smaller rooms.

Fenwick was also finding his own situation particularly difficult. Other officers, with less responsibility he claimed, were being paid twice as much and, as he reported to the Board of Ordinance in August 1804, he, the commanding engineer, was sinking into a 'state

Commanding Officer's residence, Royal Artillery Park, rear elevation

of Inferiority ... hardly [able to] maintain his family.' The authorities in England must have been listening, but, as with most bureaucracies, the response did not come swiftly. Two years later, almost to the day, a grateful Fenwick left for England.

Charlton lived in the handsome, partially papered house for only three years. He was followed by a succession of commanding officers, most of whom stayed for anywhere from one to four years until posted elsewhere. One of these soldiers, Lieutenant-Colonel Alexander Cavalié Mercer, had spent a peripatetic career in Ireland and South America, and in Belgium at the Battle of Waterloo. Posted to Canada in 1823, he served there intermittently, returned to England, and finally came back once more to Halifax in 1837. He returned to England in 1842 and, after a lifetime of loyal military service, attained the rank of general in 1865. He died three years later, at Exeter. Mercer is remembered today more for his ability with a paintbrush than for his military exploits. In his extensive tours through the province he recorded the landscapes of Nova Scotia and New Brunswick in charming and instructive watercolours. Most of his sketches can be found today in the National Archives.

The commanding officer's residence has undergone a variety of structural changes since 1805. It continues to present the welcoming mien that, for nearly two centuries, greeted a succession of military men and their families. These people watched from its windows as the history of Halifax unfolded before them.

Although highly visible and often beneficial, the military presence in Halifax was sometimes seen as a mixed

Artillery Park in 1842, painted by Alexander Cavalié Mercer; the Commanding Officer's residence (front elevation) is at the right

blessing. But, to one woman, the profusion of military men was nothing short of wonderful. In *The Novascotian* of 6 January 1851, 'A Disconsolate Mother' voiced her views on the subject, views that differed substantially from those of her husband, who had earlier written to the paper:

Mr Editor – I deeply regret that my poor foolish husband should have made such a show of himself by abusing the harmless officers of the British Army. I am the unfortunate mother of seven very accomplished daughters who can sing and dance, and make footstools and cushions. They are more than ever attached to their birth place in Hollis Street. But deary me, Mr Editor, if these Red Coats are so naughty, what will my poor girls do. Oh! ... I cannot believe that they are so bad. But dear Mr Editor, you see that my husband is troubled with the gout ... One of these defenders of our country, trod upon his toe, and laughingly told him to 'keep his boot out of that' so my husband sat down, and between you and I, Mr Editor, made himself the laughing stock of the whole place ... perhaps the city authorities might be prevailed upon to billet one or two of them in our house, and then the dear girls could get the length of their feet, and work slippers for them? ...

In the late 1830s Royal Artillery Park was expanded and nearby Dresden Row extended, thus creating an odd point of land, a triangle facing Citadel Hill. Here stands a house that began life as a modest Georgian structure, and then assumed a curious configuration by squeezing itself farther into the triangle's point. It is locally known as the Bollord house because for seventy years, starting in 1903, it was owned by Charles Bollord and his descendants. (It is also known as the 'Bollard' house, for the two granite posts at the pointed end of the property, like the bollards which are used to secure ropes on a ship or a quay.) The building's associations date back to the founding of Halifax. In 1764, Lieutenant-Governor Belcher granted all the land between the present Sackville Street and Spring Garden Road to Richard Wenman, one of the settlers who immigrated in 1749 with Cornwallis.

Wenman's first move on his arrival in 1749 had been to obtain a tavern licence. This enterprising decision led to a series of successful and varied ventures, including ownership of a brewery. He acquired land at every opportunity, much of which he leased, and by 1776 was known as one of the ten richest landholders in town. Position came with wealth. Wenman became a justice of the peace and represented Halifax Township in the Legislative Assembly from 1765 to 1770. His most controversial activity was his management of the 'Orphan House.' He was criticized for the cost of its operation. The orphanage drew most of its inmates from the illegitimate offspring of the military garrison (a point that 'A Disconsolate Mother' might have considered when she yearned to billet those 'Nice Red Coats' in her home with her daughters).

In 1770, Wenman gave the land on which the Bollord house now stands to his stepson, John George Pyke, and the area eventually became known as Pyke's Fields. In 1834 six and one-quarter acres were sold to barrister James Scott Tremaine (or Tremain), who subdivided it and sold the lots, including the triangle formed by the expansion of Royal Artillery Park and the extension of Dresden Row. This was bought by William Flinn, a mason from Cashel, Ireland, who built the south part of the house now standing at the intersection of Sackville Street, Queen Street, and Dresden Row. It is seen as a rectangle on an 1835 map. His investment was a good one. In 1845 he sold this and two adjacent lots to one Jacob Currie for £300. He had paid only £60 for them just seven years earlier.

By the 1860s, when the city was enjoying an economic boom, the house was owned by a Scottish builder, John McVean. In 1872 he was listed in a city directory as

The Bollord house makes full use of the triangular lot at the intersection of Sackville Street, Queen Street, and Dresden Row.

an architect, a principal in the firm of McVean/Dumaresq. Certainly the building and the lot on which it stood provided a challenge to any architect. But, undeterred, McVean enlarged the house, squeezing an addition onto the triangle's point, thus creating a structure both visually interesting and structurally intriguing. About one-third the size of the original, the new section opened to the old only through a doorway on the main floor. Thanks to sympathetic detailing, the completed building presented a pleasing and unified appearance. For the next fifty years the two connected buildings operated with street numbers on both Dresden Row and Queen Street. Then, in 1903, shipwright Charles Bollord moved in. The exsiting structure, its exterior unchanged since the 1860s, still invites puzzled glances.

Back in the early 1840s, at about the time that William Flinn was starting to build the Bollord house, another building was going up on the west side of the Common, at the corner of Robie Street and Jubilee Road (1714 Robie Street). It too had an Irish owner. Neighbours must have watched with interest as the house took shape, for it was one of the first Regency cottages to be built in Halifax. Low, massive, and hip-roofed, the house featured the requisite tall, decorative chimneys. A verandah, supported by fluted Doric columns, wrapped around three sides of the house. Henry Hill, the architect, kept faithfully to principles of classical symmetry in the placement of tall windows balancing the front door. But in order that symmetry be maintained, the centre window on the south side was blind, painted to resemble glass. Typically, Hill seemed

1714 Robie Street, one of the city's earliest Regency cottages

little concerned about light and air for the upper storey, for in those days bedroom windows were frequently kept closed, since night air was suspected of being malarial. Light was provided to the ground floor by an oval skylight through a well in the second storey.

Ideally, Regency buildings were to be situated in romantic, pastoral settings – nestled in the woods, overlooking a gentle stream, or perched on some dramatic site in the wilderness. Such was not the case, however, with this cottage. It stood not 300 yards from the spot where, in unmarked graves, soldiers who had been executed on Camp Hill's exercising grounds lay buried.

The house was called Camp Hill Cottage by its owner, William Caldwell, son of an Irish immigrant, John Caldwell, who had settled first at Windsor, then at Grand Pré. In 1851, in what was a significant milestone in the history of Halifax, William Caldwell became the city's first elected mayor. From the time of incorporation ten years earlier, mayors had been appointed by the Executive Council from among its own members. It was a self-perpetuating system which invited abuse and, of course, rankled reformers. Thus, Caldwell's election was a cause for celebration.

He was a popular mayor. At his death in 1854 *The Halifax Morning Chronicle* recalled that Caldwell's maxim had been 'I want every man to be my friend; and I want to be every man's friend – if he will only permit me.' At his funeral,

The Firemen of the City ... preceded the Hearse to the Cemetery at Camp Hill, at the Eastern entrance of which they halted, opened ranks, and uncovered while the remaining portion of the Funeral procession, consisting of the Corporate Body and their respective officials, the St George's Society, and a numerous concourse of other Citizens, wended their way into the Burial Ground ... The estimation in which the deceased was held was evinced in the City by the colours of most of the shipping in port being lowered half mast, while many of the Public Buildings, including the County Court House, Engine Hall etc. wore the ensign at half staff ... William Caldwell [the paper concluded] never forgot in prosperity those friends with whom he was intimate while in comparative poverty.

History was repeated when one of Caldwell's three sons, Samuel Richard, was elected mayor of Halifax from 1859 to 1861. And Camp Hill Cottage itself achieved recognition. When the Dominion of Canada was born on 1 July 1867, the first volley in honour of the occasion was fired from the Caldwell residence, then occupied by William Caldwell, Jr. They kept it up 'for over an hour-and-a-half from the old cannon that [had] in its time so often awakened the echoes around the city on the mornings of former festivities.'

Farther down Robie Street, in the direction of the present Point Pleasant Park, was an area known as the Ropewalk Field, where the heavy rope for sailing vessels was laid out and twisted. The site was first owned by a New York Loyalist, Jonathan Tremain. A rope maker by trade, Tremain came to Halifax in 1786, having fled first to Quebec, where he spent two or three years. Thanks to his connections with the lieutenant-governor, Sir John Wentworth, he soon became a member of the ruling élite. Not long after his arrival, he purchased fifty acres in the south suburbs near the Freshwater River, off the road that led up from the 'Kissing Bridge,' a popular trysting spot where the Freshwater River emptied into the harbour. (Inglis and Barrington streets meet there today.) Tremain also brought in fine new rope-making equipment and, at the rear of his property, he built an 850-foot ropewalk that stretched along what is now South Bland Street. In 1805 Tremain's sons, John and Jonathan, Jr, took over the ropewalk from their father and for the next thirteen years operated the business successfully. John purchased his brother's share sometime around 1818.

Their father, in the meantime, had carefully divided his property into eleven long, narrow lots – one for each of his eleven children. John, who already owned the ropewalk, received lot 3. Business was prospering, so it seemed that the time to build a house was at hand. This he did, on the ropewalk property, and in 1823 John Tremain and his family moved into their fine new home, now part of the Universalist Unitarian Church at 5500 Inglis Street. There, two years later, the marriage of his daughter Catherine took place. But Tremain's optimism was short-lived. Within a few short years he encountered two major problems. The first was free trade. The second was Enos Collins.

In 1822 John Tremain had taken out a mortgage of £1,600 to help finance the construction of his house. Four years later the British government declared Halifax a free port, and almost immediately a flood of American goods appeared. Halifax merchants were delighted with this development for it meant more products for them to ship to the West Indies. But for Tremain it spelled disaster. He was forced to compete with cheaper American rope. He petitioned the assembly, stating that he would go bankrupt and jobs would be lost to the United States. Nevertheless, ever optimistic, Tremain bought more property and took out another mortgage.

Enter Enos Collins. Collins, well on his way to becoming 'the wealthiest man in British North America,' was one of those to whom Tremain was heavily indebted. He demanded a guarantee on his loans by way of a mortgage on the ropewalk property. Tremain provided the mortgage and promissory notes. Now he had no way of raising further money. The matter ended in court, and Tremain was sued by most of his other creditors. In the end he lost everything and left Halifax in 1837.

Enos Collins thus acquired Tremain's fine house. It appears in a watercolour sketch by Mercer, then commanding officer of the Royal Artillery, a painting now in the National Archives. In 1843 Collins, concerned because the house was falling into disrepair, sold it to John Bayley Bland. With some relief he wrote the new owner: 'I am glad to see it in the hands of some Gentleman who will improve upon it. As it is now it shows to great disadvantage.'

But no sooner had Bland purchased his new home than his wife, Joanna, died – as did their infant son six months later. Bland was left to raise two older sons. Not until 1855 did he remarry. His bride then was Mary Maude Porter, a daughter of the Rev. Charles Porter, the second president of King's College, Canada's oldest university, located initially in Windsor, now in Halifax.

Mary Maude's arrival signalled the start of renovations. The Tremain house was renamed Dorset Cottage, a ballroom wing was added, as was a library. The Blands purchased adjoining land and continued to improve the property until Dorset Cottage was considered one of the finest properties in that part of Halifax. In 1869 Bland's older son, James, died from a 'disease of the spine,' and the following year John Bland himself died after a lingering illness. Nearly a century after his death, the building, having been altered many times, was purchased by the Universalists, renovated, and later denoted as a provincial heritage property.

Of the eleven lots divided for Jonathan Tremain's children, Henry Tremain received lot 5. But Henry predeceased his father and so his lot passed to his sisters,

Abigail and Phoebe. They sold it in 1832 to Philip Letson, a tanner. It was he who shortly thereafter built the elegant Thorndean (5680 Inglis Street), another fine example of a modest dwelling whose builders knew as much of proportion and balance as did the owners of the grand houses on Hollis and Morris streets. Thorndean's history includes tales of tragedy, deception, and, not to be outdone by the commanding officer's residence in Royal Artillery Park, more than one ghost.

During a recent restoration of Thorndean, the date '1834' was found on a basement wall. Since Philip Letson mortgaged lot 5 that year for £400 it seems likely that this was the year in which the house was built. It was designed in the Greek Revival style, its central door flanked by two windows, a broad pediment above, and, in the upper storey, Scottish dormers, a feature both aesthetically pleasing and functional, in which three sides provided ample light and allowed for a view in three directions. First seen in the province in Pictou and Halifax, they became fashionable and were built in various other areas. Inside Thorndean, double rooms opened off the central hall. The kitchen was in the basement. Six fireplaces provided heat.

Letson sold the property in 1838, advertising it in *The Novascotian* of 26 April 1838 as a 'new building of nine finished rooms, excellent kitchen and frost-proof cellar.' It was purchased by James Forman, Jr, who lived in the house for thirty-two comfortable years. He might have lived there longer had he not been forced to sell the property in order to repay some of the money he had, for more than twenty-five years, systematically

Thorndean, 5680 Inglis Street

embezzled from the Bank of Nova Scotia while serving as its first general manager.

Forman began his business life working for his father, James, Sr. The elder Forman was a formidable figure – a successful merchant, justice of the peace, and justice of the Inferior Court of Common Pleas for Halifax County, and one of those involved in selling privateers' captured booty. He was known as well for his habit of swimming daily in the ocean, even on days when he had to break through a layer of ice to do so.

James Forman, Jr, was one of the prominent Haligonians, along with James Boyle Uniacke and William Blowers Bliss, who petitioned the House of Assembly to incorporate a public bank, to be called the Bank of Nova Scotia. It would compete directly with the Halifax Banking Company, which was run by and for the city's conservative oligarchy. When finally incorporated in 1832, the bank named James, Jr, then thirty-seven, as its cashier, a position we would today call general manager. He was a cultivated gentleman with good social connections. His salary: £300 per year. As president they chose the Hon. William Lawson, age sixty, a respected reformer and a man of action.

Five years later, a new man took over the president's office. He was Mather Byles Almon, one of the original petitioners, and a close friend of James Forman, Jr. By the following year, Forman and (presumably) the bank were doing well enough that the cashier was able to purchase Thorndean, a home eminently suitable for a man in his position and with his lofty expectations.

James Forman, Jr, and (opposite) Margaret Ann, his wife

Almon remained as president for the next thirty years, during which time Forman had privileged status. He was considered a leading citizen of Halifax and acknowledged as a contributor to many organizations. But, in July 1870, all came crashing down around him. Alman and the bank discovered with horror that the man who had been its trusted cashier for thirty-eight years had defrauded it of $310,000 – an enormous sum for the day. An alert junior clerk had noticed a discrepancy in the books, having been puzzled perhaps by Forman's habit of taking the bank's records home with him every night.

Almon resigned a month later. Forman transferred Thorndean and all his 'household furniture, plate, horses, carriages, harness, stock, cattle, farming implements, goods, chattels and effects of every description' to the bank. Finally, on 23 December 1870, he wrote from Londonderry, Colchester County, to the bank's new president and its directors. In a banker's flowing script, he formally acknowledged 'discrepancies' in the bank's accounts:

Gentlemen
When Cashier of the Bank of Nova Scotia on 30th July last I made out a memorandum and balance sheet of the accounts of the Bank and it has since then been represented to me that the said balance sheet ... shows discrepancies amounting to Three hundred and ten thousand dollars ... and in this acknowledgement, I desire to admit such discrepancies, and at the same time to state that I have made all the reparation in my power by transferring to the Bank all my property real and personal which will go a great way in reduction of the deficiency.   I am
Gentlemen
J. Forman

He then fled to England, a broken man. The bank decided not to prosecute since he was by then in failing health. He died in London a short time later. His wife, Margaret Ann (née Richardson), died at the home of a son, in Acadia Mines, Nova Scotia, 14 January 1878.

Thorndean remained a banker's home. It was purchased in 1870 by John S. Maclean, a Halifax merchant, shipowner, and president of the Bank of Nova Scotia from 1874 to 1889. Maclean had just joined the bank's board when the theft was discovered. In 1967, after several subsequent owners and a series of unfortunate 'modernizations,' it was bought by a Montreal architect and his wife. With foresight, determination, and hard work they restored the house to its original gracious form. The house now contains five apartments. Halifax's Heritage Advisory Committee has named it a Registered Heritage Property, as has the Province of Nova Scotia.

Thorndean, they say, is haunted. Imaginative stories suggest that the ghost of James Forman, Jr, appears now and then. The house boasts a well, set in the flagstone floor of what was once the basement kitchen. A male figure in a top hat is reported to have emerged from the old well and departed outside. Today the well is securely filled with earth and, at floor level, a colourful display of plants.

CHAPTER SEVEN

Wier and the Tallahassee

The carnage of the American Civil War had an immediate impact on Nova Scotia. And there were strongly held opposing loyalties. Some 10,000 men, most of them from rural areas, left to fight for the Union side. The Northern states had been home to many, and strong family ties still existed in spite of the rift caused by the American Revolution. But, for a pragmatic Halifax merchant, profit rather than patriotism was the motivation. Most took the British side and supported the Confederate cause. A piece of the cotton trade between the Southern states and England was worth the risk of being actively involved. Confederate officers were confined in Halifax, and some men helped them escape capture, or refitted their vessels. Benjamin Wier was one such man – a man who started his business career as a country shopkeeper near Windsor and, by the time of his death, had amassed a fortune and was living in one of the finest houses in Halifax.

Born in 1805 to Benjamin and Phebe Wier, the young Benjamin grew up in Newport Township, Hants County, and married his cousin, named Phoebe Wier. In 1830 the junior Wiers departed for Halifax, where Benjamin hoped to find a place among the prosperous Water Street merchants, then enjoying the rewards of a business boom. But his timing was poor. Recession followed, and for several years Benjamin Wier barely kept his head above water. He became an indignant grumbler, never hesitating to take offence or to air his complaints. Even when his fortunes improved, his disposition, seemingly, did not. Wier gained a certain notoriety in October 1858 for what was called the 'great editor-whalloping.' He had, with a 'stout cudgel,' attacked Alpin Grant, editor of *The Colonist*, in Hollis Street – this because the paper had had the audacity to print a report that Wier, while in Boston, had engaged in a brawl, been taken to police court, and charged with assault. Eye-witnesses to the Hollis Street 'whalloping' said that Wier 'knocked down Her Majesty's Printer and ... placed his knee upon Mr Grant's chest and continued to beat him after he was down.'

Wier's animosity initially focused on Halifax's moneyed élite. Thus, in the 1840s, he entered politics. As a Liberal reformer and proponent of elected municipal government, Benjamin Wier became a member of the Legislative Assembly and, from 1856 to 1863, sat on the Council. Business improved, as did his political career. His formidable bulk and his notorious bombast made him eminently noticeable. He was, according to one contemporary, a man of considerable girth, with a 'great massive face ... and a harsh expression of countenance which he improves the wrong way by scowling.'

As Wier's wealth increased, however, his liberal views, in inverse proportion, began to wither. Prosperity had arrived in the form of a thriving trade with New England and the growth of his own sailing fleet. Along with wealth came increasing social acceptance. Gradually he moderated his passion for 'power for the people' as he himself entered the ranks of the establishment. As the reporter for *The Acadian Recorder*, a newspaper that had never been among his admirers, noted on 31 May 1856:

Upon every leading political question which has been under discussion, for the last fifteen, or twenty years, he has been very forward to express his opinion, and to express it in the broadest, loudest most emphatic manner; and he has always manifested a great desire to force his opinions upon others. I have been thinking ... that within the last four, or five, years – that is since he became a member of the House – he has contradicted every political opinion expressed by him in his previous life. For instance he formerly preached in favour of the most ample and complete civil and religious liberty of the people, and that the members of Governments were, in the fullest sense of the term, the people's servants, appointed to administer for the people; he now contends ... that the members of the Cabinet are the masters appointed to administer for themselves and that the people should have only so much liberty as is compatible with their entire subservience to the will of their masters, no matter how capricious that will may be. Mr Wier was once eager to have the Ballot crammed down the throats of the people; he would not now give it to them if the whole body implored it on their knees.

In 1862 Charles Tupper, a bitter political enemy, accused Wier of using inside information to speculate in gold-mine property and of selling worthless land to unsuspecting British investors. Wier survived the resulting inquiry, but the scandal brought an end to his political career. He hardly noticed its absence. By then, business was booming, and Benjamin Wier had become a wealthy man, happily enjoying his new respectability.

Wier's true moment in history came during the American Civil War. He acted as an agent for blockade runners, offering to refit and repair Confederate vessels in return for cotton, which he then re-exported to Britain. It was a lucrative, if hazardous business. The incident which resulted in notoriety for Wier involved the elusive, infamous *Tallahassee*. She had been playing havoc with Yankee shipping all along the east coast and had already captured fifty vessels when she lost her mainmast, then ran low on fuel. With thirteen Yankee vessels in pursuit, she headed for Halifax to refit. *The Evening Express* of 19 August 1864 reported her arrival:

She was built in England about two years ago for a blockade runner, for which she was in every way suited, being capable of steaming 18 or 20 miles an hour. The T. is commanded by Capt. John Taylor [Wood] and has a crew of a hundred and odd men who are subject to the order and discipline of a man-of-war. All the officers are Southerners.

Wier undertook what seemed an impossible task. International law allowed Captain Wood only forty-eight hours to provision and leave. Union gunboats were waiting anxiously outside the harbour. Capture seemed inevitable. But Benjamin Wier somehow managed to have the vessel speedily refitted and supplied with coal within the alloted time. The *Tallahassee* had an iron hull and was twin-screwed to ensure good manoeuvrability and, on the night of 19 August, with her 180-man crew aboard, she slipped silently through the Eastern Passage, between McNab's Island and the mainland. This was the narrowest and shallowest part of the harbour. Captain Wood later described her escape:

In looking over the chart of the harbour with Pilot Jock Flemming, who had been recommended to me, I asked him what water we would carry out through the Eastern passage. He said it was the spring tides and fourteen feet might be found,

but the channel was narrow and crooked and with a long ship
he would not advise it. I told him if he could find water
enough I would keep her in the channel with the double
screws. 'All right,' he said; 'I have never been ship-mates with
such things, but if you keep her pinted right I'll take you out.'
Flemming was as fine a specimen of an old water man as I
have ever seen. He was of herculean proportions, with a large
head set well down between broad shoulders. A shaggy suit of
brown hair covered not only his head but his neck and face as
well ... He said the tide would serve at 10 that evening. I cautioned him to say nothing of our intentions ... The enemy's
cruisers, the *Nansemont* and *Huron*, which were in sight off
Chebucto Head, in the main ship channel, were kept fully
posted as to our movements by their friends in the city ...

The night was very dark and overcast. Going down the harbor to the westward of George's Island, we steamed slowly
over to the Eastern Passage. All lights were extinguished. It
was a case of feel, not sight ... Only once, off Lawlor's Island,
did [Flemming] hesitate, and there I sent a boat ahead to
mark the turn. We touched nothing except the eel-grass. By
midnight Devil's Island lights were abeam and we felt the pul-
sations of old mother ocean ... Off to the westward could be
seen the lights of the Federals watching for us. When the island lights bore north, Flemming dropped into his flat and
wishing us God-speed was soon out of sight ... Years afterwards I would meet the old man and over a glass of beer at
Capt. Birds' he would love to talk of taking the *Tallahassee* out
the Eastern Passage [on] the darkest night he ever saw.

Captain John Taylor Wood

The *Tallahassee*'s Confederate captain, John Taylor
Wood, returned to Halifax after the war to set up business. His house (since demolished) stood at 5251 Morris
Street. One of his sons was the first Canadian officer
killed in the Boer War. Flemming, the pilot, lived at
146 Lower Water Street.

Thanks to the *Tallahassee* incident, everyone soon
knew of Benjamin Wier, and he became something of
a Halifax legend. In keeping with his new-found prestige, he decided to build for himself a suitably splendid
house, a dignified Italianate structure at 1459 Hollis
Street, close to Government House. Built of brick with
sandstone trim, it had elaborate detailing inside and out.
Sandstone-hooded windows on the ground floor, more
delicate and ornate windows on the second floor, and
a Palladian window on the roof level provided the façade with an air of refinement and quiet dignity. Inside,

a spacious entrance hall led to high-ceilinged rooms with large windows that overlooked the harbour.

The new house was magnificent, but Wier had little time to enjoy it. He had been named a senator at Confederation, and it was in Ottawa the next April that he died 'of congestion of the lungs.' *The Novascotian*, in a never-speak-ill-of-the-dead obituary, proclaimed that he had been 'esteemed and respected by all parties for the energy and independence of character which at all times distinguished him ... Occasionally warm in temper and hasty in expression, he was at heart generous in feeling, steadfast in principle, a firm friend, and a frank, fearless and yet kindly opponent.'

And kindly he may have been. In his will, Wier left the bulk of his estate to his beloved wife, Phoebe, but he also remembered with generous bequests his brothers, sisters, a niece, and servants. (The Wiers had been childless.) Phoebe Wier stayed on in the house until 1875.

After she left, the house had various occupants for the next ten years, including the illustrious Judge William Henry, a Father of Confederation, member of the Supreme Court, and former mayor of Halifax. In 1885 one of the province's elder statesmen, Sir Adams George Archibald, purchased it.

Archibald's ancestral roots went deep into Truro Township. His great-grandfather, Samuel Archibald, was one of four New Hampshire brothers (David,

Benjamin Wier's house, 1459 Hollis Street

Samuel, James, and Thomas) who settled there seven years after the expulsion of the Acadians. The vessel that brought them to Truro on a cold December day in 1762 had also carried thirty-eight other Archibalds – their wives, children, and various other relatives. The Archibalds were nothing if not prolific. Nor did relocation do anything to slow their rate of proliferation. Samuel, the second brother, had been born in Ireland in 1719. He and his Irish wife, Eleanor Taylor, in keeping with family tradition, had twelve children. (The eldest of these, Matthew, was apparently so dedicated to his Bible readings that the site of his farm was called Bible Hill.) Samuel's fourth son, James, had a son, also Samuel, who married his cousin Elizabeth; their family consisted of ten children – five sons and five daughters. The second of their sons was Adams George Archibald, future lawyer, politician, judge, and, eventually, lieutenant-governor of both Manitoba and Nova Scotia.

Adams Archibald studied at Thomas McCulloch's Pictou Academy. By 1839 he had been called to the bar in both Prince Edward Island and Nova Scotia, after which he practised law in Truro. He was ambitious and claimed that 'In our province we all know that every young gentleman who studies law hopes to be at least Chief Justice.' It may have been the only goal he failed to achieve.

Archibald was elected to the assembly from Colchester in 1851 as a proponent of reciprocity with the United States, state schools, railway construction, and elected municipal governments. He opposed universal male suffrage, however, claiming that political change, while necessary, must come only after the economic and moral development of the people had improved sufficiently for them to benefit from it. (The question of offering the vote to women did not, of course, enter the discussion.) A brief political skirmish erupted in May 1860 when his recent election and appointment as attorney general was challenged on the grounds that voters had been bribed. During the vicious debates that followed, *The Acadian Recorder* let fly with a new title, calling Archibald the 'Briber-General.'

But Archibald was in fact a man of principle. He represented Nova Scotia at the Charlottetown and Quebec conferences which led to Confederation, and became devoted to that cause. He was, however, far from being a stirring speaker. On one occasion, just before Confederation, he tangled valiantly with Joseph Howe, but

Adams Archibald

was no match for Howe's eloquence and cutting wit. *The Truro News*, in a series of Centennial articles about Archibald, recalled a Confederation debate between the two. Archibald was on his home turf but received a resounding verbal drubbing from Howe. He began on the defensive by responding to derisive comments Howe had previously made about him – and remained on the defensive for the rest of his two-hour oration, through which 'no enthusiasm was manifested' by the audience. Howe followed, 'warmly cheered' through his two-and-a-half-hour speech. Charles Tupper, the next speaker and no mean orator himself, received only sporadic applause, suggesting that the audience was uninterested in the premier's views or, more likely, exhausted after five hours of political haranguing.

As leader of the Liberal party, Archibald was its only advocate of Confederation, supporting Charles Tupper in the assembly, against Howe's heated opposition. After Confederation Archibald served as a mediator between Howe (who led the faction seeking better terms) and the federal government, until Howe was mollified.

Archibald became secretary of state for the provinces in John A. Macdonald's first post-Confederation cabinet. Asked to accept an appointment as lieutenant-governor of Manitoba, he agreed, on condition that when the term was over he be appointed to the Supreme Court of Nova Scotia. The years in Manitoba were fractious and there was continual conflict with the Métis, the early settlers of mixed Native and European ancestry. Archibald signed two treaties with the Ojibways and Crees in which Indian claims to all lands in Manitoba and adjacent lands to the north and west were relinquished for reserves and money. His wife and daughter, Lilly, who was living with her parents in Manitoba, were witnesses to the agreements.

In 1872 Archibald resigned and awaited the long-sought appointment to the Nova Scotia bench. He was made a judge in equity the following year but held the appointment for only ten days. He resigned to become lieutenant-governor of the province.

Archibald and his wife did not move into the Hollis Street house until after he had completed two five-year terms as lieutenant-governor. Their children were grown by this time, but Archibald, then in his early seventies, was still actively involved in public pursuits.

Adams and his wife, Elizabeth (née Burnyeat), were first cousins. They had four children. Their only son,

George, died in 1861, in a hunting accident near Truro. Their daughters were Joanna, Elizabeth (Lilly), and Mary Lavinia. One of these daughters was a bridesmaid when John A. Macdonald married Agnes Bernard, his second wife, in London, England, in 1867. The other attendants were the daughters of Tupper, McGee, and McDougall, delegates to the London Conference. Joanna, the eldest, married Colonel Francis Duke Laurie, who later became mayor of New Glasgow. Lilly, the second daughter, was married while her father was lieutenant-governor, in what was deemed to be 'the social event of the season.' She married the Rt Rev. Llewllyn Jones, Bishop of Newfoundland.

Adams Archibald died in Truro in 1892. He had been an able diplomat, highly respected by his contemporaries. An incident during his term as lieutenant-governor typified his skills. In November 1878 Canada's new governor general, the Marquis of Lorne, and his wife, Princess Louise (Queen Victoria's daughter), were due to arrive in Halifax by ship. The prime minister, John A. Macdonald, was in Halifax to greet them. All was in readiness for their arrival when it was announced that the ship had been delayed for some hours. The welcoming party prepared to relax. Sir John retired to his room – with some good brandy for company. By the time the royal couple arrived, Macdonald was so relaxed that it took all of Archibald's skill and that of his secretary to get the prime minister in shape to greet the royal guests.

After the death of Sir Adams Archibald in 1892, the Hollis Street house was sold to Dr William Wickwire, a former medical partner of Dr Charles Tupper, and later manager of the A. Keith and Son Brewery.

*Elizabeth Archibald
(née Burnyeat)*

CHAPTER EIGHT

The
Northwest Arm
SHIPPING, STATECRAFT, AND SURVEYING

Although a Hollis Street address such as Benjamin Wier's was impressive in 1864 (and had been since Government House opened its doors in 1805), the south suburbs had long been fashionable as well. There, in the 1830s, merchant Richard Tremain built a stately home on his Oaklands estate. But in the summer of 1848, flames engulfed the house and, as *The Novascotian* reported on 18 June, 'soon after the announcement of the catastrophe by the Fire Bells, a large number of citizens and military visited the scene of conflagration, and rendered valuable assistance in removing the furniture etc. With all their exertions, however, the building itself could not be saved, but with the exception of the bare walls is entirely burnt.'

That loss was yet another in the seemingly unending misfortunes that had plagued Richard Tremain, scion of one of Halifax's leading Loyalist families.

Tremain's life had been one of comparative privilege. A son of Jonathan Tremain (and brother of John Tremain of the ropewalk near the present South Bland Street), Richard had married Mary Boggs in 1801. He owned a profitable export-import business that flourished during the War of 1812 and into the 1820s. He also owned a flour mill and bakehouse in Dartmouth with an exclusive contract to supply the local garrison with flour. He was civic minded as well, serving as a lieutenant-colonel in the militia, church warden of St Paul's, director of the Nova Scotia Bible Society, president of the Chamber of Commerce, and magistrate. Life was good for Richard and Mary Tremain, their seven daughters, and five sons.

But his successful career was to end in a way he could never have anticipated. It was he who indignantly charged Joseph Howe with printing libel after Howe published a letter in which the writer insinuated that those magistrates in control of the poorhouse (Tremain was one) were profiting by selling inferior food to the inmates. In the ensuing uproar and trial, Howe emerged triumphant. Tremain gradually lost his wealth, and his influence waned. The destruction of his home was a near-final blow. Six years later, on 30 July 1854, he died.

In 1861 the Oaklands property was bought by William Cunard, son of the legendary Sir Samuel Cunard, a man whose name had become synonymous with shipping and entrepreneurial genius. The senior Cunard was living in England at the time, and managing his commercial empire from there. William and other family members took care of the Canadian operations.

Samuel Cunard was the quintessential local boy who made good – and exemplified those virtues that popularly make such success possible. He was honest, thrifty, and hard-working. Never a minute was wasted in idleness – Haligonians remembered that even as a boy he could be seen knitting industriously as he drove the family's cow to pasture.

Born in 1787 in a cottage just below Brunswick Street, Samuel Cunard eagerly absorbed business know-how while working on the wharves in the town's north end. There he would buy goods to sell in town. Soon he became involved in the West Indian trade, importing rum and molasses; an agency for tea shipped from China by the East India Company; the timber business; whaling; coal; iron; and, eventually, shipping. He won the contract to carry mail by steamship between British ports and New York via Halifax and Boston. This was a boon to nearly everyone in the province. Exuberant crowds were there to meet him when he arrived on his steamship *Britannia* on 17 July 1840, on the first of the faster mail deliveries.

Along with the equally ambitious Enos Collins, Samuel Cunard was a founder of the Halifax Banking Company. A widower at forty-one (his wife, Susan Duffus, had died in 1828 after bearing nine children in their thirteen years of marriage), he was customarily seen on Sundays escorting 'to the front pew of St George's Church on Brunswick Street a graduated procession of seven daughters and two sons.' By the time he was in his forties he had amassed a substantial personal fortune. He moved to England in 1858 and was made a baronet the following year, a reward for the services of his vessels in the Crimean War.

Samuel Cunard

A few years later, William Cunard began building a splendid brick house on the Oaklands property while the local citizenry watched with interest. On 30 May 1864 *The Halifax Evening Express* noted with enthusiasm:

The beautiful building in course of completion at Oaklands, near the N.W. Arm, for William Cunard, Esq., will be ready for occupation in about two months. The improvements on the grounds, such as laying out walks and making roads, are fast being completed, there being a number of men at work. We notice that Mr C. has purchased from the Hon. J.W. Ritchie, a small portion of the 'Belmont' property, through which he is making a fine, substantial road. At the entrance to the grounds there will be a very neat gate-way and a Porter's Lodge, and when the whole is completed it will equal anything of the kind in the Lower Provinces.

William's house did indeed seem equal to anything of its kind, even including a conservatory where he grew hundreds of pounds of grapes. It remained one of the most impressive houses in Halifax through the rest of the nineteenth century. Not long before his death, Samuel, on a visit from England, was driven along the mile-long road that led from the entrance gate through extensive grounds – they stretched from the Northwest Arm to Robie Street – to view with approval his son's grand Italianate villa.

Sharing Cunard's life at Oaklands was his wife, Laura Charlotte Haliburton, whom he had married in 1851. The third daughter of author, jurist, and historian Thomas Chandler Haliburton, Laura had been a girlhood friend of Ann Cunard, one of William's six sisters, and the families had been friends for years. Laura was a talented artist and her work had been exhibited at the Royal Academy in London, England. There one writer described her as 'a remarkably handsome, talented, and witty woman, and ... of a most generous and talented disposition.'

His mansion at Oaklands was not the only house to concern William Cunard in 1864. As a man with a social conscience, he was involved with the purchase of another Halifax house on Lockman Street – a half-way house, it would be called today. It was to serve as a refuge for women recently released from prison, to help them avoid being 'obliged to return to the house from whence they had been condemned to Rock Head [prison].' Some of the neighbours complained, but Cunard had pru-

William Cunard

dently secured the agreement of the owners of the adjacent properties, T.A. Anderson and W.B. Fairbanks, both of whom had no objections. Cunard then defended the home in a letter to *The Evening Express*, 4 May 1864:

The writer in the Express, asks how I should like to have had such a place nigh my own residence. I answer him that it would have been there, had a suitable house been found, as the locality would have been a more convenient one for the ladies who visit the institution ... He also objects, to use his own words, to place such an establishment under the eyes and noses of your wives, daughters and sons. I presume he takes the daily papers into his house, and that his wife, daughters and sons sometimes read the police reports, from which they will learn much more than they will from walking past this establishment.

Oaklands was to remain with the Cunards for only a short time. They moved to England, where they enjoyed life in houses every bit as splendid as their Halifax home – a town house on Eaton Square in London; a country place, Orleans House, 'once the home of Louis Phillipe and the Orleans family,' and a villa in Nice, where they spent their winters.

By 1871 Oaklands had become home to a man who had been a mayor of Halifax and who would shortly become premier of Nova Scotia – Philip Carteret Hill. His wife, Margaretta, was a daughter of Enos Collins. Philip Hill's father, a military man, had arrived in Halifax with the Royal Staff Corps in 1815. His mother, Hannah Binney, was a second cousin of the Rev. Hibbert Binney, bishop of Nova Scotia.

The Porter's Lodge at Oaklands, 1124 Robie Street

Philip Hill became premier in 1875, but three years later his Liberal government went down to defeat and he left politics. Four years later he too moved to England, where he spent the rest of his life. In later years the Oaklands estate was owned by Lord Alexander Russell, commander-in-chief of Britain's troops in Canada, after whose family Russell Square in London was named.

In the early 1900s, fire once again destroyed the elegant dwelling on the Oaklands estate. Today the 'neat gate-way' and the Porter's Lodge (1124 Robie Street) are all that remain. The iron gates and stone pillars by the lodge still stand as sturdy sentinels as they did when, for the better part of a century, carriages carrying the first families of Halifax passed between them.

In 1863, while William Cunard was busy formulating plans for Oaklands, another family member was moving to new, if less exalted, quarters. She was Margaret, widow of Edward Cunard, one of Samuel Cunard's younger brothers. Her new home, at 5270 Morris Street, built in 1834, was a typical 'Halifax house' – narrow, with a three-bay façade, pitched roof, off-centre door, and Scottish five-sided dormers. This last-named vernacular feature, popular from the 1820s and 1830s, had been introduced to the province by Scottish craftsmen.

Margaret Cunard's husband, Edward, had held various responsible roles in the family business, with registered vessels of his own. He had been in charge of the Halifax office before William took over the reins. He worked well with his two other brothers: Henry, quiet and retiring, and the flamboyant Joseph, both of whom directed the family's flourishing timber business and shipyards on the Miramichi in New Brunswick.

In 1864, the year that William Cunard moved to his Oaklands estate, another prominent Nova Scotian moved into a new home. Dr Charles Tupper had come to Halifax from Amherst seven years earlier, having established a fine reputation as a physician and subsequently doing the impossible – defeating the undefeatable Joseph Howe in Cumberland County in the election of 1855. (This setback gave Howe only momentary pause. He quickly relocated in another riding.) Tupper was handsome, articulate, financially secure, and a man endowed with great personal magnetism. He was popular with both sexes – known by opponents and supporters alike as the Ram of Cumberland County.

A year after Tupper so spectacularly humbled Joseph Howe, the Liberals were defeated and James W. John-

Five-sided Scottish dormers top Margaret Cunard's house at 5270 Morris Street

ston became premier. Charles Tupper was appointed to the cabinet as provincial secretary in 1857, and he and his wife moved with their young family to Halifax. Frances Tupper was known for her 'sweetness of disposition and high character.' She too was an Amherst native.

In 1864 Tupper became premier of Nova Scotia. That year he bought thirty acres (now the corner of Tupper Grove and Armview Avenue, at the foot of Quinpool Road) on the beautiful Northwest Arm, where the homes of Halifax's affluent families dotted the shore. By the following year, their new house, Armdale, was ready, and the Tuppers moved in. Armdale stood near the village which later adopted its name. From its windows they could see Melville Island, a military prison built during the Napoleonic Wars. Naval, then army prisoners, both French and American, had been held there.

Shortly after Tupper became premier, the province, as one local paper announced, extended an 'At Home' to Canada. On a bright summer day in August 1864, 'the cream,' the delegates who were en route to Charlottetown for the September conference on union, attended an outing on Bedford Bay:

After a perfect round of success in New Brunswick, the Canadians, 97 in number, arrived at Windsor on Wednesday last ... The admirable arrangements of the Hodge Podge and Chowder party of the Halifax Yacht Club, gave the whole party yesterday an opportunity of witnessing our matchless

Sir Charles Tupper's home, Armdale, in 1885

harbor and basin in all its glory. Under the flag we all love, on board the Dartmouth steamer, the Revenue Cutter, and half a dozen beautiful Yachts, three or four hundred British Americans, Canadians, New Brunswickers, and Nova Scotians, assembled on the shores of the Bedford Basin, on the grounds familiarly known as the Prince's Lodge, where the day passed delightfully in sport and feasting, and song, eloquence, and good fellowship, until the shades of evening came. (*The Acadian Recorder*, 13 August 1864)

Another account noted that the picnic had taken place at The Music Room of The Prince's Lodge,

formerly owned by H.R.H. Duke of Kent when he resided in this Province, and is now, or lately was, the property of Mrs Gore, the novelist ... On a grassy plot close-by there stood three or four long tables covered with the 'good things of this life' and towards these an eager multitude whose appetite had been merely stimulated on board ship wended their way in procession, two by two, with the band of the 16th at their head. Arrived there, leap-frog at once became the order of the day and a lively scene ensued. Members of the Upper House backed members of the Lower House with an agility perfectly wonderful. Blue-noses sprang over Canadians with a shriek of delight. Canadians bounded over New Brunswickers and tripped over Nova Scotians ... After leap-frog came racing on the green sward and again considerable distinction was won by Canadians, though the palm was carried off by Nova Scotia. (*The Halifax Evening Express*, 13 August 1864)

Speeches followed the athletic endeavours. First, Charles Tupper, representing Nova Scotia, welcomed the visitors. Then (for half an hour) D'Arcy McGee spoke, extolling the virtues of union, followed by Joseph Howe who praised 'the beautiful women of our colonies' – a subject on which Howe could speak with genuine enthusiasm. Suggesting that he praise Confederation would have been asking for trouble.

The reporter (who must have been 'from away') went on to explain the festive meal served to the honoured guests: '"Hodge Podge," ... is a very peculiar dish supposed to be made of mutton boiled with all sorts of vegetables till it becomes a very palatable soup. Chowder is composed of haddock sliced and boiled until a rather suspicious mixture is produced which obtains but little favour with those not accustomed to it.'

Everyone claimed the event an unqualified success,

with the exception of one soldier, a Sergeant Bull. It was his duty to tour the visiting Canadians around Citadel Hill, perhaps against his wishes. He brought the tour to an abrupt finish by informing his company that a light from one of their cigars 'had fallen on the magazine, which would probably blow up. Whereupon Canada made a hasty retreat' (*The Halifax Evening Express*, 19 August 1864).

Tupper was premier of Nova Scotia during the stormy period before Confederation. He led the Nova Scotia delegation to both the Charlottetown and Quebec conferences of 1864 at which the principles and terms of union were hammered out, and then won the subsequent hard-fought debate within the province against the anti-Confederation forces marshalled by Howe. (These years were not altogether without their lighter moments. When Tupper and three other Fathers of Confederation arrived in Charlottetown for the historic meeting, no one was on hand to greet them. A circus was in town – the first to visit Prince Edward Island in twenty years – and everyone preferred it to the Confederation debate, including some of the delegates themselves.)

Tupper's management of the union debate was the cause of much bitterness. Some felt he had bludgeoned Nova Scotia into Confederation. Whether a man with a more conciliatory nature would have managed better is uncertain, but his wishes carried the day. He firmly believed that Confederation would bring financial security, an industrial base, and, most important of all, the railway. Wilfrid Laurier, no admirer of Tupper's, had his opinion of Tupper's handling of the all-important issue of Confederation, as recorded by Joseph Schull in *Laurier*: 'Few men in the House had much respect for Tupper, the man who had bludgeoned Nova Scotia into Confederation, the eternal egoist and self-seeker, the politician's politician, who had none of the grace, none of the saving humour that had won Macdonald forgiveness for so much.'

Then as now, politicians had to deal with constituents' problems, even in the midst of more weighty, pre-Confederation concerns. One such letter, from a former patient, arrived on Tupper's desk in 1865:

Respected Friend: As you are aware my health has failed me and I received some medicine from you also that you kindly requested me to inform you of its effect. I am sorry to say that it done me but Little good. And I continue to be in rather an

unhealthy state. Still hoping that you can inform me as to
what will be best for me I take this opportunity of describing
as nearly as I can the features of my complaint at present ...

The unhappy man continued with a detailed list of
his every ailment: headaches, frothy spittle in the day-
time, matter gathering about his teeth at night, his disagreeable smell, his cough, and his constipation. He
closed by asking Tupper for a job – preferably with no
physical labour involved – suggesting that ticket-taker
for the railway would be his first choice. Tupper's reply
is not recorded.

In 1867 Charles Tupper left provincial politics and
won a federal seat as the only supporter of Confederation from Nova Scotia in the first federal Parliament.
That same year he was created a Companion of the Bath,
an appointment which he acknowledged from Armdale
on 16 August. In 1879 he was named Knight Commander of St Michael and St George and, in 1886, of
the Grand Cross of the same order. By 1884 he was
in London as Canada's High Commissioner to the
United Kingdom. In 1888 he was created a baronet. On
1 May 1896 he became prime minister of Canada.
Tupper had reached the pinnacle of his career, but the
following month, almost before he had time to settle
himself at the prime minister's desk, he suffered a stun-
ning general-election defeat. He resigned on 8 July, after
only ten weeks in office.

But the year had its high points, too. On 8 October
1896 Charles and Frances Tupper celebrated their
Golden Wedding Anniversary. It was, *The Ottawa Daily
Free Press* effused, the social event not only of the year,
but of the century (forgetting, perhaps, the Prince of
Wales's memorable tour in 1860). They were attended
by their surviving children, James Stewart, William Johnston, Sir Charles Hibbert, and Emma Cameron Gray,
as well as numerous grandchildren. Conservative
members and senators presented the couple with a
golden salver, made in Ottawa at a cost of more than
$1000; the family gave them a service of gold plate,
the Senate, a gold centre-piece. The Liberals, including
Wilfrid Laurier, sent good wishes.

Indomitable as always, Tupper continued as opposition leader but was defeated in the election of 1900
and retired to Vancouver. In 1907 he was made a
member of the Privy Council for Great Britain. Tupper
had been living in England for two years when he died,

at Bexleyheath, on 30 October 1915. He had outlived every other Father of Confederation.

Armdale was sold to MacCallum Grant, who was later to become lieutenant-governor of the province. Grant lived there until 1916, moving out just before cuts were made through Armdale's extensive grounds for what would become the Canadian National Railway, virtually destroying the estate. But Armdale itself survived. In the ensuing years the house was considerably altered, with unsympathetic additions sprouting in various directions. Its main identifying feature, however – a spectacular, steep central gable enhanced with decorative bargeboard – remains intact.

In 1866, when Armdale was newly completed, one of Tupper's closest friends, the brilliant Sandford Fleming, settled in Halifax in a frame house on Brunswick Street (now 2549-2553). The Flemings eventually moved to Ottawa, but they enjoyed Halifax so much that, in 1872, they decided to purchase a summer home by The Arm. In Ottawa they lived in a house they called Winterhome. Not surprisingly they called their vacation house in Halifax (1260 Blenheim Terrace) Summerholme. In later years it became, simply, The Lodge. A light-hearted, many-gabled villa, it had been the home of a successful and flamboyant merchant, William Duffus.

The Duffus saga in Canada began with the arrival in 1784 of William's grandfather (also William Duffus), then a young man of twenty-two. A native of Banff, Scotland, Duffus had spent a few years in London before

Armdale today, at Tupper Grove and Armview Avenue

embarking for Canada. (While in London he witnessed the Lord George Gordon Riots and was always eager to compare his account with that of Charles Dickens in *Barnaby Rudge*.) Little is known of his first wife, Mary, other than that she died at age twenty-eight, in 1792. Four of her five children died as infants and are buried with her, as is her son, James, who survived her.

The second Mrs Duffus was the attractive Susannah Murdoch, age twenty-one, one of eleven children of Rev. James Murdoch. She and William Duffus were considered the most handsome couple in Halifax as they rode out each day, she dressed in scarlet with a white beaver hat sporting a feather. No mention was made of William's attire, although he was described as a 'Taylor and Habit Maker,' so he too may have been a fashion plate. William's firm prospered in those halcyon days in Halifax, but when his London agent absconded with company funds, Duffus was unable to satisfy his creditors. Susannah of the scarlet cloak now advertised 'that she has fitted up the House formerly occupied by Mr Barney, No. 25 Granville-Street, as a genteel Boarding and Lodging House.'

Susannah took care to keep her family well away from her boarders and vice versa. The boarders, related a granddaughter, 'never by any chance saw her daughters, and the gentlemen were years in the house before they knew she had a family.' Two of those Duffus daughters married into the Cunard family – Susan, the up-and-coming Samuel in 1815, and Elizabeth his brother Henry, of Chatham, New Brunswick, five years later. Thanks to financial assistance from Samuel Cunard, Susannah Duffus was able to give up her boarders, and her home became 'the place above all others which her grandchildren loved to visit.'

William and Susannah had four other children. Their second son, John, headed the family's imported dry-goods business at the southeast corner of Granville and Buckingham streets. Duffus and Co., along with eight other drygoods firms, catered to the refined tastes of Haligonians, providing stylish wear from England and the continent. John and his wife, Jeannet Gronton, had four children, the youngest being William, born in 1841. He married Mary Elizabeth Davis of Pictou and built a house for her on the Northwest Arm.

The Duffus house, completed in 1871, is unique, with twenty-two small gables that dot the roof like the points in a crown, their windows brightening the bedrooms on the second floor. A verandah on two sides of the house encloses projecting bays. The elevated site adds importance to this fine house, and, when it was built, provided an unobstructed view of the waters of The Arm. In 1872, after only one year in his home, Duffus sold the house to Sandford Fleming.

When William Duffus died in 1916, an obituary in *The Acadian Recorder* noted that,

he was a lover of good horses and dogs. No one man probably did as much for 'the sport of kings' in this country as Mr Duffus; he was a promoter and one of the largest shareholders in the old Riding Ground, where officers of the army and navy and prominent citizens raced their horses and ponies, and where the present King George played polo ... [Duffus] imported valuable thoroughbreds, which took part in races against the best in the Maritime Provinces. In a word he was a great patron of sport, and his memory will long live among those who followed the turf in the Provinces years ago.

The new owner of the Duffus house, Sandford Fleming, and his friend Charles Tupper strode through nineteenth-century Canada. In an age of individualists, they stood apart. Both were intelligent, bold, farsighted,

Sandford Fleming's home, 1260 Blenheim Terrace

and blessed with boundless curiosity. Fleming had a vision of his country still shared by many today. In the summer of 1864, as delegates prepared for the Charlottetown Conference, he remarked to his friend D'Arcy McGee: 'Let the Canadians [from Upper and Lower Canada, now Ontario and Quebec] see that Maritimers are not covered with barnacles and let the Maritimers see that the Canadians don't wear horns. Its just silly notions like that which are holding up the union of British North America.'

Fleming was never short of creative ideas, and applied them with pragmatic precision. During a long and productive life he became Canada's foremost railway surveyor and construction engineer – surveyor for the railway that would link the country coast to coast. He promoted, until it became a reality, cable communication across the floor of the Pacific to unite Great Britain with her colonies around the world. He also advocated universal standard time, which, eventually, was adopted world-wide. And he designed and engraved Canada's first postage stamp, the threepenny beaver.

When he moved to Halifax in 1864, Sandford Fleming was supervising the construction of the Intercolonial Railway, and travelling along the line when necessary. By that time he had been nearly twenty years in Canada. He had emigrated from Kirkcaldy, Scotland, at age eighteen, with some background in engineering and surveying and a few letters of introduction. The voyage out with his brother David, on the *Brilliant*, seemed likely to be their last when, during a raging storm, iron bars restraining the cargo broke loose and crates tossed back and forth, crashing continuously against the hull. With each contact the ship was expected to shatter. In the midst of this turmoil, a cool-headed Fleming wrote a farewell note to his parents. The note was tucked in a bottle, the bottle corked then tossed overboard. The *Brilliant* survived the storm, as did the bottle. It was picked up by a fisherman on the Devon coast and forwarded to the Flemings in Kirkcaldy. Fortunately by the time it arrived they knew their boys were safe. It was the first of Fleming's many successful efforts at communication.

Young Sandford was tall and good-looking, with a shock of auburn hair. He stayed initially in Peterborough, Ontario, with a relative, Dr John Hutchison, but in spite of letters of introduction to some of the colony's most influential men, the only advice he received was

Sandford Fleming as a young man

that he would be wise to return to Scotland. Yet Fleming was determined to succeed. He had already made a survey of Peterborough, then engraved and printed it. The maps sold quickly, so he followed with others. Finally he moved to Toronto to survey there and study for the exams which would qualify him as a provincial land surveyor.

During his stay in Peterborough, Fleming met young Jeanie Hall; the daughter of a friend, James Hall, she was the woman who was to become his wife. One day in January 1854, when both had been in Toronto on separate visits, Sandford offered to accompany Jeanie on the return trip to Peterborough. Near home their sleigh overturned. Sandford was thrown against a stump and knocked unconscious. Later, he recalled in his journal:

upset passing farmers sleigh ... heads among horses feet ...
traces lose – horses ran away – furious! dreadful upset –
against stump – insensible – lay in snow some time – thought
ribs and breast bone broken. Fortunately Miss H. not
hurt ... managed to crawl up – met two highland women –
showed us to the nearest house – great pain all night. Miss H.
and Doctor very very attentive ...

Jeanie stayed to care for Sandford, and those few days of unplanned proximity worked wonders. One year later, on 3 January 1855, a happy Sandford Fleming wrote in his journal:

Preparation for our wedding, beautiful morning. Walked
from town to get Licence ... Rev. Mr. Rogers expected in two
or three minutes. It is now 11 o'clock. All ready to start off in
an hour, ceremony to take place at noon. 12 O'clock. Now
married to Jeanie Hall. After breakfast started off in spring
wagon back to Toronto. Clear sunshine. Stopped at Hotel in
Lindsay all night, spent the evening in same room that we did
exactly 12 months ago under different circumstances, afterwards quietly retired.

Fleming was a romantic. He returned to the site of the accident, recovered the stump that had caused the carriage to overturn, and carried it back to town. According to legend, he fashioned from it a cradle for their first child.

By 1852 Fleming had become assistant engineer, then chief engineer, responsible for the construction of the

Ontario, Simcoe and Huron Railroad, and its successor, the Northern Railway. It was completed in 1862. In the process he formed a vision – an idea that Canada would someday be linked by railway from sea to sea. He envisioned new communities, with communication between them, and new job opportunities, all following in the path of the rails. A year later the Intercolonial Railway beckoned and he was on his way to Halifax as its chief engineer. When complete, the line stretched from the south shore of the St Lawrence at Rivière-du-Loup, across the Gaspé, through Bathurst, New Brunswick, down to the Miramichi River, and across into Nova Scotia to Truro, where it linked up with lines to Halifax and Pictou.

Sandford and Jeanie Fleming moved into their beloved Summerholme on the Northwest Arm in 1872. Even when business took Fleming elsewhere in the winter, they happily returned every summer. The design of the house placed comfort as a priority, with a warm and elegant library directly off the large entrance-hall. Yet it was the perfect house for entertaining, with large living and dining areas and enough other rooms to house a growing family, a host of friends, and the requisite servants. And the year that the Flemings moved into Summerholme was the year that Sandford began the survey which led to the fulfilment of his earlier dream – a rail link from coast to coast.

Sandford Fleming left Halifax on the Intercolonial, travelling to Toronto, where the survey party assembled. Among them was Fleming's son, Franky, and a friend, Rev. George Monro Grant of Halifax, a leader in the

As Donald Smith drives the last spike for the Canadian Pacific Railway at Craigellachie, 7 November 1885, Sandford Fleming towers behind him

Presbyterian Church, described by one biographer as a 'muscular Christian.' He acted as secretary and later wrote of the expedition in his book *Ocean to Ocean.* The party, headed by Fleming, travelled on foot, by canoe, in wagons, and on horseback, across 2,000 miles of often treacherous terrain, across northern Ontario and the Prairies, and through the Rocky Mountains to the Pacific coast. It took them 103 days. Thirteen years later, on the morning of 7 November 1885, Donald Smith, whose financial backing had been crucial in the gigantic undertaking, drove the last spike on the Canadian Pacific Railway line. Behind him stood the towering figure of Sandford Fleming, his square grey beard a focal point in one of Canada's most famous photographs.

It is thanks also to Fleming that the world operates on one standard time. Until late in the nineteenth century, time systems were chaotic. Travelling on the Intercolonial line, Fleming found that every town and village had its own time, a few minutes different from that of the last stop. Frequent travellers carried a variety of watches, each showing the time at different locations. When the situation was compounded world-wide, total confusion resulted. Fleming advocated a system based on a prime meridian at Greenwich, with twenty-four time zones that circled the globe. In 1879 he presented the idea to the Royal Canadian Institute (which he had founded) and his paper was then circulated. An immediate and positive response came from the Czar of Russia. After stubborn objections from the usual nay-sayers, the plan – still in use today – was adopted around the world on 1 January 1885.

Many honours were heaped on this remarkable man, not the least of which was a knighthood. But perhaps the most meaningful tribute was his appointment as chancellor of Queen's University, in Kingston, Ontario, where his old friend George Grant was principal. Fleming had never been to college, and this great honour affected him deeply. He remained in that position from 1880 until his death in Halifax in 1915. Not long before he died, he reflected on his life, and on his 'good fortune to have [had his] lot cast in this goodly land.'

Fleming left the citizens of Halifax a generous bequest of land at the Dingle on the Northwest Arm. (The origin of the name Dingle has never been determined: some claimed it was named after Dingle Bay in Ireland, but more likely it is because the word means a deep wooded valley or dell.) Now called Fleming Park, it boasts a tower designed by Fleming to commemorate the institution of representative government in Nova Scotia in 1758. It can be seen from a window in one of the many peaked gables that crown Fleming's Summerholme.

In 1914, a year before her father's death, the Flemings' daughter, Lily Enshaw, bought the house. It remained in her hands until 1939. During some of those years it was leased (for a time to a Dalhousie University fraternity), but it withstood the vagaries of various tenants. Now restored, it shows the results of meticulous attention.

When railways were built in Canada they changed the face of the country forever. Their arrival was greeted with enthusiasm in most quarters, but certainly so in Halifax, where an item in *The Morning Chronicle* of 8 July 1854 cheerfully announced:

Good News For The Ladies. It is said that upwards of Forty connubial Co-partnerships were entered into in this city during the last 'leafy month' of June. This beats by all odds any previous performances of Hymen, in Halifax, for a corresponding month. If such happy results have attended the commencement of the Railroad, what may not be expected from its consummation!

CHAPTER NINE

Dartmouth

FORGOTTEN PATRIOTS, LEGEND, AND SONG

Land on the spectacular Northwest Arm where Cunard, Tupper, and Fleming built their estates had been, for one brief period, home to a group of people for whom 'home' was an elusive concept. These were refugees from the United States, escaped slaves who had hoped to obtain their promised freedom by siding with Great Britain during the War of 1812.

The summer of 1815 saw seventy-six of these refugees huddled in makeshift dwellings on 5,000 wooded acres near the present Armdale Rotary. This location, like so many others for the blacks, would be only temporary. The land was theirs legally by a grant from Queen Victoria, but none the less these homeless ones were soon forced to move on. They were only a few of nearly 2,000 black refugees who came to Nova Scotia after that war, settled, and, with the inspiring leadership of an escaped slave, Richard Preston, established more than twenty churches in the province – churches that proved to be their mainstay in a less than welcoming environment.

While the black refugees of 1815 came north of their own free will, black slaves and indentured servants had been in the province for years. Slaves were brought to Nova Scotia in the 1760s as 'possessions' of the New England Planters (settlers). Advertisements for the purchase and sale of slaves appeared in the newspapers of the day:

WANTED, to purchase, A NEGRO WOMAN, about 25 or 30 years of Age, that understands Country work and the management of a Dairy, she must be honest and bear a good character. Enquire of the PRINTER. (*The Nova Scotia Gazette and Weekly Chronicle*, 28 May 1776)

The main influx of blacks, however, came following

the American Revolution. During that war, escaped slaves were promised their freedom if they agreed to fight for the Crown. It was said that up to 100,000 slaves, one-fifth of the total black American population, fled to the British army. When the British evacuated Boston in 1776, an entire black regiment known as the 'Company of Negroes' was taken to Halifax. In all, nearly 3,000 black Loyalists came to Nova Scotia after that war; almost half landed in Shelburne in 1783 along with the thousands of white Loyalists who were settling there. Birchtown, a settlement near Shelburne, became one of the largest black communities outside Africa.

For the newly free blacks, the promises of land proved hollow. They received the poorest land – and less of it. (In Shelburne County, the average land grant to blacks amounted to less than half that given to the white Loyalists.) The best land and supplies went first to those who had lost the most, and to the military. Free blacks were last in line. Isolated in separate communities, they waited years for their land, such as it was. Even so, free blacks were somewhat better off than were the slaves – 1,232 of them – brought to Nova Scotia by their Loyalist owners.

In 1792, after years of discouragement, about 1,200 free blacks left for Sierra Leone to settle in a British-sponsored colony of their own. Those who remained in scattered black communities were the less skilled, the weak, and the infirm.

Four years later, in July 1796, 550 Maroons arrived on the scene from Jamaica. Fierce mountain fighters, the Maroons were the descendants of escaped slaves who had disappeared into the hills of Jamaica when their Spanish owners were driven from the island by the British in the 1650s. In the ensuing years they hid in remote mountain regions, making daring raids on the island's sugar plantations, and welcoming to their ranks increasing numbers of escaped slaves. Nothing the English did could dislodge them. For much of the eighteenth century they remained a problem to Jamaica's white settlers until, in December 1795, they were finally defeated; when they were expelled the following summer, their support was guaranteed by the Jamaican government.

Proud, capable, and in splendid physical condition, the Maroons were initially welcomed to Halifax with uncommon respect. Governor John Wentworth put them to work rebuilding fortifications on Citadel Hill. Four years later, discouraged by the harsh, unfamiliar climate, and unwelcome since the Jamaican government had stopped paying their expenses, they asked to be sent to a place where the climate was more like Jamaica's. Soon they were on their way to Sierra Leone to join the black Loyalists already there. But there was a more sinister reason for this choice of locale. The Loyalists already in Sierra Leone were protesting further unkept promises, and this simmering revolt had to be put down. Who better to accomplish this than the Maroons? As historian Pearleen Oliver has related: 'It proved disastrous for the Loyalist black Nova Scotians, but all in the line of duty for the Warrior Maroons who now had not only the joy of fighting and killing, but the hot climate of Sierra Leone to put down their roots.'

This was the situation when Richard Preston and other refugees arrived after the War of 1812. The first black settlers had come, and already half had gone. Richard Preston's arrival in 1815 was connected with an event considered to be a miracle. Back in Virginia he had been separated from his mother – a common practice among slave-owners, who deliberately broke up families – but he had heard that she had been taken to Canada by the British. When he escaped from slavery he set out with nothing more concrete than this knowledge, but he was determined to find her. Discouraged, he had almost given up his search when he discovered his mother living near Dartmouth in a township called Preston, named for an English settler. To celebrate his gratitude, he adopted the name as his own.

Rev. Richard Preston

Richard Preston was a mulatto, six foot one inch tall and 'of regal bearing.' He had taught himself to read and write, although education of slaves was virtually forbidden in the Southern states, and a slave caught with even the smallest piece of printed paper was subject to severe whippings or mutilation – 'for to educate a Negro was to unfit him (her) for a slave.' Preston was later chosen to be trained for the ministry in England. He often told his parishioners of this 'miracle,' and no doubt the story was well known in his first church, the African United Baptist Church (now the Cornwallis Street United Baptist Church) at 5475 Cornwallis Street in Halifax.

A simple frame building, with pure, classic lines, the design of the church indicates that the funds available for its construction did not extend to unnecessary ornamentation. It was 1832, and Preston, then in his early forties, had just returned from England, newly ordained and with £50 in his pocket to help build the little church – funds donated by English Baptists. He petitioned the House of Assembly for support in buying land on which to build, citing 'circumstances of an unpleasant nature' that existed between 'white and coloured members of the Baptist Church in Halifax.' In fact, black people were not generally permitted to worship in any church unless they sat in especially built galleries. The assembly pried open the public purse a trifle and offered £25, a recommendation subsequently overturned by the Council. Nevertheless, Preston's church was completed in time to joyfully celebrate Britain's abolishment of slavery on 1 August 1834. Exultant voices soared in the little church as parishioners sang:

> Sound the loud timbrels
> O'er Egypt's dark sea,
> Jehovah hath triumphed
> His people are free.

(Some consolation could be taken in the fact that, by the time slavery was abolished in British North America, there was little slavery left to abolish since most blacks had by then obtained their freedom. Many owners had already granted freedom to their slaves in their wills. They were influenced by society's growing disapproval of slavery, and the anti-slavery stance of public figures such as Chief Justices Andrew Strange and Salter Blow-

Cornwallis Street United Baptist Church, 5475 Cornwallis Street, Halifax

ers of Nova Scotia and Ward Chipman of New Brunswick, all of whom had made their views well known.
Not coincidentally, slavery in Canada had also become
uneconomic.)

Behind Preston's church was a small parsonage where
he lived with his wife, Barbara Mapleby. A spellbinding,
witty orator, Preston literally walked the province, helping blacks establish churches, serving as the pastor of
many, and working tirelessly for emancipation. In 1844
he helped found the Beech Hill church, erected for the
refugees who, nearly thirty years earlier, had spent a brief
sojourn on the Northwest Arm after the War of 1812.
He served as its pastor until his death in 1861.

In the same year that he helped the Beech Hill people
build their church, Richard Preston assisted the Baptists
of Dartmouth in a similar enterprise, a 'meeting house
and cemetery' on Crichton Avenue. But it was too small
and in an inconvenient location, so in 1906 the congregation accepted an offer by the Anglicans of Christ
Church to use their Sunday-School building. It was
moved to its present location on Victoria Road, where
it is now known as the Victoria Road United Baptist
Church.

In spite of problems for some, Nova Scotia was indeed seen as a haven for the persecuted at the end of
the war-torn eighteenth century. Adversity brought another group of settlers to the colony after the American
Revolution. These were whalers from Nantucket Island,
part of a population of 5,000 to 6,000, mainly Quakers,
who, until hostilities began, had operated the greatest
whaling fleet in the colonies, supplying England with
sperm oil for street lamps, medicine, and cosmetics.
Choosing from faith not to fight, they had become in-
creasingly uncomfortable in the United States during
and after the war. When peace returned, their trade with
Britain was crippled by high tariffs imposed against
goods from the new United States. They then looked
to Nova Scotia, their British neighbour to the north.
The move seemed inviting and, with Nova Scotia's offer
of a large subsidy for housing, irresistible.

Thus, in 1785, about twenty-four Quaker families left
their Nantucket homes for Dartmouth, where 150 acres
of harbour land were waiting for them, plus extensive
property outside the town. That the site was sparsely
settled was not because it was unattractive but the result
of an event that had taken place thirty-four years earlier.
The *Alderney*, an old but roomy naval vessel bought by

a London merchant and converted into a transport ship (with the relative comfort of five-foot headroom between decks), had brought 353 passengers to Halifax in 1750. Governor Edward Cornwallis and his council, after considering sites on the Bedford Basin and the Northwest Arm, decided to settle them across the harbour, now the site of Dartmouth.

A town was laid out in eleven oblong-shaped blocks, lots were apportioned, and a blockhouse built. But in May 1751 a ferocious Indian attack took place, with reports that men, women, and children were butchered. Accounts of the carnage varied, some claiming that half, others that nearly all the population had been massacred; Cornwallis's official report, however, listed only four dead and six taken prisoner. Two things resulted: a palisade was erected around the whole town plot, and many of the surviving settlers departed. From that time until the arrival of the Quakers, only soldiers and a determined population (193 in 1752) remained. Among them was one John Connor, who, on 3 February 1752, was allowed to begin a ferry service from Dartmouth to Halifax. It continues to this day.

The assembly, eager for a fine new source of revenue, was happy to welcome the Quakers. They came with brigantines, a schooner, and the equipment for whaling. This potentially lucrative industry lived up to expectations by bringing in nearly 15,000 barrels of oil in its first year of operation, fitting out 9 vessels and employing 126 men. Members of the assembly, rubbing their hands in delight, accommodated them with the prom-

Victoria Road United Baptist Church, Dartmouth

William Ray house, 59 Octerlony Street, Dartmouth

ised subsidy, a magnanimous £1500 to build twelve two-family homes. Governor John Parr wrote enthusiastically that 'The affairs of the Quakers of Nantucket is of the greatest moment in this province.'

One of the new arrivals was William Ray, age thirty-eight, whose occupation as a cooper made him a significant member of the whaling community. Ray, with his wife, Elizabeth Coffin, and their children, was among a group of sixty-eight, the first to arrive from Nantucket. His double house (59 Octerlony Street) was built with framing supplied by the government, on a foundation of split stone and brick. The house, nearly forty square feet in size, was built as a 'salt box,' but the roof was later lifted and bedrooms added to the second floor. The kitchen and living rooms were warmed by a central fireplace. The house was completed by 1786. Two years later Elizabeth Coffin Ray died. William remarried in short order. His new wife had the same name: she was Elizabeth Coffin (née Swain), the widow of fellow whaler David Coffin.

Soon the Nantucket whalers became victims of their own success. It sent them packing. They had, in their second year of operation, taken more than 22,000 barrels of spermacite oil, but the British government was watching with a covetous eye. First, it barred any further immigration of whalers from Nantucket Island. Then, with pressure from British mercantile interests, it insisted that a reluctant Governor Parr remove the whalers, allowing them to resettle in Milford Haven, Wales, where they would be under British control, their whaling profits filling Britain's coffers. By 1791 they were leaving Dartmouth. Ray sold his Octerlony Street house and departed for Wales with the second Elizabeth Coffin Ray and their family. Two hundred years later, after many subsequent owners, the old Quaker house was purchased by the City of Dartmouth and is now part of the Dartmouth Heritage Museum. It is open to the public.

Evergreen, on Newcastle Street, Dartmouth, dates back to 1867 when it was completed for Alexander James, a teacher, lawyer, and judge. He had purchased the property from James Creighton, Jr, in 1862. (Creighton, who had settled in Dartmouth in 1800, was the son of a settler who had arrived at Halifax with Cornwallis.) The property stretched down to the harbour. James retained Henry Elliot as architect.

Evergreen combines Victorian and vernacular Nova

Scotian styles. The south (or harbour) side has the appearance of a Victorian mansion, while the north side, facing Newcastle Street, is an unadorned two-storey frame building with a central gable on a three-bay façade. Seen from the Newcastle Street side, the house appears to be of modest size, while in fact it is a substantial twenty-room dwelling.

Evergreen stood in solitude at the top of a hill overlooking the harbour. After Judge James's death in 1889, his widow, Harriet Hawthorne, stayed on for a time. By 1921 Evergreen was the home of Charles E. Creighton. His daughter, Helen, born in 1899, lived there from 1921 until 1978, when she sold it to the City of Dartmouth. The house is now part of the holdings of the Dartmouth Heritage Museum.

A year before moving into Evergreen, Helen Creighton settled herself at the wheel of a Red Cross ambulance and travelled to isolated towns and villages in Nova Scotia, delivering medical supplies. Then, after a few years of social work in Toronto, and a sojourn with one of her brothers in Mexico, she returned to Dartmouth, making the first contacts in what was to become her life's work – listening to songs and stories in the kitchens and parlours of the province. In a life-

Evergreen, Newcastle Street, built in 1867, later the home of folklorist Helen Creighton

time's labour of love, Helen Creighton captured and recorded the oral tradition of Atlantic Canada, preserving it through folklore and song.

By the time she was twenty-seven, Helen Creighton was a 'radio aunt,' telling her stories to 'radio nieces and nephews' across Canada. Having received three Rockefeller Foundation scholarships and with experience collecting for the Library of Congress, she joined the staff of the National Museum of Canada, where she remained for twenty years. She recorded an incredible 4,000 songs in English, French, Mi'kmaq, Gaelic, and German. In her autobiography, *A Life in Folklore* (1975), Helen Creighton described how she rescued from oblivion the lilting words and music of 'Farewell to Nova Scotia,' a ballad loved today by Nova Scotians, and those who wish they were.

Helen Creighton wrote twelve books, the most popular being *Bluenose Ghosts*. She told of 'forerunners' – mysterious happenings such as the three knocks foretelling imminent death; a buried treasure and the ghost of the sailor who was buried alive to guard it; phantom appearances on land or at sea; and other strange phenomena.

Creighton claimed that she had a sixth sense for such happenings. One day, when she was just eighteen, it saved her life. On the morning of 6 December 1917 she was asleep in a room with a friend when suddenly they were awakened by an immense explosion. As Rosemary Bauchman records in *The Best of Helen Creighton*, Helen shouted to her friend, 'Duck, Doris, duck.' A moment later the ceiling collapsed. Glass and nails from a heavy window lay where Helen's head had just rested. Later, she mused, 'Was it the sixth sense inherited with my caul, my guardian angel, ... that caused me to shout?' At 8:45 that morning the Belgian vessel *Imo* had collided with the French munitions carrier *Mont Blanc*. Benzol, picric acid, TNT, and guncotton were ignited, and the munitions ship blew sky high. It caused what was at that time the world's greatest man-made explosion. The north end of Halifax was destroyed. The blast, subsequent tidal wave, and fire killed 1,600 people and injured 9,000. Hundreds were blinded by flying glass. Helen Creighton had survived the Halifax Explosion.

THE SOUTH SHORE

CHAPTER TEN

Chester and Mahone Bay

It is said that the waters of Mahone Bay and the land around them are haunted. Maybe they are. Certainly there have been enough ships and men lost in the fog, on the rocks of its 365 islands, or through attack by foreign vessels to make the legends of phantoms in the night seem as real as the fog through which they move. And is there buried treasure on Oak Island, the mile-and-a-half-long island forty-five miles southwest of Halifax in Mahone Bay? (Captain Kidd's gold perhaps? The Holy Grail? Marie Antoinette's personal fortune? Blackbeard's booty? All have been subjects of speculation.) The search has brought death to some but fortune to none since the discovery of shafts and tunnels there in 1795.

But if the area is haunted, it is also haunting, and that is simply because of its beauty.

Mahone Bay stretches from the Aspotogan Peninsula to Lunenburg. In 1759, ten years after the founding of Halifax, a Crown grant of 100,000 acres was made to Captain Timothy Houghton of Massachusetts in the area then called Shoreham, now known as Chester, on Mahone Bay – 100 acres for each settler he brought and 50 for every member of his family. It signalled the government's intention to fill the area west of Halifax with reliable, hard-working New England Planters (the old English word for settlers).

Houghton arrived with his wife and three children on 4 August 1759, accompanied by twenty-one other settlers, Captain Robert McGown, his son Robert, his first mate, and one seasick preacher, Jonathan Seccombe. They had sailed from Boston six days previously. Seccombe kept a diary during that six-day voyage, entering on its pages in graphic detail his daily struggles with his heaving stomach:

30 July 1759: Set sail from Boston between 11 and 12 Clock
AM ... Began to vomit at 5 Clock PM.

For the remainder of the voyage Seccombe made note
of every mouthful of a diet of tea, broiled pork, and
cucumbers. He also managed to record other notable
events, such as when, on their second day, 'Mr Houghton's Calf jumped overboard, but was saved.'

Jonathan Seccombe was an articulate and gifted Congregationalist minister whose vocation was the last that
would have been expected when, as a student at Harvard
College, he had distinguished himself for his pranks and
wit, his stealing and lying, and not much else. His or-
dination as a minister of a Congregationalist parish in
Harvard at the age of twenty-five did nothing to curb
his natural zest for cards, food, and drink. Even marriage to a wealthy and religious young woman, Mercy
Williams, the daughter of an eminent clergyman, could
not keep his spirits down.

The Williams family wealth was not spared in providing the young couple with a mansion renowned for
having the longest row of elm trees in New England,
a stand that extended from their estate to Jonathan's
meeting-house. But in short order both Seccombe's ministry and his marriage were in trouble. A variety of accusations, from infidelity to vague criminal matters,
pursued him, with Mercy one of the most vocal in pursuit. He made public apology in church but then seemed
to offend with his style of preaching, which some found
to be New Light (an evangelical ministry, later spread
through Nova Scotia by a charismatic preacher, Henry
Alline).

Finally dismissed from his parish, Seccombe decided
to leave Harvard and establish his ministry in Nova Scotia among the New England Planters. Mercy, having said
her piece to all and sundry, elected to follow when he
was established. Thus Seccombe found himself, in August 1759, seasick and on his way to a new home. The
arrival was memorable:

August 4 [1759]: A Fine morning. we saw divers islands –
Cathartic – at 10 clock a.m. arrived at Chester and wieghd
Anchor in a most beautifull Harbour; a hot day – many
guns fir'd at our arrival.

By the following Sunday he was preaching, his seasickness forgotten, if not his diet:

August 9: Lords day. Fair pleasant day. same Breakfast as yesterday. [Tea, Cake, Apple pye, and Gooseberry Tart]. Preach'd A.M. 2 Sam. 7 10 P.M. Luk 7.34 Din'd on fresh Cod fish. Dutch people from Mushee-Mush. about 12 miles bro't to sell, Turneps and Beans; and Butter at 6s/2d. pr. pound. – Fir'd Guns at going off. – supp'd on Fresh fish, apple pye, Goose berry Tart, Cake and Cheese.

By all accounts, Jonathan Seccombe became a new man in his new home. He was a gripping preacher. In 1776 he was charged with preaching a seditious sermon, but he must have satisfied the authorities, for he was soon preaching again in Halifax. By 1779 he had achieved such renown for his preaching that his printed sermons sold for a shilling. He was widely respected by all in the dissenting churches for his devotion and self-sacrifice.

Mercy and the five children joined Jonathan at Chester in 1763. Either domestic bliss reigned or Mercy ceased to make her complaints public. Seccombe built a home for his family on Wake-Up Hill the year they arrived. The name originated from the Mi'kmaq 'wecob,' meaning 'wigwam'; from this came 'Wake-Up,' but then the name was changed again, full circle, back to 'Wecob.' The Seccombe's house and the hill are known by this name today.

The house is a 'three-quarter Cape,' with a full two-window section on one side of the door and a single-window portion on the other. The building's framing was brought from Cape Cod, assembled and pegged. The main floor had a parlour and a kitchen divided by

Seccombe house, 'Wecob,' Wake-up Hill, Chester

a wall with back-to-back fireplaces. Two bedrooms and a tiny 'borning,' or 'birthing' room made up the first floor. Stairs led to the loft above where Wecob's ghost resides – a girl who stands in one corner, then quietly disappears.

At his death in 1792 Seccombe left the house and buildings – 'My house lot Number sixty-nine (commonly called Pleasant Point) with all the buildings thereon and all such livestock as shall remain undisposed of' – to Mercy. He wrote this will in 1779, but he also wrote a more entertaining poetic version. In his *History of the County of Lunenburg*, M.B. DesBrisay includes thirteen verses of Seccombe's last wishes in doggerel:

> To my dear wife,
> My joy and life,
> I freely now do give her
> My whole estate
> With all my plate –
> Being just about to leave her.
>
> My tub of soap
> A long cast rope,
> A frying pan and kettle
> An ashes pail
> A threshing flail,
> An iron wedge and beetle.

Jonathan, leaving nothing to chance, was determined to mention his every possession, even including his beetle (a heavy tool used for ramming, crushing, etc.).

At Mercy's death, Wecob was inherited by her children, Mercy, Hannah, John, and Willis. Hannah; her husband, Ebenezer Fitch, and their six children lived in the old homestead. The house then passed to their son, John Seccombe Fitch, who married Mary Hawbolt. Then, in 1840, Wecob came into the hands of one George Hawbolt, probably a relative. It stayed in his family for the next 129 years.

In 1969 the house, empty for several years, was sold and restored. It was discovered that little had changed since 1763. Some shingles were original, as were the wide floor boards, beams, frame, birch-bark insulation in the walls, and sections of hand-painted wallpaper. It stands today in trim simplicity, typical of the many such houses built by Nova Scotia's first settlers.

One of Seccombe's legacies was his diary. It provides

fascinating glimpses into life at Chester in 1759 (along, of course, with a record of his every mouthful of food):

3 September ... Arrived at Mrs. Clap's at Goreham's point at 12 – din'd on a Pudding with Raisons and Plumbs in it – Boild Pork and Pigeons – Cariots, spinish, Potatoes, Beans, Squash, Cucumbers, new Cheese, Boild corn – Good Claret and Beer. Current jelly etc.

16 September. Cloudy, cold. Wind East. Paul Labadore an Indian, brought 5 Patridges to Mr Bridges, who lately killed four Moose, and two Bears. brot also Dry'd Moose and Tallow. din'd on salt Fish, Cariots, Eggs and Spanish Potatoes.

27 September. Lords day ... Preached all day from Tit. 2 11. For ye Grace of God etc – Fresh Bever for dinner, fry'd.

And he ministered to the particular needs of the time:

20 December. Visited James Morrison in the morning being under Sentence of Death for Desertion.
Monday. Visited the Prisoner again.
Tuesday. Visited the Prisoner again.
Wednesday. Visited the poor Prisoner, and attended him to the place of Execution where he was shot about 12 Clock.

On his arrival in 1759, Jonathan Seccombe recorded that, after a salute by gunfire, the party 'went on Shore and refresh'd our selves at Mr Bridge's.' Benjamin Bridge, a surveyor, had been living at Shoreham for eight years. Others who entertained, and undoubtedly fed, Jonathan Seccombe were Philip Knaut, established in Lunenburg for eight years by then, and Jonathan Prescott, formerly of Littleton, Massachusetts, the area's first doctor.

Prescott had taken part in the British siege of Louisbourg in 1745 as a young volunteer and, after the French fortress was captured, received grants along the south shore of Nova Scotia. Part of his new land was in Chester, 300 acres at Prescott Point and two nearby islands. By the time Seccombe landed, then thirty-six, Prescott had been there three years. He and his second wife, Ann Blagden, raised five sons and five daughters. (One of the sons, Charles Ramage Prescott, settled in the Annapolis Valley, at Starr's Point, and brought the first Gravenstein apple trees to the valley.)

Soon after they arrived, those first settlers in Chester

built a blockhouse to protect their community from attack by French or Indians. Little did they realize that it would later protect them from attack by their former countrymen. Privateers knew the coast of Nova Scotia well, and the sight of an American vessel rounding a point was part of life during the years when wars legitimized these attacks. The towns of the South Shore got frequent unpleasant surprises, but they rose to defend themselves with remarkable bravado and ingenuity and were usually successful in repelling the assault. In one such assault, legend holds that it was Jonathan Prescott who saved Chester.

Prescott's house had been burned three times by raiders of one sort or another. As a result, in 1782 the Crown awarded him the right to live in the blockhouse and be in charge of the town's defences. He moved into the building which had been completed in the late 1760s, and which had since served as barracks and haven to the community.

That June, a local fisherman was kidnapped and forced to guide three American privateers through the islands of Mahone Bay to the harbour at Chester. There they fired on the village. The timing was bad. Chester's militia (every man between the ages of sixteen and sixty) was away from town and therefore out of reach, leaving Prescott and a son in charge of Chester's security. Help from Lunenburg would take a day to arrive. To make matters worse, when Prescott checked the gunpowder he found it was bad. After sporadic firing the Americans called out, saying that one of their men had been killed and they wanted to discuss a burial. Prescott told them

The blockhouse, Chester

to lay down their arms and come to the blockhouse.

What followed became the stuff of local poetry and song. Prescott had his son hail him in the middle of the conference and announce that a hundred men would soon be arriving from Lunenburg and needed billeting. When he left to attend to the billeting, his American 'guests' made a quick exit. Next day, realizing that this ruse would not hold water for long, Prescott called on the women of the village to help save their homes. Customarily these women wore grey cloaks lined in red. Prescott had them turn their cloaks inside out and parade in front of the barracks, broomsticks at the ready. From a distance, their brooms looked like rifles. The privateers, it is said, were duped and departed, the next day turning their fire on Lunenburg.

The original blockhouse that was Prescott's home forms only part of the blockhouse which stands today. Quarters were cramped. A cooking fireplace dominated the small main room, used for cooking, eating, and work. That, and an adjacent bedroom comprised the first floor. Stairs led to two bedrooms above, each with its own fireplace.

In 1885 the blockhouse was purchased by John and Sarah Wister of Philadelphia. They more than doubled its size. The main floor of the addition included two parlours with back-to-back fireplaces connected to a central chimney, as in the Seccombe house, and bedrooms above, each with a fireplace. At one time, cannons on the hill in front of the house pointed out to sea.

If there was any doubt about the accuracy of shots lobbed into the fledgling village of Chester by American privateers, one present owner found proof by his front door – a three-inch cannonball buried a foot deep. For Simeon Floyd, who in 1764 built the house now known as The Quarterdeck, as for most other New Englanders, this missive from home was decidedly unwelcome. Family divisions during the wars with England were painful and long lasting, and relatives frequently found themselves on opposite sides of the independence fence. Simeon Floyd now thought of himself as a Nova Scotian. A cousin, William Floyd, was a relative who remained in New York. He later was a signatory to the Declaration of Independence.

The Floyd house on Queen Street, a Cape Cod cottage, has had only four owners in the last 200 years. One of them operated a small boatyard on the property, and built boats in a shed where a garage now is situated.

There is evidence of this activity in the construction of the house. The drawing-room wall curves a full ninety degrees: the wainscoting is solid wood but has been bent in a manner which indicates that a steam box, such as would be used in boat building, was available. The house was constructed of hemlock boards covered in birch bark for insulation. In the basement the owners found gingham, of the type used in petticoats, substituted for the birch bark.

One of Chester's ghosts is connected with a tall frame house known as White Cottage. It had been standing for more than fifteen years when, in June 1813, an American privateer, the *Young Teazer*, exploded in Mahone Bay. Its inhabitants had front-row seats for a maritime drama, a chase connected with the War of 1812.

The *Young Teazer* had become a terror along the eastern seaboard. On 25 June, its crew had sailed brazenly into Nova Scotia waters, and before long five local vessels gave chase, pursuing her from Halifax towards Lunenburg. She was finally surrounded in Mahone Bay – when she exploded. Presumably the magazine had been ignited intentionally. The suspect was Frederick Johnston, first lieutenant of the *Young Teazer*. He had been captured in an earlier encounter and removed to Halifax, and there had taken an oath never again to attack one of the king's ships. He knew that, should the *Young Teazer* be taken, he would be hanged.

Only eight of the crew survived the explosion. According to local legend, the bodies of two of the dead sailors were carried to the basement of White Cottage and the 'Yankee sympathizer who retrieved the bodies' was shot. The house stands today, on Water Street, little

The White Cottage, Water Street, Chester

changed, its dominant feature a large door with side-lights and transom. One can assume that the bodies were not carried into the house through this fine door, but at night through some basement entrance, since any favour shown to a Yankee, living or dead, could bring a charge of treason. The ghost of the dead Yankee is said to walk the house, and a pale blue light is sometimes seen through an attic window – another of the tall tales that all began when the *Young Teazer*'s brief life came to an end and it joined the ghost ships that legend says still sail the bay.

At the western end of the bay is the town of Mahone Bay, instantly recognizable by the trio of churches that stand at the water's edge: the Anglican St James, with its painted steeple, the chaste white St John's Lutheran, and Trinity United, also painted white but notable because, somewhere along the way, it has lost its steeple.

On a hill overlooking Mahone Bay stands a Cape Cod cottage whose current pristine condition is owing to a careful and well-researched restoration. It was built by one of three German brothers, tenant farmers who came as 'foreign Protestants' in the hope of becoming landowners in 'Neu Schottland.'

Theirs was a story typical of the many men and women who settled in the Lunenburg/Mahone Bay area. The Eisenhauer brothers – Hans Adam, Johannes, and Johan George – had taken up an offer of free land, free passage, and provisions for a year tendered by John Dick, agent for the Lords of Trade and Plantations for England. The offer was intended to entice good German settlers to Nova Scotia.

If land ownership was the up side for the brothers,

George Eisenhauer house,
Mahone Bay

there was a down side as well: crossing an ocean that was fourteen weeks wide, jammed in with 264 other men, women, and children (32 of whom were buried at sea); their first look at Neu Schottland ('Gott in Himmel. Das ist ein forst!'); a year in rowdy Halifax, then two years old and a town of huts, brawls, and debauchery. But they found there new and close associations with other Germans, most of whom gathered at the Little Dutch Church.

Their reward came in 1753. George Eisenhauer (then only nineteen), Hans Adam, and Johannes drew lots in Lunenburg. George left Halifax at the end of May that year, with a pouch of Spanish silver saved for a rainy day. (He never spent it, although there were many such days.) What followed was a year of desperate hardship, cold, and hunger – so difficult that, when their shoes wore out that winter, they had to wait until the government issued one pair of boots per household before venturing very far from home in the snow.

The hardships, however, were worth it. They still owned their land. In 1759 George sold his Lunenburg acreage and bought a beautiful site on a hill overlooking Mahone Bay, at a spot called Oakland. Here he moved with his wife, Catherine Margareta Morizar, originally from the Palatinate, whom he had met in Lunenburg. Nine sons and four daughters were born to them.

The Eisenhauers built a house of pine, well seasoned on their own property. The house had a large cooking fireplace with a bake-oven, ornamental carving on the wall cupboards, and, through a door off the parlour, a borning (or birthing) room – a tiny bedroom, put to good use it would seem, given the thirteen babies who arrived on the scene. The family also enjoyed one particular extravagance, a luxury that harked back to George's long Atlantic voyage and the putrid, contaminated water he had been forced to drink. He dug three wells close by his home so that his family would never thirst for pure, sweet, water.

George died at age seventy-two, in 1805. His son, George, Jr, then twenty-nine, inherited the house and part of the property. He and his wife, Anna Barbara Lantz, filled it with eleven children and the smell of German cooking – turnip kraut, hodge podge made with fresh vegetables and cream, and corned beef or mutton.

The oldest son of George and Anna's brood was John George Eisenhauer. In due course he inherited the homestead and married a cousin, Mary Ann Lantz. John

George and Mary Ann had no children, but they lived close to three of his brothers, Benjamin, John, and Emmanuel, and their families, all of whom had built houses on the hill nearby, copying the Cape style of the comfortable house in which they all had grown up.

John George was a pillar of the local Presbyterian church, which he ran, according to one account, 'almost single-handed, except, of course, for the assistance of the Almighty.' One year, when the church needed some means of lighting for evensong, a meeting of the elders was called. John George presided. One timid soul suggested that they should purchase a fine new chandelier. George is credited with jumping to his feet to shout 'The hell ve vill, ve haven't anyvon who can play vun.'

Although illiterate, John George was a shrewd man. He prospered both as a farmer and also as a shipowner, with his schooner, the *Bessie L.* By the time of his death in 1892, he had amassed an impressive estate of $10,000. The schooner was inherited by an adopted nephew, Augustus Lantz, but Mary Ann received all his money and most of the house: the beds, bedding, furniture, 'two stoves and the pipes belonging to them for herself,' along with 'two rooms and three bedrooms on the first floor and two rooms up in the attic on the north west part of my house during her natural life.' By specifying exactly what she would receive, John George was making sure that his wife would be well provided for. Women then had few legal rights and so, in order to protect his wife's interests, a conscientious husband left nothing to chance.

At her death, the house came into the hands of Augustus Lantz, but then, for unknown reasons, it was abandoned. It stood deserted for forty-eight years until it was rescued by a far-sighted woman who carefully restored it to its original condition. In the course of the restoration she found treasures – old furniture and Spanish doubloons, one dated 1787.

Mahone Bay has always been memorable, a distinction owed in part to George Ramsay, 9th Earl of Dalhousie, lieutenant-governor of Nova Scotia from 1816 to 1820. Dalhousie, a general who served under Wellington, was an intelligent administrator with a keen interest in agriculture. A man of contradictions, he combined an aristocratic demeanour and haughty and testy nature with a genuine interest in the poor. His inquiring mind took him on a continuing series of jaunts through Nova Scotia, where he inspected the agricultural efforts

The Earl of Dalhousie,
1834

of the local farmers, after which he lectured them on the merits of hard work and the demerits of laziness. Happily for posterity, he also kept a journal.

It is through the Dalhousie journals that the early days of Zwicker's Inn, in Mahone Bay, come to life. It was a post house, a place where stage coaches could get fresh horses and their passengers could relax, and as the first such inn between Chester and Lunenburg it was a favourite stopping place. Opened in 1800, Zwicker's was known for its good fare and its German innkeeper. Lady Dalhousie found it so pleasing that she requested a summer's sojourn there.

25th June. [1818] The fine season being now set in, my public dispatches closed for some weeks, I am now preparing to set

Zwicker's Inn, opened in 1800 and still operating

Zwicker's Inn and Mahone Bay from the northwest, sketched by John Elliott Woolford

out on a long ride into the distant parts of the Province I did not reach last year ... As Lady D. had very much admired the Mahone Bay when we visited Lunenburg, she wished to go there during my absence, and Miss Cochrane having agreed to accompany her, Sir John Louis offered them the forth, and accordingly we embarked last night ...

29th June ... a fresh breeze from S.W. carried us up to our anchorage in Prince's harbour (or more properly Mush a Mush by the Indian name) an hour before sunset. After breakfast next morning, 27th, we landed the ladies at a near Country Inn, kept by Zwicker, a German original settler. We spent the day with them, and seeing everything most comfortable we returned on board late at night ... The admiral with his usual kindness, has sent down to remain with them a small Yacht with a midshipman and 20 men; they have also a rowing boat with which they may go to all parts of that beautiful bay.

On one of several stays at Zwicker's, Dalhousie asked John Elliot Woolford to sketch the inn. Woolford was an artist and architect who had served with Dalhousie during the Napoleonic Wars. Dalhousie became his patron and, when he came to Nova Scotia as lieutenant-governor, brought Woolford with him to serve as draughtsman. When Dalhousie left Nova Scotia in 1820 to become governor general of British North America, Woolford did not move with him to Quebec, but stayed on in Halifax. He was supervising the construction of Dalhousie College, sponsored by the earl as an alternative to the Anglican presence of King's College. Dalhousie then procured for Woolford an appointment as barracks-master at Fredericton, where the talented artist spent the rest of his life, leaving an invaluable historical record in his sketches. The sketch of Zwicker's Inn, the favourite of Lord and Lady Dalhousie, shows the old hostelry positioned as it is today (restored and once again operating as an inn), serenely looking out to sea, its plain but classically beautiful lines another landmark in a town of landmarks.

CHAPTER ELEVEN

Lunenburg

Halifax. [Last Monday] also arrived here Capts. Rogers and
Cobb, with the Transports under their Convoy, who had
been to Merleguish and landed their first Freight of German
Settlers etc. for that Place; who inform us that they met with
no Obstruction at all; that it is a fine open Country, the Soil
exceeding good, the Grass almost as high as a Man's Knees,
the Fruit Trees all in Bloom etc. They left the Settlers in high
Spirits, and we hope soon to hear of a fine Settlement there.
And Yesterday the said Capts. with their Convoy sail'd from
hence, with their second Freight of Settlers for the same
Place, with a good Wind. (*The Halifax Gazette*, 16 June 1753)

'Exceeding good' soil was what the settlers were looking for. Called 'foreign Protestants,' they were skilled
farmers, most of them German or Swiss, part of a large
emigration from Germany to North America. The British government was still eager, four years after the
founding of Halifax, to establish a commanding presence in Nova Scotia. Enticements such as free building
materials were offered to Germans who would settle
there. Britain was determined to fortify the colony with
men and women loyal to the Crown and not to France
since attacks by French and Mi'kmaq were still feared.

The German and Swiss farmers, nearly 2,000 of them,
arrived in Halifax between 1750 and 1752. While waiting
for their land grants, they settled into a growing community that met at the Little Dutch Church. The land
they eventually received, however, made the wait worth-
while. When they arrived at the site (called Merleguisch
when it was home to fifty Acadians), they found a beautiful natural harbour surrounded by protecting hills
which rose steeply from the sea. The land was indeed
good – but the sea proved better. Descendants of these
able farmers soon became skilled fishermen and ship-

builders. Some said they were the best shipbuilders in the world. They built a self-sufficient community, where German was spoken and where the needs of the ship-builders could be met locally. They called their town Lunenburg.

Laid out as a model town, Lunenburg followed a British plan designed for use in the colonies. It called for geometrically regular streets and blocks. This plan was accomplished by running five streets up the hill from the shore to form six strips. These five streets were then intersected by eight streets laid out parallel to the harbour, creating eight blocks, numbered A to H, in each strip. Block D, near the centre and running across the whole grid, was set aside as a Grand Parade for pub-lic buildings and parks. The plan also demanded a dis-tinction between urban and non-urban areas, with an open commons around the entire grid to define its limits and an allowance for defensive fortifications. The last fortification was destroyed by fire in 1874, but the rest of the town plan is still in evidence. Lunenburg was the second model town built in Nova Scotia, the first being Halifax (illustrated in chapter 1), and it retains its original layout today. In 1991 the old town of Lu-nenburg was declared a National Historic District by the Historic Sites and Monuments Board of Canada.

When they arrived, the German settlers improvised shelter with quickly constructed huts called pole houses –quite simply, small trees, stripped of their branches and propped up side by side like soldiers, then strapped to-gether with boards and roofed in. That done, a race with time began as the settlers rushed to complete per-manent homes before the onset of winter. Each family was given exactly 500 feet of boards and 250 nails, but records show that the settlers also purchased timber and shingles from the shrewd New England merchants who arrived by ship that summer. Those first dwellings were frame, one-storey Cape Cod cottages that faced the harbour.

As soon as the essential matter of a shelter was at-tended to, these German settlers began to think of build-ing a church. That first summer, services were con-ducted in the open while funds and materials were sought – the former were found in England, the latter in Boston. The building which stands today at Church Square as St John's Anglican Church is a majestic struc-ture, rich in ornamentation and aesthetically pleasing. But beneath this embellishment is the stern frame building built by Lutheran settlers soon after their 1753 arrival. It was unadorned on the exterior and interior. A pulpit was not installed until several years after construction was completed.

In the late 1770s Lunenburg's Lutherans and Presbyterians left St John's to build their own churches. Then gradually, as the nineteenth century progressed, the simple frame church acquired its adornments – the tower, gracefully arched windows and doors, pinnacles, buttresses, and, in the interior a chancel, a beamed ceiling, surmounted by a blue 'sky' and stars, and numerous fine examples of ecclesiastical art. The simple frame structure had become a Gothic Revival edifice.

York Street, running parallel to the harbour, and second from the top on the grid, was where a cooper,

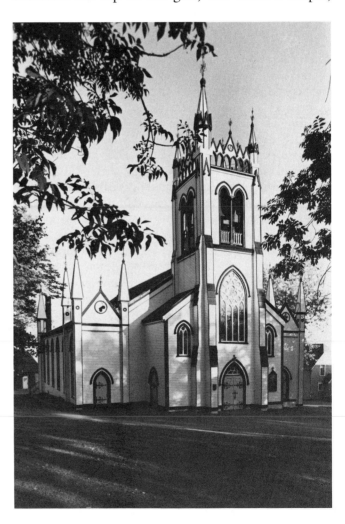

St John's Anglican Church, Church Square

George Metzler, built his house in those middle years of the eighteenth century. Described as a 'half-Cape,' the house at 57 York was a sturdy structure of simple design with no frivolous ornamentation. Two small windows and a door faced the street. Inside, a narrow staircase wound around a central massive chimney to the loft above. Later the little house took on a new life as a 'three-quarter Cape' with a small addition to one end.

The first street up from the harbour was Montague. Pelham Street was the second. The lot at 82 Pelham was initially owned by George Iristadt, but the house there may have been built by Jacob Ullshe, a mariner, sometime after 1774. By 1783 it was home, not to Germans, but to James A. Anderson and his family, Loyalists who had located first in Shelburne, then quickly relocated to the more settled town of Lunenburg. A subsequent owner, Edward Dowling, used the house as the customs office in 1860, adding another door and window to accommodate the business. The house is a single storey on the Pelham Street side, but two storeys on the side that faces the harbour. Two small dormers were originally set into the gambrel roof at the front, but they were later replaced by the five-sided Scottish dormer, when this feature became popular in the 1800s.

The fifth street up from the harbour is Townsend. Adam Wambolt, one of the 1753 settlers, first owned a lot there and possibly built a pole house on the property. In 1775 he moved on, selling to Henry Koch, who was in a position to build a sturdy but finely designed two-storey home, its two massive chimneys serving eight

82 Pelham Street, once the Customs House

fireplaces, four on each floor. Additional heat was provided by the bake-oven in the basement kitchen where the family ate their meals.

The house (now 68 Townsend Street) has been restored to its original Koch design, and the 'Lunenburg bump' – an ornately detailed projecting bay window situated above the front door – removed. The 'bump' had been added in the 1880s, when most fashionable houses in town were sporting this new and popular embellishment.

Henry Koch was a successful man. He owned more than forty lots in the town plot, hundreds of acres outside the town, mills, and a share of a fishery. In 1797 he sold the house to his eldest daughter, Elizabeth, and her husband, John Christopher Rudolph. Presumably Koch and his wife then moved elsewhere.

In his will, written a year before his death in 1814, Koch divided his substantial holdings among his wife, Elisaphronia, and their children, Elizabeth Rudolph, Magdalina Moser, Catherina Milward, Elisaphronia Clark, Anne, and John. He left 'the homestead, or family residence here in Town ... to accommodate my beloved wife, Elisaphronia, son John and daughter Anne.' He had already 'fully and amply provided for [his] eldest son, Philip Koch, and second son, Henry, by giving each of them good and ample title deeds.'

After many years in the house, Elizabeth and John Rudolph sold in 1849 to George T. Solomon, a judge who had studied with the Hon. Richard John Uniacke. George Solomon, his son, later inherited the house and on his death left it to his wife, Mary Jane, along with

68 Townsend Street, the
Koch/Solomon house

household goods – 'plate, linen, china, furniture ... gardens and out-buildings.' Their children – Edward, Kenneth, William, Janet Maria Bolman, Elizabeth Rudolph (wife of Captain G.J. Rudolph of Liverpool, England), and Charlotte – received generous bequests. The house remained in the Solomon family until 1917.

Philip Augustus Knaut, a native of the Electorate of Saxony, now part of Germany, arrived in Nova Scotia in 1749 on the sloop *Sphinx*, as part of the expedition led by Edward Cornwallis, the founder of Halifax and governor of the colony. Four years later he moved to Lunenburg with his wife, Anna, and a group of 'foreign Protestants.' He spoke French and English as well as German, and became a leader in the community and a member of the first Legislative Assembly. He represented and acted as a spokesman for his German constituents for the rest of his life. As well, he was a successful merchant, sawmill owner, and trader with the Indians.

Philip Knaut prospered. When he died in 1781 he left an estate of £9,000, a small fortune in those early days. Trouble began almost immediately. Philip's first wife, Anna Grob, had died some time after the birth of their third child. In July 1781 Philip, then in his midsixties, remarried; his bride was a Lunenburg woman, Jane Brimmer. Just five months later, he died. Within six weeks of that melancholy event, Jane, by then a rich widow, remarried. At this juncture she and the Knaut children locked horns over the estate. After a spate of legal squabbling, Knaut's eldest child, Catherine, and

Benjamin Knaut's fine home at 125 Pelham Street

her husband, John Newton, were granted letters of administration for the estate and the guardianship of her brother Benjamin, who was still a minor when his father died. Benjamin, in time, inherited a sizeable fortune.

Twelve years or so later, Benjamin Knaut was ready to build a home for himself – a handsome New England colonial house with Georgian adaptations, now 125 Pelham Street. It remains, two centuries later, a Lunenburg treasure, its serene simplicity marking it as one of the finest eighteenth-century buildings in the province.

The house was set on a stone foundation more than two feet thick, and built around two huge chimneys. In true Georgian fashion, the doorway was centred along the five-bay façade, with sidelights and a straight transom above the door admitting light to the centre hall. Every exterior detail was simple and refined, the intention being to indicate, by restrained embellishment and careful proportions, the dignity and beauty that were to be found within. Interior trim was finely detailed. In places, simulated wood-graining added an elegant touch. This involved painting inexpensive woods and then, with a combing technique, giving the finish the appearance of mahogany, walnut, or other fine-grained woods.

In 1813 the Knaut house was sold to Conrad Rhuland and then, in 1826, to John W. Creighton, a lawyer who had grown up in Lunenburg. His father, also John Creighton, had come to the province in 1749 with Edward Cornwallis and Philip Knaut, and in time became a significant presence in Lunenburg. During the American Revolution, the elder Creighton helped defend Lunenburg against a privateer raid, after several vessels landed near the town and ninety men attacked the small garrison. Creighton was taken prisoner and his home torched, but his devoted slave, Silvia, managed to save some of the family's valuables by lowering them into a well, then shielding one of their sons with her body.

John W. Creighton was educated in England and served for a time in the British army. He purchased the Knaut house during a successful career which saw him become a member of the Legislative Assembly for Lunenburg County, president and speaker of the Council, and a judge of probate. Two of his three sisters married into the Halifax establishment: Lucy married Hibbert Newton Binney, collector of impost and excise; Sarah married Lewis Morris Wilkins, politician and judge.

The Knaut/Rhuland house epitomized the Georgian

style, which followed the sturdy, utilitarian Lunenburg homes of the eighteenth century. As the nineteenth century progressed, restraint went out. Excess – and the 'Lunenburg bump' – came in. The ubiquitous five-sided dormer, imported by immigrant Scots and first seen in Halifax in the 1820s, became stage one in what was to become Lunenburg's trademark. Whereas the Scottish dormer initially sat modestly on the roof, in Lunenburg it moved forward by degrees, then grew until it became a projecting bay dominating the façade, skilfully embellished by the craftsmen who built 'the best ships in the world.' Men who carved fanciful figureheads on seagoing vessels also created architectural wonders in wood. They turned Lunenburg's sedate Georgian houses into works of ornamental art.

The house at 166 Pelham Street is a fine example – a simple dwelling where the dormer took on a life of its own, creeping forward to overhang the door, then making its way to the ground. The door, with fanciful sidelights and transom, was embellished in the process.

The owner of the house, David Smith, could afford to enjoy the results of skilled woodworking, for he was also owner of a shipyard where more than 200 ships had been built. After his death in 1899 his son, with George Rhuland, formed Smith and Rhuland, a partnership that built the 285-ton racing schooner *Bluenose*, the pride of Lunenburg and Nova Scotia. It was launched in 1921. *Bluenose II*, launched in 1963, was built there as well.

David Smith house,
166 Pelham Street

When 'the bump' took on a vivacious mien, it transformed even larger houses than Smith's modest home. Lawyer Charles Bolman's house, for instance (13-15 King Street), built in the 1830s, had once been an example of Georgian simplicity and one of Lunenburg's finest houses. John Zwicker, a prominent merchant, bought the building from Bolman in 1836. Forty years later, the Zwicker family decided to update the place. Windows were enlarged and elaborately framed, and a two-storey projecting bay with round-topped windows and bracketed eaves was built on the front. Topping it all was a splendid new dormer, five-sided this time, with a curved, mansard roof.

Lunenburg bumps were frivolous, but they also had a practical aspect. As well as providing a degree of protection to front doors, they could offer an unparalleled view of the town, the bay, and the busy waterfront. And there, at the waterfront, stood Henry Koch's 'Red Store,' a building he bequeathed to his youngest children, John and Anne, in his 1813 will. It foretold the future colour of many of the buildings along Lunenburg's waterfront. Red they were, and red they remain. These buildings stand out so vividly that the scene has become one of the most photographed spots in Canada. Lunenburg's picturesque waterfront was, until recently, depicted on this country's 100-dollar bill. It has since been replaced by a Canada goose.

15 King Street: the 'bump' was added some forty years after the house was built

*The sheer delight of
Lunenburg bumps*

CHAPTER TWELVE

Liverpool and Mill Village

When Simeon Perkins came to Liverpool in May 1762, he was twenty-seven and 'disconsolate.' In 1760 he had married Abigail Backus in Norwich, Connecticut. Within a year he was both a father and a widower. Abigail had borne a son, Roger, and had died one week later at the age of eighteen. A year and a half after this tragedy, Simeon Perkins left for Nova Scotia. Baby Roger remained in Norwich, presumably to be raised by relatives.

Although the pull of his birthplace was strong, Perkins remained in Liverpool, and made a comfortable living from a combination of mercantile, lumbering, trading, and privateering ventures. In so doing, he became a respected and responsible citizen – a justice of the peace, a judge of the Inferior Court of Common Pleas, lieutenant-colonel of the militia, and, for more than thirty years, a member of the Legislative Assembly. At his death in 1812 he left his province an invaluable legacy – a journal that he had kept for forty-six years, and described as 'one of the most valuable and interesting records, that ever perhaps, came into the province.'

In looking to Nova Scotia for new prospects, Perkins was not alone. He was one of 8,000 New England Planters, settlers who came north to the old colony of Nova Scotia, bringing with them lumber, house frames, sawmill frames, animals, and household goods. There was land for the taking, and the free grants offered by Nova Scotia's Governor Charles Lawrence were enticing, now that the colony was British, not French. Halifax had been founded as a British military garrison thirteen years earlier, and the French influence had waned since the expulsion of the Acadians in 1755, the capture of Louisbourg in 1758, and the fall of Quebec in 1759. Twenty-one years after Perkins's arrival, thousands of Loyalists would follow, further entrenching the English character of much of the South Shore and the Maritime region. Simeon Perkins, like most Planters, had ties to Britain as well. His ancestors had emigrated from Gloucester, England, to Massachusetts around 1630.

By the time Perkins arrived in Liverpool, the initial land grants had been allocated, and so he faced a waiting period before he became a landowner. He immediately set up as a merchant, however, and became involved in the fishery, still in partnership with relatives in Connecticut. Over the years his fortunes rose and fell like the tide, as was true of most of the colonists. Many left when the difficulties they faced seemed insurmountable, but others were more tenacious, and in time the merchants of Liverpool developed a brisk trade with the West Indies. Warehouses appeared on the docks, and churches and houses soon dotted the streets of the town.

The most visible signs of Perkins's success in Liverpool were the many vessels that he built or bought. From sloops to full-riggers, his ships plied the coast from Labrador to the West Indies, and even across the Atlantic. He was unquestionably among the province's most highly regarded citizens, and his ownership of privateering vessels did nothing to sully his reputation, privateering being both legal and commendably patriotic in wartime. He owned some of the best-known privateers, ships that fought for England and brought home 'prizes' under a licence, or letter of marque, from the governor.

Many of the vessels that Perkins's privateers attacked sailed from his American homeland. His loyalties were initially divided, as were those of many expatriate Americans. Nova Scotia's neutrality during the American Revolution was received with disbelief in New England, for by 1775 three-quarters of the colony's population was of New England background. But, when American vessels attacked, the choice became easier. By the end of the war neutrality had frequently turned to support for Britain. Perkins lost five privateers during the American Revolution, but his own privateer, the *Lucy*, outfitted in 1779 at a cost of £2,000, captured six enemy vessels. *The Nova Scotia Gazette and Weekly Chronicle* of 4 January 1780 listed prizes taken by Liverpool privateers since July 1778. In that year and a half, thirty vessels had taken prizes of £800,000.

By 1798 there were more opportunities for Nova Scotia's merchants to profit from privateering. Britain was

Simeon Perkins

at war with France and her ally, Spain. Eager privateers saw rich gains awaiting in the waters of the Caribbean, and wherever the vessels of Britain's enemies sailed. In 1798 Perkins and two partners built a privateer, named her after the governor's son, Charles Mary Wentworth, persuaded the governor to pay for sixteen guns, and then got the government to provide the shot and powder. Within two years she had taken ten prizes worth £16,000.

Simeon Perkins had been a widower for fifteen years when he married a Liverpool widow, Elizabeth Headley, mother of a seven-year-old daughter, Ruth. Perkins's first son, Roger, arrived two years later to live with them. He was then a young man of seventeen. The house that Simeon had built in 1766 (on what is now Main Street) grew to accommodate six daughters and two sons, plus a black couple, Anthony and Hagar, from Shelburne; Simeon's slave, Frank; and a continual stream of visitors. Even women hired to tutor the children lived in, one of them bringing her own furniture with her. Visiting clergymen came and stayed for weeks, soldiers and members of shipbuilding crews were frequently billeted with the family, and any dignitary arriving in town was sure to be welcomed. Small wonder that, by 1781, Simeon and Elizabeth decided to enlarge their house.

The original 1766 house had visible roots in New England, for, like most colonists, Perkins had chosen a style that reminded him of home. His modest storey-and-a-half clapboard dwelling was one of the ubiquitous Cape Cod cottages found along the eastern seaboard.

Perkins house, Main Street

The usual layout had a central door flanked by windows (placed symmetrically or not, at the owner's whim), a steeply pitched roof, a large attic with partial full-headroom, and a central chimney or, in later versions, two chimneys, one at each end. The style combined sturdy Georgian symmetry with colonial pragmatism.

The front door of the Perkins house opened to a small, cramped, dimly lit hall, with steep stairs leading to attic bedrooms above. The present stairs are not original but replaced earlier versions, the first of which may have led up from the rear of the house. To the right of the stairs was the parlour, the room where anything of a public nature took place. An open fireplace did its best (with little success) to dispel the winter's cold, which penetrated the thin, poorly insulated walls.

To the left of the front door was a large kitchen that extended to the back of the house. It was dominated by a large cooking fireplace and bake-oven. Here Mrs Arnold, the Perkins's housekeeper, prepared the meals and slept when her duties were over. The 1781 extension transformed the room. It was divided, and part of it became the keeping-room, with a fine new fireplace and mantel. The family's best china, silver, or pewter was displayed here, meals served, and housekeeping chores attended to. A new kitchen was built, formed from part of the original kitchen and part of the extension. A ground-floor bedroom was added, and would have derived heat through the wall on which the kitchen fireplace and oven backed.

Behind the parlour was a small office. Speculation has surrounded a blocked door in this room. It may have served as an office door, built so that business associates or militiamen could enter without disturbing the family. If this is true, it may have been through this door that Perkins first heard, on 13 September 1780, that privateers had successfully taken Liverpool's fort and were in command of the town. Perkins roused those militiamen not yet captured, and took the fort again.

While the Perkins diaries contain invaluable and detailed information about shipping concerns and politics, along with news from Halifax and abroad, personal items are frustratingly intermittent. He did, however, record some family events:

1776. Thursday morning, Oct. 3d. About 3 o'clock my wife called the woman, and about 3 o'clock p.m. was delivered of a daughter, and by the goodness, both mother and child are as well as common. We call the child Abigail, after my first wife.

In 1790 Perkins described a treatment prescribed for his four-year-old daughter:

May 17. I begin this morning to plunge my Daughter Mary in Cold well water, for a Ricketey complaint, by the advice of Doctor A. Timothy Miller. He gave us an Ointment, which is to be Apply'd the evening before dipping and to be Continued Untill the whole of it, about one Gill, is used. the dipping is to be three mornings and then omit three, untill She is dipped Nine times. We only Dip her in and directly out again (not three times in one morning), the Child Bears the dipping to admiration.

Dec. 31st. Wind S.E. We trim away the Ballast that was taken out yesterday, the East Side of the King's Store. Sets in to Snow, and in the Course of the day the wind backens to the North East. Mrs. Perkins was taken Ill last evening, had very little rest, and is Very Ill this morning. Her Face is much Swelled, on the Right Side, and Looks Very Red. She complains of Violent pains in her Back, and much Distress in her whole frame. I Judge the disorder to be the Erisipelas, or St. Anthony's fire. She Sends for Mrs. Parker, who has been used to the Disorder. She thinks best to take advice of the Doctor. We Send for him towards evening. He has ordered Some Balm, and Hisop tea for Drink or rather Barley Water, if Barley was to be had.

Elizabeth recovered and outlived Simeon, who died in their home on 9 May 1812, aged seventy-seven, having contributed with vigour to the business, political, legal, and military life of the province that he had at first so tentatively adopted. His large family, however, seemed ill-fated. His oldest son, Roger, died in a storm at sea, during a visit to Connecticut. ('He was a promising young man,' Perkins wrote in his journal, 'and the Loss of him was a very Sore Stroke and great Disappointment.') Elizabeth Perkins stayed on in their home for ten years, but they were fraught with tragedy, as four of their eight children died within that decade: Eunice, Mary, and Abigail died in Liverpool before 1819, and Simeon Leonard died there in 1822. John Perkins, the eldest son, moved to his father's old home, Norwich, Connecticut. After the death of Simeon Leonard, Elizabeth sold the home and left for New York with her surviving daughters, Elizabeth and Charlotte. She received £600 for the house from the new owner, Captain Caleb Seely.

Seely was part owner of the most famous privateer of all, the *Liverpool Packet*. The schooner's varied career began in the slave trade, in which service she was called, with a singular lack of humour, *Black Joke*. In 1811 she was purchased in Halifax by Enos Collins and his Liverpool partners. The ship was filthy, thanks to the contemptible conditions that the slaves had endured, and the schooner had to be fumigated before embarking on further voyages. She sailed to Liverpool, was renamed the *Liverpool Packet*, and set off to make a better reputation for herself along the eastern seaboard. She was a speedy craft, and could be handled by very few men, so that during the War of 1812 the rest of the crew could acquire 'prizes.' And prizes she took – a quarter of a million dollars in two years. The Boston papers bemoaned the fact that she was stealing from right under the noses of furious Boston merchants. Caleb Seely himself took command of the privateer in 1813.

By the time that Caleb bought the Perkins house from Elizabeth nine years later, he had retired from privateering and had become a trader, exporting timber and fish. He had been married for seven years to Phoebe Collins, a sister of his partner Enos. When they moved into the house, they were parents of two children. Three were born later. He became, like Perkins, a judge of the Inferior Court of Common Pleas. Phoebe died in June 1847. Within six months Caleb Seely remarried, this time to Desire Grieve, who, upon her death in 1855,

Liverpool harbour in the 1890s

was promptly replaced by Jane Sancton. She died the next year.

Caleb lived for another thirteen years. At his death he bequeathed to his heirs (Ellen, Edwin, and Charles Seely) 'all that Building situate on Main Street in the Town of Liverpool to be divided equally among them.' Ellen Seely Agnew and her husband, Moore F. Agnew, lived in the house after Caleb's death, and it stayed in the family until 1936, when it was taken over by the Queen's County Historical Society and opened to the public. During its 169 years it had been owned by only two families.

Among Simeon Perkins's many business connections was an Irishman, Patrick Doran, who operated a sawmill and supplied lumber and fish for Perkins's trading ventures. Doran had been Perkins's chief clerk in Liverpool, but had moved to Mill Village, about ten miles away, to work for Samuel Mack, a Connecticut merchant who had come to the area in 1764 and bought mills established by two New England settlers twenty years earlier. Mack developed a thriving West Indies trade. He died at age forty-one, leaving a widow with the inviting, if not uncommon name, Desire.

Desire Mack was from Massachusetts, and had come to Nova Scotia with her father, William Cohoon, a descendant of an earlier William Cohoon who had settled in Rhode Island in 1662. Desire's father was one of the first landholders in Liverpool Township. When her husband died, Desire was left to raise five children – Samuel, Stephen, Solomon, Elizabeth, and William. Mack's effects were sold at auction, but records of the sale showed that articles 'sold fairly to the highest Bidder' sometimes went to the widow Mack herself. Desire Mack's purchases suggested that she knew her way around the farm and their mill, for she bought two dozen narrow axes, four new mill saws, two yoke of oxen, one black cow, and one scow boat – all for a little more than £22. Also attending the sale was Patrick Doran, who left with a yoke of red and black oxen for which he paid £11 – the highest price spent on any one item. But his yoke was soon to be linked with Desire's.

In addition to her name, Desire Mack had other charms. She was the proud owner of two sawmills at nearby Port Medway Mills and a 200-acre lot in the village. She had purchased land from her father in 1784, a year after her husband's death; a witness to that deed of sale was Patrick Doran. One year after that Patrick became her husband. Adding to his good fortune was his appointment, shortly thereafter, as magistrate – a position which, the Perkins diaries suggest, he secured with the help of his friend Simeon Perkins.

According to a family history commissioned by his grandson, Patrick Doran was 'an Irishman of the Saxon stock, he ... was employed by Mr. Mack being a man of education and possessing good abilities with liberal and tolerant views ... he had seen John Wesley before he left Ireland and he had been favourably inclined towards his views and no doubt it was by his demeanor and assistance that the methodist principles were so extensively propogated throughout the village.'

When Patrick Doran and Desire were married in January 1785, they moved into a fine house near Mill Village. The house had a serenely simple exterior belying the architectural flights of fancy found within. Finely detailed wood trim on china cupboards, mantelpieces, cornices, and wainscoting delighted the eye, adding interest to rooms otherwise marked by chaste simplicity. Three rooms, each with a fireplace, surrounded a massive chimney. The dining-room was the scene of the many social events for which the Dorans were known. Patrick and Desire had four children: Catherine, James, Edmund (who lived only one week), and Eleanor.

Eleanor Doran married Samuel Davison. Their son, Edward Doran Davison, inherited the extensive family business. Both his parents had died before he was twelve, and so, while still in his teens, he was successfully managing operations. He expanded by building a steam sawmill, damming the La Have River, and buying up land and bankrupt mills. Eventually he and his sons owned the largest lumbering concern in the province.

Doran house, Mill Village

CHAPTER THIRTEEN

Lockeport to Seal Island

At Ragged Islands, in the spring of 1829, the vessel *Myrtle* struck rock. Her captain wrote in his log: 'April 3. P.M. Moderate breezes and hazy weather. At 6 struck West Head near Shelburne. So ends this day. Hard up on a sharp rock and a hell of a sea going.' Within a year or so, the *Billow*, from Bermuda for Halifax, was also wrecked off Ragged Islands in a gale. One hundred people drowned, sixty-eight of them children. The *Myrtle* and the *Billow* were only two of the many hundreds of vessels that were wrecked on the jagged shoals around Nova Scotia when fierce gales made the ocean heave and churn, and the vicious undertow took countless lives.

Ragged Islands is now called Lockeport. A picturesque fishing town, it was settled in 1755 by families from Massachusetts who landed, first, in Liverpool, but later discovered a bay with abundant fish, just east of Green Harbour, and decided to settle there instead. The first to arrive, Josiah Churchill of Plymouth, Massachusetts, found Mi'kmaq and a few French refugees from the Acadian expulsion.

Next to come, in 1761, was the couple who gave the town its new name – Jonathan Locke and his wife, Abigail Perry. Marion Robertson, author of *King's Bounty*, relates that Locke came first to Liverpool, where he worked as a carpenter for Simeon Perkins. Some sources refer to him as 'doctor,' but Robertson surmises that this was a courtesy title: 'he may have known old home remedies, and to the early settlers this would have been a source of comfort in their illnesses.'

Locke was the great-grandson of Captain John Locke of Yorkshire, England, who emigrated in 1644 and settled in New Hampshire, at Jocelyn's Neck, which was later called Locke's Neck. Captain John was killed by

Indians in 1696 while working the fields of his farm in Rye, New Hampshire. The third of his eleven children, Nathaniel, married Dorothy Blake and, tradition maintains, fathered nineteen offspring. Remarkably, for the time, fifteen grew to adulthood. Jonathan Locke was the twelfth. He died soon after his marriage, and his son, Jonathan, born in 1726, after his death, is said to have studied medicine for a while. At the age of thirty-five he left for Nova Scotia, where he founded Lockeport.

The inhabitants of Lockeport had strong emotional ties to their New England birthplace, and thus the sympathies of many lay with the Americans during the Revolution. Such sentiments were common throughout Nova Scotia, but were particularly predominant in the southwest of the province, where there was easiest access to New England. Lockeport's deep bay thus became a haven for American privateers, and rebel prisoners who escaped their British captors were often taken stealthily back to their American homes. As a result, the people of Lockeport assumed that their community and others along the southwestern shore would be spared attacks by American ships. The rebel forces assumed that they would have active military support from Nova Scotia. Neither was to be the case.

There were several reasons for Nova Scotia's position: the colony's close historic links to Britain and the strength of the British presence in Halifax; the isolated nature of settlement in the province owing to its myriad secluded bays, poor roads, and the consequent lack of communication; and a lack of inspired rebel leadership in the colony. Most compelling, however, was the attitude of the settlers themselves: their very survival was challenge enough. They wanted peace.

Such was the situation when, on 20 August 1779, an American privateer appeared in Lockeport harbour and the village was plundered. The sympathies of the good people of Lockeport towards Americans took an abrupt about-turn. Their reaction was made abundantly clear in a letter to the Council of the State of Massachusetts written by Jonathan Locke and three of his neighbours.

These lines Comes with my respects to you, and to acquaint you of the Robery done to this Harbour. there was a guard of men put upon every house and the houses stript. very Surprising to us. they came in here Early in the Morning on the 20th day of August last, and said they were from Penobscot and were torries bound to Halifax. they Come to my house first and wanted some refreshment, accordingly we let them have what they wanted; and then they went away and stayed on an Island till the tide run so that they could Come at my Boat, then they come and took my Boat and put a Guard upon my House and went a Robing. They took about 19 Quintals of Cod fish and Four Barrels of Salt, three Salmon Netts, 60 lbs of Butter, one Green Hyde, five dressed Skins and some Cheese, and a Great many other Things. The Boat Cost me fifty pounds Halifax Currency. They then went to Mr Matthews and there Robed him then went to Mr Haydens, and Robed him, then went to Mr Locks and Robed him. These things are very surprising that we in this Harbour that have done so much for America, that have helped three or four hundred Prisoners up along to America and Given part of our Living to them, and have Concealed Privateers and prizes too from the British Cruisers, in this Harbor. All this done for America and if this be the way that we are to be paid I desire to see no more of you without you come in Another Manner, but I hope the America Gentlemen that Grants out Commissions or are Bondsmen would take these Notorious Rascalls in hand for this Robery. Sir, be so kind as to Inform some of the Council of the affair, that we might have some restrictions otherwise we shall not be able to help the American prisoners, and more Sir, if you find out who these be, and whether we are like to have anything, be pleased to write.

William Porterfield   John Matthews   Thomas Hayden   Jonathan Lock. Raged Islands, Sept. 25, 1779

There is no indication that restitution was ever paid. In any event, Lockeport and the Locke family thrived. Five of their houses stand today on a waterfront that has been designated a heritage streetscape: four were built for great-grandchildren of Jonathan Locke and the fifth for a great-great-grandchild.

The Lockes, Jonathan and Abigail, had five children, the last of whom was also named Jonathan. He married Mary Ryder of Rhode Island, who bore him seven children. Their second child, Samuel, married Letitia McKillop and prospered in the fishing and West Indian trade. Eventually, he owned most of Locke's Island.

Of the five houses that line the waterfront, the oldest is a simple frame building with three narrow dormers and a central door topped with a fan transom. It was built in 1836 for Samuel Locke's daughter Elizabeth

The earliest of the five Locke family homes on the Lockeport waterfront: Elizabeth's, built in 1836

The home built for Elizabeth's sister Mary in 1841

when she married William Stalker, a shipbuilder. Two doors away stands the house built in 1841 when her sister, Mary Locke, then sixteen, married the local blacksmith, Gurden (or Gordon) Bill. Five years later, in 1846, brothers Jacob and John Locke each built a home near their sisters'. Both chose classical detailing to add refinement to the almost identical designs. John's house differed from his brother's in the addition of a projecting enclosed porch at the front. Finally, in 1876, Samuel's grandson, Henry Locke, built his impressive Second Empire house. He later sold it in 1892 to his cousin, Churchill Locke, whose successful fish business, under different owners, later became National Sea Products.

The next major centre down the coast is Shelburne, originally settled by French colonists who called it Port Rasoir. They were carried off when the Acadians were expelled from Nova Scotia in 1755. The village was re-settled by English-speaking colonists, but did not take its present form until 1783.

On the afternoon of 4 May that year, more than thirty sailing ships appeared on the horizon. They headed past McNutt's Island, towards what was by then called Port Roseway. When the fleet anchored, more than 3,000 men, women, and children disembarked.

Loyalists all, they were the first of a group which had named itself (with its destination in mind), the Port Roseway Associates. A year later, when the rest of their number had arrived from New York, there were some 6,000 to 7,000 of them. More than 1,500 buildings were constructed – an instant city which, for a brief period, was one of the largest in North America.

Jacob Locke's house, built in 1846

The slightly more elaborate house of John Locke, also built in 1846

Henry Locke house, built a generation later

The Port Roseway Associates, like all Loyalists who had fought for or publicly supported the British in the Revolutionary War, had been faced with a choice which was really no choice at all: they could remain in the new United States, many having had their lands confiscated, and face various forms of persecution, or they could seek a new home in a British colony. Most made the latter choice. Sir Guy Carleton, Commander-in-Chief of His Majesty's Forces in America, and Rear-Admiral Robert Digby, joint commissioners 'for restoring peace and granting pardon to the revolted provinces in America,' were instructed to assist, resettle, and provision those loyal to the Crown. Up the eastern seaboard lay Nova Scotia, a British colony with available land – and an enticing nine days' sail from New York, where most Loyalists had congregated.

The Port Roseway Associates had been established in 1782 as a Loyalist group with particularly strict guidelines: new members of the association had to be introduced by old; and all decisions had to be made by the entire group, along the lines of New England town meetings. After negotiations with government commissioners, land for the group was set aside in Port Roseway, where there was said to be abundant opportunity for fishing and farming. In keeping with the military nature of the proposed landing of thousands of people, the group was divided into sixteen companies, each one headed by a captain, two lieutenants, four sergeants, and thirty-six rank and file. Sixteen captains were chosen, then each hand-picked his own company, adding to his group by selecting other Associates and then filling it out with carefully selected 'outsiders' who would later be officially admitted.

One of the captains was Stephen Shakespear, newly commissioned by the British commander, Sir Guy Carleton, in New York. Shakespear was part of the first landing at Port Roseway. Presumably he explained to his company some recent news regarding the 500 acres that had been promised to every family settling at Port Roseway. Word was that the promise could not be fulfilled. He told them, however, that there were thousands of acres of good land available for settlement at the back of the seaside township to which they were going, lands reaching as far as Annapolis County. He may not have known that these lands were part of the unwelcoming interior – rocky scrubland, unsuitable for farming. This disappointment would surface later, along with others.

A major problem concerned the captains. There were
sixteen of them, a situation which could lead to sixteen
opinions on every question. The town meeting–style democracy favoured by the Associates led to a further multitude of differing opinions. There was too much leadership and therefore not enough. Nor was the leadership
fully qualified. 'Carleton,' according to historian Marion
Robertson, 'made a great mistake when he commissioned them captains – when few if any had had military
training … [Governor] Parr had to send a regiment
from Halifax to protect the citizens from their own un-
happiness and rioting.'

Rank had its rewards, however, and Captain Shakespear was one of the first to get his grant – 500 acres
along the Port Roseway River and a one-acre lot in town.
The river lands included lot 1, above the falls, which
was marked for a mill site. He began immediately to
build a log house on what is now the corner of George
and Water streets, and completed it amid the boom-
town atmosphere of that significant year. It served as
a home and store. Stephen was now merchant, captain,
and potential miller.

An instant city of some 6,329 hopeful souls was taking shape. By year's end, nearly 1,500 new buildings
were assembled or nearly so, built from the trees which
covered the site. Stephen's log house was a storey and
a half high and built around a huge fireplace. It was
the sort of home that one would expect a Loyalist to
build – a modest, symmetrical Georgian house with a
five-bay façade, reminiscent of the New England houses
he remembered. Carved dentils under the eaves added
a touch of ornamentation.

That first summer, when Governor John Parr came
to town, cannons roared, and Loyalists, armed, lined
the streets to welcome him. Presumably Shakespear was
among them. The four-day visit culminated in a grand
ball, with a lavish dinner, and dancing that lasted all
night. To Parr, the visit was a resounding success. But
the inhabitants of Port Roseway awakened after the festivities with a hangover, for their town had been renamed – and the chosen name rankled. It was to be
called Shelburne, after the prime minister of Great Britain, William Petty, Earl of Shelburne – the very man
they considered had let down the nation by inadequately
pursuing the 'situation' in America. Had it not been for
him, said the Loyalists, the British flag would still have
been flying protectively above their former homes. Some

Stephen Shakespear house,
George and Water streets,
Shelburne

townspeople refused to use the new name.

Meanwhile Shakespear, in spite of his senior position in the town and his responsibility for keeping the peace, was encountering difficulties. On 22 July 1784, only a year after his arrival, an event occurred which caused him to be accused of setting an 'evil Example' and offending 'the Peace of our said Lord the King, his Crown and Dignity.' He was charged with assaulting John Miller, secretary of the Associates' keeper of the House of Correction, collector of taxes, and Shakespear's partner in a milling concern. (The result of the charge is not known.)

Within three years, in 1787, the Shakespear house passed to David Shakespear. Succeeding owners included Gideon White, a descendant of the Pilgrim Fathers and a Port Roseway Associate. White arrived in 1784 and became one of the town's most prestigious residents – a politician, militia officer, and judge – and a survivor, one who remained in Shelburne when most of the others had found greener fields.

The longest subsequent tenure was that of George Dienstadt, who bought the house in 1833. He was a cordwainer (shoemaker), who had been apprenticed by his mother for six years, seven months, and nine days to learn his trade from an expert, Joseph Bell. The agreement under which the youth was to learn the 'Art, Trade and Mystery of Cordwainer' was typical of the time. George promised that he would serve his master faithfully, 'his Secrets keep, his lawful Commands every where readily obey,' and that he would not 'waste or lend his Master's Goods' nor 'commit Fornication or Matrimony contract.' If George played cards he was to avoid playing to 'his Master's damage.' Further, he promised not to haunt 'Ale-houses, Taverns, or Playhouses,' although his opportunities for doing so were limited since he could not 'absent himself Day or Night from his Master's service, without his leave.'

Bell's lessons must have stuck, since Dienstadt was able to buy the house at the corner of George and Water streets. When he died he left it to his wife, Elizabeth Jane, along with the furniture in it. Deinstadt's descendants held it into the twentieth century. After a period of decline, the house was restored. It stands now, a reminder of those early days when Shelburne and the Port Roseway Associates were full of excitement and hope.

Joseph Bell, under whom Deinstadt so diligently apprenticed, was a son of a Loyalist, also Joseph Bell, who had arrived in Shelburne the summer of 1783. That year he began construction of his home, a gambrel-roofed house with a circular staircase. It still stands in the north end of town. A subsequent owner, Captain James Cunningham, was captured by pirates in the West Indies and murdered.

For settlers in Port Roseway and elsewhere who wanted to establish an instantly successful business, there was one popular answer: they could open a tavern. Patrick McDonnough was such a man. He was granted water lots 14 and 15 on Block B and, shortly after the arrival of the Port Roseway Associates, built a tavern at the southeast corner of what is now John and Dock streets. The handsome clapboard building reflects the traditional New England colonial style. It has five bays and four windows, with a door and portico at street level. Locally the McDonnough tavern is called 'high colonial' because of its finely detailed mouldings and trim, details lacking in some of the simpler examples of the colonial style.

McDonnough's was not the only tavern in Port Roseway. In fact, thirty others served the burgeoning population. The proliferation of taverns was only one of the many problems encountered by the Port Roseway Associates, problems that made their new home far less appealing than advertised.

For one thing, the Port Roseway Associates did not have the town to themselves, nor did they have a monopoly on difficulties. There were other Loyalists, some a rather dissipated lot who were enjoying the free provisions of the king. There were disbanded regiments.

The 'high colonial' McDonnough house, originally a tavern, John and Dock streets, Shelburne

There were 1,600 free blacks who had gone to the British side in the war, trusting in a promise of freedom and land grants; in Port Roseway they had been consigned to Birchtown, a separate and substandard community where they waited in vain for promises to be kept. And then there were the rocks and forests, as intractable as the winters.

The next owners of McDonnough's tavern were James Cox and William Robertson. Then, in 1807, the business was purchased by Thomas Bingay, Jr. Affairs seemed to be prospering for Bingay. He was the co-owner of a 65-ton schooner, the *Swallow*, built in 1798, and was importing flour and corn from Philadelphia. But when he died several years later in 1822, his total estate was worth only £118, nearly half of which was represented by the tavern lots and £5 of which was the value of 200 acres on the Tusket River. His personal property consisted in entirety of '1 feather bed, 2 bedsteads, with curtains and pillows, 2 mahogany tables, 1 pair brass andirons, shovel and tongs, 2 beer glasses, 17 pictures, a mahogany bureau, 1 bed quilt, 1 pair candlesticks, 3 silver spoons, 1 silver sugar tongs, 1 set silver castors, 1 milk jug, 1 pair of salts, 1 carpet, 1 dressing glass, 1 warming pan, 6 chairs, a shaving box and a gold watch.'

The tavern building passed through the hands of a shoemaker and a lumberman, and then, in 1863, was bought by William McLean, master mariner, a colourful man who, according to legend, was a one-legged sea captain. At his death in 1890 he left what he referred

Ross/Thomson home and store, Charlotte Lane, Shelburne

to as 'my homestead situate on the corner of Dock and John Street in the town of Shelburne ... and the stone wharf and land covered with water in front of my said homestead and store' to his son Abraham, who also inherited his father's land on McNutt's Island, which he shared with his brother John and two sisters.

This was long past Shelburne's days of glory. It had, after a meteoric period of growth, declined. When the King's Bounty (provisions of food and drink supplied by the British government to Loyalist settlers) expired, many gave up the fight and decamped. A tenacious 90 families (400 people in all) stayed on, in a town that the lieutenant-governor, Lord Dalhousie, later called 'the picture of despair and wretchedness ... the large homes, rotten and tumbling into the once fine and broad streets, the inhabitants crawling about idle and careworn in appearance, sunk in poverty and dejected in spirit.'

Those houses that survived were the fortunate few that had enjoyed continuous ownership as the fortunes of the town declined. One such was the Ross/Thomson house and store on Charlotte Lane, built by George and Robert Ross about 1785, just as Shelburne's population exploded. The brothers were Loyalists who had left their homes and moved south in response to the offer of refuge extended by the governors of east and west Florida during the American Revolution. When the Floridas were surrendered to Spain in the early 1780s, they, like others who wanted a British government, came in a small company to Shelburne in 1784. The brothers lived in one end of the building in spacious and well-appointed quarters, while their store occupied the other.

Interior of the Ross/Thom-son home, now a museum

Business boomed. The brothers owned several ships. By the mid-1780s Shelburne boasted 10,000 residents and was basking in its importance.

By 1809 that market had all but disappeared. Robert Ross had died, leaving George to run the store. Their clerk, Robert Thomson, had turned to schoolteaching. George sold the store in 1815, the year before his death, to Thomson's wife, Dorcas, while Thomson continued to teach, and the 300 customers still in town were served by Thomson's son, Robert Ross Thomson, who later added a post office. The building remained in the family until the death of Robert Ross Thomson, in the 1880s, when the store finally closed. It was later purchased by a Yarmouth native, restored and operated as a museum by the Shelburne Historical Society, and, in 1971, became the property of the Nova Scotia Museum.

The Ross/Thomson house reflects in its simplicity the golden days when Shelburne's future prospects seemed limitless and its prosperity assured. For colonists such as the Ross brothers and Thomson, and for the thousands of Loyalists who flocked there, the town offered hope and a brief, if difficult, refuge. Today, 70 per cent of the town's residents trace their ancestry back to the Loyalist refugees.

Down the coast from Shelburne, nestled in a bay at the southwestern tip of Nova Scotia, is the small community of Barrington. In contrast to the mass migration that created Shelburne two decades later, settlement here began with only twelve families who arrived in 1761, mainly from the Cape Cod towns of Chatham and Harwick. Within four years, these devoted Congregationalists started to build a meeting-house. According to their New England traditions, the settlement would be incomplete without a place to serve as public forum for town meetings and religious services. The Barrington Meetinghouse stands today – the oldest non-conformist, non-denominational meeting-house in Canada.

Joshua Nickerson, a ship's carpenter, and Elijah Swaine, a Nantucket Quaker, supervised the work as construction began and a simple, dignified two-storey building took shape. Since this labour of love had to compete with the demands of survival, it took many years before the work was done. In fact, seventy-six years passed before descendants of those first builders pronounced the meeting-house 'now finished and completed.' It had opened for worship in 1767, however, though still without seats, with the Rev. Samuel Wood preaching. Men entered by one door, women and young children by the other. They remained segregated. Children and older women were placed in front of the massive pulpit facing the congregation. Their attention and good behaviour were, seemingly, guaranteed.

There was no need to demand attention, however, when, in 1780, the charismatic Henry Alline came to preach. Alline, the son of William and Rebecca Alline, was born in Rhode Island, but his family had come to Falmouth Township in 1760. After a religious conversion Henry began preaching in the Minas region. Ordained there at age thirty-one, he became an itinerant and dynamic evangelical preacher, his highly emotional sermons interrupted by conversions to 'new birth,' confrontations with disbelievers, and outbursts of spontaneous song or lay preaching. His New Light ministry became almost a popular movement, appealing to a people isolated and struggling to make a living, but his mysticism and doctrines of personal salvation brought him into conflict with established religions and New England Puritanism. Alline rarely preached in church buildings, many of which were closed to him, and so his visit to the Barrington Meetinghouse was unusual. That meeting-house, however, was open to all preachers of the Gospel.

(The meeting-house may have welcomed all preachers, but it had not always welcomed all parishioners. In his *Nova Scotia Sketchbook*, L.B. Jenson tells

Barrington Meetinghouse

of an incident that occurred during its first year, when 'Charles, the local Indian head, attended service. He was dressed rather oddly wearing a long old shirt over all his other clothes. After the service was over, he went to shake hands with Mr. Wood, the Minister – Harvard Class of '45 – but Mr. Wood declined so Charles gave him a good, swift kick.')

By 1841, the meeting-house was finally completed. Two years later, town meetings were discontinued and the building was set aside for strictly religious purposes. Nearly demolished in 1889, it was saved and now operates as a branch of the Nova Scotia Museum.

Southwest of Shelburne and Barrington, off the southwestern tip of Nova Scotia, are three remote, barren islands: Seal, Mud, and Cape Sable. They became the graves for many hundreds. Some of the rocks around them have been named for wrecks. Blonde Rock, for example, off Seal Island, recalls HMS *Blonde*, which sank in the 1770s.

Over each long winter the shoals and ledges around the islands broke ships that had been forced off course, adding to the list of men and women who have lost their lives in the treacherous waters surrounding them. Sometimes survivors in the waters around Seal Island could be seen from shore, clinging to part of the wreckage for a while. Even if they survived long enough to reach the island they were only prolonging the inevitable. The lights of a fire might be seen for a while – then darkness. One man was found frozen, still in a kneeling position, where he had tried to get the spark for a fire from a flint and a steel.

And every spring in those years, a Yarmouth lay preacher, Calvin Cann, set out by boat with other Yarmouth men on a self-appointed mission. They were headed for Seal Island to bury the bodies they knew they would find there.

Some shipwrecked sailors were more fortunate. In January 1817 the *Friendship*, bound from the West Indies for Halifax, was blown off course in a four-day gale and heavy fog. The ice-covered ship lost its rudder and crashed on Cape Sable Island's rocky ledges. Her captain, Richard Hichens, and his crew were rescued by men from Cape Sable. Hichens, recovering from yellow fever, stayed with the Crowell family in nearby Barrington, where he was cared for by their daughter, Mary. She soon became his wife.

Mary Crowell knew what she wanted from life. She

was determined to make her home on Seal Island so that she might save lives. By 1823 she had persuaded her husband; her brother, Edmund Crowell; his wife, Jerusha; Jerusha's brother, John Nickerson; and his wife to move together to Seal Island. From that time onward, although there were numerous wrecks and many hundreds lost their lives (the *Staffordshire*, for instance, went down on 30 December 1854 with 250 lost), no survivor ever froze or bled to death on that island.

The three couples had to endure that first winter in makeshift shanties. The following summer they built their homes, locating them at different vantage points

Seal Island Light

so that together they could cover the entire coast. Over the years the Hichens, Crowells, Nickersons, and their descendants had ample opportunity to prove the value of their presence on Seal Island. Countless men and women were hauled from the ocean into a lifeboat that the families themselves had designed and built. Their rescue operation was the first life-saving station in Canada. Among the many rescued were fifty men saved from the wreck of the *St George* in 1869, and sixty-three rescued from the wreck of the *Assay* in 1897. On the island are three graves marked, simply, 'Woman.' The three were pulled from the sea and buried, after the wreck of the *Triumph*, on 1 May 1861.

Four years after the Hichens, Crowells, and Nickersons took up residence, they persuaded the governor, Sir James Kempt, to visit the island and assess the need for a lighthouse. In 1827 the eight-sided Seal Island light started to take form, a shared expense between Nova Scotia and New Brunswick. The light was lit 28 November 1831 by Richard Hichens, the same day that Mary gave birth to their first daughter. That light was tended alternately by Edmund and Richard until 1839. Richard then handled it alone until 1860, followed by his son, Corning Hichens, who was there until 1880. Corning Crowell, Jr, took over from 1880 to 1899; his brother John, from 1899 to 1927; and his son-in-law, Ellsworth Hamilton, from 1927 until 1941. It was only then, after 118 years, that the lighthouse-keeping duties passed out of the Hichens/Crowell family. Today Seal Island is a two-man 'bachelor station,' with the light-keepers working on rotating twenty-eight-day shifts.

When the original Seal Island light was dismantled, it was placed on a tower built near the Old Meetinghouse in Barrington. The Seal Island light was one of the earliest in Nova Scotia. The first was built at Louisbourg in 1738. The second, a stone octagonal lighthouse 'of old world design,' was the Sambro light outside Halifax harbour, dating from 1758. It is the oldest working lighthouse in North America.

CHAPTER FOURTEEN

Yarmouth

Poor Mrs Scott.

Rev. Jonathan Scott's young wife, Lucy, had put her jaw out of joint. She had done this by 'gaping' – at least that was the reason her husband gave in his journal entry of 21 June 1774. No medical help was available in the isolated settlement at Chebogue Point, the tip of a finger jutting into the sea south of Yarmouth, so Jonathan Scott decided to take Lucy to Halifax for help. Her jaw, Scott recounted, 'was extended downward and she could not get her teeth together, and it was twisted aside also and she could not get her jaws and teeth to range with each other; nor could she speak plain, or take any Food that wanted Chewing, and the pain was tedious to bear.'

Nine days after Lucy dislocated her jaw, the Scotts set sail for Halifax. It was another four days before they arrived there. The next day, after two painful weeks, a pair of doctors 'put Mrs Scott's jaw to place,' after about 'a quarter of an hour's trial.' Lucy Scott was, at the time, twenty-three years old, the mother of four, and pregnant with her fifth child.

The trip, it seems, had been difficult – not just for Lucy but for her husband as well. Jonathan Scott had slept in the hold of the ship en route to Halifax with the result that, although he was able to preach on the morning after their arrival, he afterward felt so faint that he was 'obliged to leave My company and go to bed.' Perhaps it was the rigours of the voyage that had made him ill, or it might have been the shocking conditions he encountered in Halifax, where 'profaneness abounds ... and the breach of the Sabbath ... [is] notorious.'

The Scotts soon returned to Chebogue Point. Jonathan, originally from Massachusetts, had arrived in the settlement (formerly called 'Kespoowuit,' or 'land's end,' by the Mi'kmaqs) in 1764, when he was twenty years old. That was just three years after the first little band of New England Planters (settlers) landed at nearby Crawley's Island, lured by Governor Charles Lawrence's promise of free land. Thirteen families settled there that first year, but by the summer of 1762 only six remained. The others, discouraged by an unusually harsh winter and the challenge of enduring 'Nova Scarcity,' had returned to the political uncertainties but familiar surroundings of the New England colonies.

Jonathan Scott, called by his contemporaries the 'doughty champion of New England Congregationalism,' remained at Chebogue until 1795, saving souls and fathering children. Lucy Scott died in 1777, leaving six motherless youngsters. She was twenty-six. Six years later, Jonathan married Elizabeth Bass, who bore him another seven offspring. During these years Scott became embittered and discouraged by what he perceived to be the failure of his religious mission. In 1795, the year his thirteenth child was born, Jonathan, Elizabeth, and their younger children left and settled in Bakerstown (now Minot), Maine. He died there in 1819; Elizabeth Scott lived until 1843.

Ellery Scott house, 7 Main Street

By the time Jonathan Scott left Nova Scotia, the children of his first marriage were adults, and some decided to remain. Nearly a century later, in 1892, Scott's great-great-grandson, Master Mariner Ellery Scott, purchased a house on the east side of Main Street, overlooking the harbour.

Scott's Georgian-style frame house had been built in the early 1800s by a mariner, Thomas Dalton. The land had belonged to Dalton's grandfather, Phinneas Durkee, one of that first group of Massachusetts Planters. Soon after building the house, Dalton died. The property came into the hands of his mother, Eleanor (Durkee) Dalton, and his widow, Elizabeth (Poole) Dalton, both of whom soon remarried. In the ensuing years, the Dalton property was either owned jointly by female descendants and their husbands, or settled in the name of the husband alone. The names on the title reflected the patriarchal social mores of the day. As widows and daughters married and remarried, each new husband acquired the woman's land and buildings. By 1820 title to Thomas Dalton's house was in the name of Joseph Tupper Archer (husband to Phinneas Durkee's granddaughter, Eleanor Durkee).

Joseph Tupper Archer was from a family of twenty-two, the father of this brood being an Englishman, John Archer, who had been pressed into the British navy. He eventually escaped or was released, settled in Maine, and married the daughter of Peleg Tupper, a distant relative of Sir Charles Tupper. Joseph Tupper Archer was a mason by trade. He and Eleanor Durkee became parents of nine children. He died in 1863.

The Dalton/Archer house was similar in style to its neighbours, as most settlers from New England built houses reminiscent of those they had left behind – simple wood buildings, practical and unpretentious. For the better part of a century it served the Dalton descendants well. But when Master Mariner Ellery Scott purchased it in 1892, he demanded more. Like others who lived by the sea, he added a tower to the front of his house – a splendid affair replete with Victorian embellishments: tall windows, bracketed eaves, and a delicate balustrade surrounding the flat roof. From there he could see forever. And when he was away, his wife, Margaret, could climb to the top of the tower to watch for his returning ship.

Scott's return from one voyage seemed something of a miracle. He was one of the few survivors when Mount Pelée, on the Caribbean island of Martinique, erupted in May 1902. In his journal, Scott wrote that when his ship attempted to escape the port, 'Fire, Molten Lava and Sea with Sulpher gass overwhelmed the Ship ... [with] ... men, women and children dead in a few second's time.' Scott was badly injured and it was months before he could set sail again.

The shipbuilding and trading industry, which, by the 1880s, had made Yarmouth Canada's second-largest port of registry, began in the nearby village of Tusket. By the middle years of the nineteenth century, five companies there were producing ships for the high seas. Fishing and milling concerns were also thriving. Tusket had been settled in the mid 1780s by New England Loyalists, mainly from New York and New Jersey. Among this group were some Dutch families as well as several blacks, most of whom, within a few years, sold their land to their Loyalist neighbours and moved away.

Tusket grew quickly. By the turn of the century it had become clear that a court-house was urgently needed: judges were having to hold General Sessions of the Peace for Yarmouth and Argyle townships in private homes, churches, and schools. In Yarmouth, court convened in John Richan's tavern.

By October 1805 the trim little Argyle District Court

Canada's oldest standing court-house, built for the Argyle District, stands in Tusket

House was up and ready for business. It stood by the Old Main Post Road near the centre of the village, splendid in its simplicity and testifying by its presence to the growing importance of Tusket. On the roof was a delicate cupola, which for many years housed a bell that served as the community fire alarm. (The bell was removed from the cupola during a 1982 restoration and placed in the rear yard. It cracked overnight – and now sits inside the entrance to the building.) The Tusket court-house stands today, lovingly restored and open (in spring and summer) to the public. It is the oldest court-house in Canada.

Even when new, the court-house could not have been considered spacious. The entire building measured only twenty by twenty-five feet. Inside, to the left of the main entrance, a finely crafted staircase led to a tiny courtroom. Prisoners were held in small cells on the ground floor, in one of two 'Separate Apartments,' according to the specifications: 'one, eight feet by nineteen feet for criminals – and the other to contain Twelve feet by Nineteen feet for Debtors. The "Apartment" for criminals was allowed a window with six panes; that for debtors, one with twelve.'

By 1833 more space was needed and £42 was authorized to 'finish the court house.' The small building doubled in size. In 1870 another addition, similarly sized, resulted in a building with three times the original space. This extension allowed for a new jury room and judge's chambers, along with various decorative elements to spruce up the courtroom.

Tusket's lovely court-house would not have seemed out of place in any New England village. Its Loyalist builders had successfully adapted details of the orderly and exacting Neoclassical style to which they were accustomed: a central doorway flanked with delicately fluted pilasters and topped with a fan transom; a gently curved gable; returning eaves; dentil-like brackets under the eaves; pilasters at each corner – all elements of a style revered by the Loyalists, a style that, based as it was on Greek antiquity, exemplified for them the democratic ideals on which the American colonies were founded.

Among the first of the Loyalists to settle in Tusket were four young Hatfield men, three brothers and a cousin. They arrived in 1785 and founded a family for which the word 'prolific' might have been coined. By the end of the nineteenth century it became difficult to find a family in the Yarmouth/Tusket area in whose family tree the Hatfield name did not appear at least once, and often several times.

It was not, at the time, particularly unusual for cousins to marry cousins; it occurred not infrequently in many families. The Hatfields seemed especially inclined to the practice. Perhaps they took to heart an article in *The Yarmouth Herald* of 6 August 1858 which claimed that:

The marriage of cousins, perhaps more than that of any other persons, is likely to produce a greater amount of wedded happiness, provided the union is formed from feelings of affection and respect. The intimacy that naturally exists between their families, their perfect knowledge of each others' habits and character from childhood, the seeing one another unrestrainedly at all times ... tend to make such unions most happy when entered into advisedly.

The article cautioned, however, that both partners of the union must be healthy, stating that when

two persons, whether cousins or not, of weakly constitutions and scrofulous habit of body, contract marriage, their progeny, if they have any are sure, according to the laws of nature, to show taint in some form or other – a bad tree *cannot* produce *good* fruit ...

Take, for instance, Job Lyons Hatfield. Lyons, as he was known, was a grandson of Colonel Job Hatfield, one of the first four Hatfields who settled in Tusket.

Job Lyons Hatfield house, Court Street, Tusket

(The others were Job's cousins, James, Jacob Lyon, and Abram Marsh.) All four had come from Elizabeth Town, New Jersey; settled in Shelburne in 1783; and then, two years later, moved to Tusket. Lyons Hatfield's parents were both Hatfields; his father, John Van Norden Hatfield, had married Sarah Jane Hatfield, a second cousin, daughter of Jacob Lyon. In keeping with family tradition, two of Lyons's sisters married Hatfield brothers, sons of another cousin, and grandsons of Abram Marsh Hatfield. Lyons himself married out of the family. His wife was Martha Harding. They had no children.

What Lyons and Martha did have was one of the loveliest houses in this part of Nova Scotia. Built on Court Street about 1863, it had as its most distinguishing feature its central gable, the roof line of which slopes down in a graceful curve, framing the dormer above the front entrance. So distinctive is this curved gable that it appears to be a purely local architectural element – even a Hatfield element – for the same trademark gable is found on a storage shed which was built near the house where Lyons grew up, on the homestead of his father, John Van Norden Hatfield. The house has been demolished, but the shed remains. The roof of Lyons and Martha's house projects beyond the façade and forms an open porch, supported by six sturdy columns. Above the porch, a delicate balustrade stretches along the base of the dormer. The house has changed little since the Hatfields lived there.

Lyons was a businessman with interests in many local concerns, but financial reverses in the early 1870s forced him to sell his house only ten years after it was built. Records then described him as 'Job Lyons Hatfield, merchant, an insolvent.'

The oldest house still standing in Tusket also has, not surprisingly, a Hatfield connection. Known as the Lent house, it is a simple homesteader's home, built in the 1780s or 1790s by Abraham Lent, a Loyalist who arrived in Tusket in 1785, the same year as did the four Hatfields. After some fifteen years in the village, A-braham Lent returned to Orange County, New York, and sold the house to his brother, James Lent, Sr, another of the original settlers. James Lent became one of the community's leading citizens – justice of the peace, justice of the Inferior Court of Common Pleas, and a member of the legislature. James Lent may never have lived in the house himself, as he had his own house

Job Lyons Hatfield

elsewhere in Tusket. In any event he deeded the house to a son, Abraham, in 1835; by then, Abraham and his wife, Mary Hatfield (a daughter of Jacob Lyon), had been living in the house for some time. Abraham (also a member of the legislature) and Mary spent their married lives here. They were childless, and when they died the property passed to Mary's nephew, James Adolphus Hatfield, and two Hatfield cousins.

James Lent, Sr, was known as a man who maintained a good relationship with his black servants, one of whom had acted as a wet nurse to several of his children. Another, a man servant, was trusted by Lent to return to New York after the Revolution to bring back a valued family chest. Several black Loyalists built homes in Tusket. One of them, a splendid, well-maintained, and quite elegant house, still stands – an exception to the rule regarding the poor treatment accorded black Loyalists. The first owner was listed on the deed as 'Abigail Price, black woman.' So it would seem that, for one family at least, promises were kept. But this was an exception, and soon nearly all had moved away.

In Yarmouth, at 405 Pleasant Street, stands a house nearly identical to the Lent house, and built just a few years later. It is one of the oldest houses in Yarmouth. This was the home of Ebenezer Corning, Jr, a member of one of the original Planter families. He was a boy of six when his parents brought him to Nova Scotia in 1764. When he was twenty-one he married Elizabeth Foote, daughter of Zachariah Foote, also a Planter.

Abraham Lent

The American Revolution was well under way by this time, and both the Cornings and the Footes found themselves caught up in the conflict, and like so many of their neighbours, torn by divided loyalties. They suffered at the hands of American privateers, in spite of the fact that they had harboured and transported American prisoners back to New England. Indignantly they protested to the Massachusetts courts for redress.

Ebenezer and Elizabeth Corning had been married for many years and had a grown family before they built their house, shortly after the turn of the century. In 1821 Ebenezer divided the property among his four daughters and their husbands, his three sons either having predeceased him or having received other land from their father. Four years later one sister, Elizabeth Baker, and her husband, Amos, purchased all the lots from her sisters for £160. Amos Baker, member of another Planter family, left the property to Elizabeth. They were childless, so at her death it went to his nephew, Amos Baker Brown. It remained in the Brown family for many years.

Just as there were countless Hatfields in Tusket and Yarmouth, there were a goodly number of Browns as well. The founder of one such family was John Brown, an enterprising Scot who had arrived in Yarmouth in 1813. His wife of fourteen years, Janet, and their two sons, Robert and Stayley, eleven and twelve, respectively, had stayed behind in Glasgow to await word that John had a place for them to live and a means of supporting them. Janet Balfour Brown had been a widow in her mid-thirties and the mother of two infant children when John met and married her. She was, he said approvingly, 'a cleanly prudent, Industrious Woman.' In 1800 twin girls were born to them, but they died in infancy. The following two years saw the birth of their sons. John was ecstatic: 'I received with joy these most Precious Gifts of Providence as Pledges of present and future Happieness.' Their marriage lasted until Janet's death, forty-five years later. (Other than a brief mention in his reminiscences written in 1840, John made no further mention of Janet's children by her first husband.)

Ebenezer Corning house,
405 Pleasant Street

As soon as he arrived in Yarmouth, Brown set out to establish a business. He opened a shop, selling woollens and homespun from Scotland. Within two years he had a viable operation and a solid, two-storey house beside the harbour, on land where the town's first settler, Sealed Landers, had camped. He was thus able to send for Janet and their sons. On 28 October 1815 an excited John Brown met his family when they docked in Halifax. That evening, he later recalled, 'with my Wife and Two sons at my Side I was as Rich and Happy as any Man in Nova Scotia.' By 14 November the family was 'Snugly lodged at Home in Yarmouth.' That snug home, sturdy and unpretentious, still stands today at One Market Lane, Milton Corner.

The Browns' house, a colonial-style structure, served as both home and, it seems likely, John Brown's store. The main door, sheltered by a small portico, led to the family's quarters, while a second door beside it led to the store. Goods that arrived at Market Wharf behind the house were stored in the huge stone cellar below.

With his family safe in Yarmouth, John Brown soon enrolled the boys in school and, as well, had them studying church music with a local teacher. But he wanted more than scholarly pursuits for them so that they might adjust happily to their new, quiet, surroundings – so different from the crowded streets of Glasgow: 'I wished for a Dancing School both to cheer them and this dull-spirited place Where an Ignorant grovelling Supperstition has laid a Blight on social joys and laid Reason Prostrate at its Feet!'

The boys grew to manhood. Stayley, the elder son, was industrious and dependable, moving steadily from success to success, the pride of his father's life. Robert, the younger son, was a constant worry. 'I had a strong apprehension that my son Robert would never be a merchant,' John Brown later recalled. The young man tried farming, and an apprenticeship as a carpenter, but neither appealed. Next, his parents sent him back to Scotland for the winter, to see if work could be found for him there, but he returned to Yarmouth, jobless, the following spring. In desperation Brown bought a store for Robert when the young man turned twenty-one. But before long, and in spite of his father's contribution of more than £200 worth of goods, he managed to fail in that career as well. To make matters worse, a serious rift had developed between Robert and Stayley: the brothers 'were nursing a violent antipathy to each other ... and spoke in terms of Sulky Contempt.'

One can only imagine his parents' reaction when, in 1824, the son who was causing them such concern decided to marry. Robert's bride was twenty-year-old Sarah Harding, a woman as 'young and inexperienced as Himself and with wonderful levity they resolved not to take up House where they were at Home but to remove to

John Brown house,
1 Market Lane, Milton

Prince Edward Island and leave his own store empty. [The newlyweds] scarcely known to each other, went off to seek Bread and Comfort among Distant Strangers!!'

Sarah Harding's parents lived close to the Browns in the hamlet of Milton. Sarah's father, Harris Harding, was a well-known minister of the New Light evangelical persuasion, who travelled and preached in remote communities along the South Shore. According to historian J.M. Bumsted, scandal touched the young preacher's life when, in 1796, he publicly confessed to having impregnated Mehitable Harrington of Liverpool. (Or, as was said in those parts, 'he came in the fog and left in the morning.') But Harding did the honourable thing and married Mehitable six weeks before their child was born. The following year, when Harding returned to preach in Liverpool, Simeon Perkins noted disapprovingly that 'I think it not too much to the Honor of the town to allow a man of His Character and principles to preach in a publick Meeting House.' Harding seemed devoted to Mehitable. Years later, in his memoirs, he mentioned that she was recovering from an operation. The unfortunate woman had undergone a mastectomy (surely one of the first of its kind performed in Nova Scotia) and had had 'one entire brest removed, to stop the progress of a raging cancer therein.' Harris Harding lived to the age of ninety-two, having become 'one of the beloved figures of his denomination.'

Sarah Harding and Robert Brown eventually matured, owing, as John Brown had predicted, to the necessity of providing for their growing family. Their first son, named John Brown for his grandfather, was born in Prince Edward Island, but the succeeding ten children were Yarmouth-born. Robert and Sarah had come to recognize that 'Bread and Comfort' were more readily found close to hearth and home.

Robert Brown died at sea in 1854, his father nine years later at the age of ninety-two. Stayley Brown lived out his long and successful life in Yarmouth; married Charlotte Fletcher, daughter of family friends; and, in time, became a member of the legislature and treasurer of the province.

A prosperous shipowner, merchant, and politician, Stayley was respected by all who knew him. 'No man in Nova Scotia ... enjoyed a larger share of the public confidence and esteem,' said *The Yarmouth Tribune* at his death. Although still in his teens when he left Scotland, he never lost his love for his first home and for all things Scottish. According to Isabelle Owen, a family friend (and daughter of Yarmouth historian J.G. Farish) who remembered Stayley in his later years, he was

a fine looking old gentleman with ruddy complection, bright blue eyes, [and] white hair standing straight up from his forehead … many a gold bit he gave me as a reward for playing the accompaniments to his Scottish songs … He imported his own goods and my mother's firm belief was that if she bought anything from him it was the best of its kind.

Stayley's life, however, had not been without tragedy. Charlotte, mother of their three daughters and three sons, died in 1843, when the youngest child was then only three. He raised them alone. In 1864, by then in his middle years, Stayley married Ellen Grantham Farish, and built a handsome home for her at 12 Vancouver Street. The house, a spacious two-and-a-half-storey frame structure, had a three-bay façade with a central gable above a triangular Palladian window. Venetian windows on the first floor were topped with triangular heads, all part of the detailing that characterized the house. It quite obviously belonged to people of substance and refinement.

By the time of his death in 1877, all three of Stayley Brown's daughters and one son had predeceased him. And, as his will made evident, history was repeating itself. Of his two surviving sons, one had evidently been causing him concern.

Stayley Brown house, Vancouver Street

That son, George Stephen 'Stayley' Brown, was a businessman and politician who, in his later years, became a noted Yarmouth historian. His success in both business and politics was short-lived, although, in 1863, he did win a seat in the assembly (with signs that read: 'George Stayley Brown is the man for the Town'). Although his middle name was Stephen, he was known locally as George Stayley, in order, he later recounted, to distinguish him from the 'half-dozen other George Browns then living in Yarmouth town.'

George and his wife, Elizabeth Bond, lived in Rock Cottage, a many-gabled house on a lane south off Forest Street. Elizabeth was a daughter of Deborah Tooker and Hon. James P. Bond, who had been appointed to the Legislative Council in 1837. Elizabeth inherited the house after his death in 1854. Two years later Elizabeth, then a 'spinster' of thirty-six, married the up-and-coming Brown, who was seven years her junior. Their home, 'among the most attractive private residential properties in the town,' occupied a historic site; an octagonal fort had stood there during the War of 1812 when the townspeople lived in fear of American attack.

George and Elizabeth Brown were socially prominent. In August 1858 they caused a stir in town when they entertained the 3rd Earl of Mulgrave, George Augustus Constantine Phipps, who had recently been appointed lieutenant-governor of Nova Scotia. The earl and his lady arrived one August day by steamer, and *The Yarmouth Herald* reported excitedly their every move: 'The Countess was assisted to a carriage by Dr Bond and His excellency took his seat by her side ... They drove immediately to Rock cottage, the residence of Mr George Stayley Brown. We need hardly say that there was a general turn out of our citizens in their holiday attire.'

Next morning, the distinguished visitors arrived for an eleven-o'clock reception at the flag- and flower-bedecked Masons' Hall, accompanied by their hostess, Elizabeth Brown. That afternoon, Lady Mulgrave held a 'drawing-room' at Rock Cottage, an event which was undoubtedly the highlight of Yarmouth's 1858 social season. Unfortunately, the morning reception had to take place without George 'Stayley,' who was, reportedly, 'not well enough to attend.' The family was represented by his brother, Charles Brown, and Elizabeth Brown's sister, Ann Murray.

By the time he reached his mid-forties, George 'Stayley's' real estate holdings were being liquidated, and he was in debt to his father, the real Stayley Brown. He and Elizabeth were forced to sell Rock Cottage in 1877, the year his father died. Stayley, in order to protect his daughter-in-law and her children, left half his estate to Elizabeth, her two daughters, and one son. (The couple's first son, three-year-old 'Georgie' Fletcher, had drowned in a pond near the house in 1860.) The other half of Stayley's estate was left to his younger son, Charles. George 'Stayley' was not included. He and his family moved to Boston, where, for the rest of his life, he continued to record Yarmouth history and the complex genealogies of its citizens. He died there in September 1915. His lengthy obituary included no mention of his wife, the long-suffering Elizabeth Bond.

Charles Edward Brown, the younger of Stayley Brown's sons, inherited all his father's real estate, including the house on Vancouver Street. Charles, a Harvard graduate at nineteen, was, like his father, a prominent and respected member of the community. He was a commissioner of schools for Yarmouth County and a founder of the Agricultural Society, who did much to improve the stock and fruit trees of the county.

Herbert Huntington house, 593 Main Street

All told, John Brown and his descendants left a lasting legacy to Yarmouth. Like so many other Nova Scotia families, they lost sons to the sea. Robert Brown, who so worried his father, was lost in 1854, as was Robert's son, Captain Herbert Huntington Brown, in 1892 when his new steel ship, the *Thracian*, was lost off the Isle of Man. His wife and the twenty-two crew members died with him.

Herbert Huntington Brown was the namesake of another prominent Yarmouth figure, Herbert Huntington, the only man other than Joseph Howe to have a monument erected in his honour by the legislature – governments (and politicians) being prudently aware that today's hero may well end up as tomorrow's scoundrel. But such was not the case with Yarmouth's Herbert Huntington. His sterling reputation remains untarnished to this day.

Huntington's home at 596 Main Street was built early in the century, possibly by his father, Miner Huntington, a Connecticut Loyalist, surveyor, and prothonotary (chief notary). The house, like its owner, was unpretentious – a straightforward, colonial-style structure, forgoing ostentation but adequate for the family's needs.

Herbert was barely in his teens when the War of 1812

broke out, but he mustered with the local militia and
was, on one occasion, involved in repelling an American
vessel during an attempted landing. For a while he
taught school, farmed, and, not surprisingly, developed
interests in shipping. When he was twenty-two, Huntington, along with his brother-in-law, James Starr, his
close friends John and Stayley Brown, and about sixteen
others, helped form the Yarmouth Book Society. They
were like-minded men, intellectually honest and mindful
of the importance of education. Their first library was
housed in James Starr's modest home that still stands
(much altered) on Main Street.

In his early thirties Huntington plunged into politics, representing Shelburne County; when Yarmouth
County was carved out of Shelburne County, he served
as its representative until his death. From the beginning
the voters knew their man, and in the Legislative Assembly his intellectual powers, his integrity, and his political ability immediately won him respect. He became
a friend of other reformers such as James Boyle Uniacke
and Joseph Howe – a close-enough friend that he acted
as second for Howe in March 1840, when Howe had
his duel with John Croke Halliburton, a son of Chief
Justice Brenton Halliburton. Yet he parted company
with these men on many occasions when he saw their
efforts as compromise and a betrayal of principle. Huntington's goal was responsible government, and he
pursued this with unflinching determination throughout his career. One biographer, A.A. MacKenzie, remarked: 'political reform in his native province was
largely brought about by his single-minded tenacity and
political subtlety.'

Herbert Huntington

At home in Yarmouth with his wife, Rebecca (née
Pinkney), and their five children, Huntington lived
quietly and unpretentiously. At his death in 1851 he left
'half of [his] late dwelling house' and an annuity to Rebecca. The remainder of his estate was divided equally
among four sons, James, John, Charles, and Herbert,
and one daughter, Agnes. Herbert Huntington died respected by all who knew him.

Huntington's house was simple and unassuming, as
were most of the town's buildings during its early years.
As the nineteenth century wore on, however, and prosperity increased, Yarmouth's growing wealth was reflected in the homes of its citizens. To one degree or
another, virtually everyone there was dependent on the
sea. Ships from Yarmouth sailed to ports around the

world, and the masters of those schooners brought back treasures which they proudly displayed in the imposing houses they built as symbols of their status in the community. As in most seaports, houses were situated overlooking the sea. They boasted towers and turrets, 'widow's walks' and 'widow's peeks' (tower windows) – built so that those who feared and loved the sea could watch over it.

Yarmouth had become a commercial and administrative centre. Shipbuilding enterprises that had begun with the New Englanders at Chebogue and the Loyalists at Tusket now grew rapidly in the harbour. Ferries ran daily to and from Maine, because many families had ties and business interests there and along the eastern seaboard. Many Yarmouth men owned or had a financial interest in one or more vessels – a risky business at best, but with the potential of handsome returns. One such man was John W. Lovitt.

In his extensive genealogy of the Lovitt family, George 'Stayley' Brown wrote that John Lovitt was a descendant of a distinguished family which traced its history back to one Richardus de Louet, who had arrived in England from Normandy in the company of William the Conquerer. Richardus's son, William, was 'in high favore with the king' and renowned for his great strength. William had married a French woman and upon her death had accompanied her body to France, buried her there, and retired to a nearby monastery. From there he 'every day until the day of his death paid a visit to her tomb and on that day caused himself to be carried and laid upon this grave, where he expired.' The story became a family legend and resulted in a nursery song:

> May my child be as stout
> May my child be as strong
> May my brave boy live as long
> As Willie of Normandy.

The following generations did indeed prove themselves stout and strong. Centuries later, one descendant settled in Salem, Massachusetts, and thus began the American branch of the family. Many became mariners and, of those who did, many died in foreign ports, were lost at sea, or sailed from port and were never heard from again. Seven master mariners named Lovitt died in one year alone.

With such a family history, it was not surprising that one intrepid member, Andrew Lovitt, landed near Yarmouth in 1766, shortly after the arrival of the first Planters from the American colonies. Here, the Lovitts' seafaring traditions carried on. Almost a century later, in 1863, Andrew's grandson, Captain John Walker Lovitt, was writing to his seafaring son, also Captain John Lovitt, sending news of Yarmouth and sharing his concerns about the family's shipping business. The father mentioned in passing that the son's new house at 10 Parade Street, the construction of which he was supervising, was 'finished complete and ready for Elizabeth to move into when she has a mind to.' Lovitt also implied that it was high time for his son to return home.

But Elizabeth Lovitt (née Guest) had a mind to be at sea with her husband. Six months later, in March 1864, John Lovitt again wrote his son, reporting that the new house had been leased for a year to a Mr Brown. At the time Elizabeth was on board the *Frances Hillard* with her husband and their children. The final bills for the house were in; it cost $2,800. The letter ended with: 'Your mother is very lonesome,' and a postscript: 'Write as often as possible.'

That request, it seems, fell on deaf ears. One year later, 13 March 1865, the senior Lovitt scolded: 'I have been despaired in not hearing from you before. I do not like such treatment when there is so much property

Lovitt house, 10 Parade Street

at stake ... it was your duty to have let me know how you was progressing with the ship business.'

In due time, John and Elizabeth Lovitt returned to Yarmouth and settled into their new home, a simple, Georgian-style frame house, pleasant in appearance, but architecturally quite unremarkable. Not for long, however, did the house remain ordinary. The younger Lovitts had ideas of their own. Specifically, they wanted a tower – a place from which they could see out to the ocean and a place which would, as well, provide a dramatic spot to house Elizabeth's plants and flowers. So add a tower they did – an addition so distinctive that it set the house apart from any other domestic dwelling in Nova Scotia.

The new tower was a glassed-in, three-storey, prow-like structure, thrusting out from the façade. Its pointed, domed roof was topped with a finial, the end of which was shaped like a fleur-de-lis. Built into the roof were several portholes which enabled the Lovitts to see across Yarmouth, over the harbour, and out to the horizon. In later years the portholes and the finial were removed, but the house remains today one of the town's most unusual buildings.

Captain Lovitt, his seagoing days behind him, settled down in the Parade Street house and went on to become a wealthy shipowner and politician, first in the provincial legislature and then as a federal member of Parliament. In 1896 Lovitt was appointed to the Senate. He died

Sen. John Lovitt, June 1897

The home of George and Mary Ellen Guest, 12 Parade Street. The cupola has been removed since this photograph was taken.

in 1908, survived by Elizabeth and five of their eight children.

John Lovitt was also survived by a sister, Mary Ellen Guest, who had a handsome house next door. It, too, had been built by their father. Mary Ellen's husband, George Hutchinson Guest, was a brother of Elizabeth Lovitt and so their children were 'double cousins.' Guest was also high sheriff of Yarmouth County. George and Mary Ellen's house, likely built at about the time of their 1874 marriage, was in the then-popular Italianate style, with tall, paired windows, bracketed eaves, and a playful, pagoda-like cupola (since removed). Signalling the family's seafaring background were pilasters at each corner of the house outlined with carefully carved mouldings which looked for all the world like rope. Small 'portholes' added a decorative touch to the entablature above the second-floor windows. It was, like its neighbour, a quietly elegant house. But then the Lovitts built their 'glass tower,' an addition so prominent that it tended to dwarf the architectural details of every other building on the street – and, in particular, the Guest house next door.

George Guest's (and Elizabeth Lovitt's) father, Robert Guest, had been a merchant in St John's, Newfoundland, but left there in 1827 to seek his fortune in Yarmouth, where he soon became involved in the town's shipping industry. George, born there in 1849, and educated at the Yarmouth Academy, was also involved in shipping, as a shipowner and in the marine insurance business. As well, he had good political connections, not only by marriage but through his mother's family, who had been in Yarmouth since the town's earliest days. Guest's maternal great-grandfather, Norman Utley, had represented Yarmouth in the provincial legislature from 1800 to 1806. When the position of high sheriff came vacant in 1887, George Guest's family connections added weight to the influence already exerted by his brother-in-law John Lovitt, next door.

The fanciful cupola that once topped the Guest house may have been copied from a similar building at 3 Sycamore Street. This house, according to local legend, was once used to store illicitly imported rum brought from the West Indies. It was owned by a Yarmouth merchant, Norman J.B. Tooker.

The Tooker house exemplifies the intricate family connections woven and interwoven throughout Yarmouth's history. The land on which it was built was first owned by a sailmaker, Hiram Betts, and next by a shoemaker, Samuel Purdy. Then, in 1847, the name 'Norman James Bond' appeared on the title. He was a son of the Hon. James Bond who built Rock Cottage, and a brother of Elizabeth Brown. At the time he was single; by the time he was married in 1854, to Jane Moody, the property had passed to its next owner and the builder of the house which stands there today.

This was Captain Thomas Stowe of Bermuda whose wife, Eliza Moody Bingay, was undoubtedly related to the future Jane Bond. They lived there from 1852 until his death in 1866. The house was inherited by his three daughters and his son, Thomas, Jr. Early in 1872, the latter, in a distinct departure for a Yarmouth man, married someone 'from away,' one Julia Leaycraft of Quebec.

By 1875 the house on Sycamore Street had changed hands again. This time the owner was Norman James Bond Tooker, who, it is said, hauled illicit rum via a dumb-waiter up to the attic for safekeeping. Adding another strand to Yarmouth's tangled family relationships was Tooker's wife, Jane Hatfield, a sister of J. Lyons Hatfield of the beautiful Tusket house. She, coincidentally, was christened with the same name as her husband's mother, Jane Hatfield, daughter of one of the first four Tusket Hatfields, Colonel Job Hatfield.

Sudden death at sea was not the only threat faced by citizens of Yarmouth. On land there was an ever-present danger from epidemics that took young lives overnight. Few families escaped both kinds of tragedy. George Bond (a brother of the Hon. James Bond and an uncle of Elizabeth Brown and Norman Bond) and his wife, Frances Carter, were among those who suffered the heart-breaking but common loss of children. Their first baby, Eliza Carter Bond, born 14 October 1833, died less than a year later. The Bonds then named her sister, born 17 July 1836, Eliza Carter. Two more children, Sarah and John, followed, and then, on 21 December 1841, another baby, Anna Ritchie Bond, was born. She lived only three and a half years. Less than a year after Anna's death the family was blessed with another girl baby. She too was named Anna Ritchie, after her dead sister. This practice of 'replacing' children who had died seems strange today but was not unusual for the times.

George and Frances lived in Murray Manor (at the corner of Main and Forest streets). Built for them, probably about the time of their marriage in 1832, it was hip-roofed, with Gothic and classical features. There were lovely Gothic windows on the first floor, and above them small 'eyebrow' or 'kneeling' windows. It was a style in which exterior appearance was the main concern, with the availability of light of secondary importance.

For reasons now unknown, the George Bonds moved to Centreville, California, some time before 1854. Their house came into the hands of George's niece, Ann, the daughter of James Bond, and her husband, James Murray. They lived there until 1899.

Directly behind Murray Manor, at 17 Forest Street, lived the Rev. John Thomas Tidmarsh Moody, who, for forty years, served as the revered rector of Yarmouth's Holy Trinity Anglican Church. Moody's wife bore two solid Yarmouth names: she was Sarah Bond Farish, daughter of Dr Henry G. Farish and a niece of James and George Bond. (Had any one of the Bond, Brown, Tooker, Farish, or Hatfield families ever attempted a family picnic, one can only assume that the entire town would have turned up for the event!)

Born in Halifax in 1804 of Loyalist parentage, John Tidmarsh Moody studied at King's College, Windsor, and in 1834 was ordained by the Rt Rev. John Inglis. For the next twelve years he served the area around Liverpool until, in 1846, he was appointed to Yarmouth, and there he spent the rest of his life – a life of devotion to his family, his parishioners, and the town.

Three years before his death on 18 October 1883, he and his wife celebrated their fiftieth wedding anniversary – a landmark occasion that we today recognize as notable, but in the days when only a fortunate few

Murray Manor, 225 Main Street

lived to see a seventieth birthday it was an even more exceptional event. The marriage, however, had not been without tragedy. Of their nine children, five predeceased them. *The Yarmouth Herald* of 25 October 1883, in a lengthy obituary, described him as 'singularly attractive' in character: 'among all denominations he was beloved and reverenced for his high-mindedness ... His manner was dignified, but winning; old and young alike were attracted to him, recognizing instinctively that he was a Christian and a gentleman, and that his kindly interest in them came from the sincere depths of a genuinely good nature.'

Dr Moody's widow survived him by four years.

The Moody house, an unusual structure, was built about 1855, and originally stood on Main Street at Cumberland. It replaced the first building on the site, which had been the home of Sarah's father, Dr Farish, and subsequently that of the Rev. T.A. Grantham, an early rector of Holy Trinity. The building was moved to its present location on Forest Street in recent years.

The house began as a typical vernacular centre-gabled cottage, but finished as a somewhat eccentric collage of unrelated architectural details. Off-centre windows, heavy door and window mouldings, and porthole windows in both gables (an unusual feature, even for Yarmouth) suggest that the house, like Topsy, 'just growed.' Certainly it seems likely that the Moodys were more interested in matters spiritual than architectural.

Soon after Dr Moody's death, parishioners at Holy Trinity began the search for a new rector, and a furore erupted in the congregation. The curate, Rev. Richmond Uniacke Shreve, age thirty-three, seemed to many the logical choice, but many others favoured appointing someone new. When the final vote was taken, Shreve's supporters lost by eight votes. They were furious.

The Shreve contingent included some of Yarmouth's most influential citizens. They appealed to the Bishop of Nova Scotia, Hibbert Binney, asking that the parish be divided so that they could be given their own church and, by extension, their own rector. That approach met with immediate disfavour. Undeterred, they then suggested setting up a completely new parish. But the Anglicans of Yarmouth didn't know their man. The stern, authoritarian Bishop Binney held that the church must remain steadfast against local whims and fashions. The dissidents were out of luck, and the unfortunate Rev. Shreve found himself looking for a new post. Eventually

The front door of Murray Manor

he settled in the United States as rector of Holy Innocents Church in Albany, New York.

From all accounts, Richmond Uniacke Shreve handled the situation with grace and good humour. In later years, a granddaughter described him as 'gentle, somewhat stocky, smiling and cheerful.' Her most vivid memory, she recalled, was seeing him one summer day 'in his clerical robe and flat hat, standing in the stern of a rowboat among the bullrushes and flycasting for trout.'

Shreve was not fond of his middle name, Uniacke, and never used it. His granddaughter wrote that 'it was long after his death that we learned what the suppressed "U" stood for.' The most likely namesake was the feisty Richard Fitzgerald Uniacke (1797-1870), an evangelical clergyman much admired by his contemporaries – one of whom was Richmond Shreve's father, the Rev. Charles Jessen Shreve. Richard Fitzgerald Uniacke was frequently at odds with Bishop John Inglis and his successor, Bishop Binney. Just possibly Richmond Uniacke Shreve's career in Nova Scotia came to an end because of his middle name. Other careers have foundered on more trivial circumstances.

About a year before the death of J.T.T. Moody and the ensuing uproar at Holy Trinity, Richmond Shreve (who had evidently expected to stay in Yarmouth for a while) built a house for his family at 59 William Street. Like most houses in town it was built of wood, but, befitting its owner, it was more restrained than its flam-

Home of the Rev. Richmond Uniacke Shreve, 59 William Street

boyant neighbours, depending only on some delicate bargeboard and a small bracketed portico for ornamentation. Shreve; his wife, Mary Catherine Parker Hocken; and their four children lived in their new home for only a year before their departure for the new parish in the United States.

Shreve had acquired the lot on which he built his house from Robert Sargent Eakins, a local businessman who had already built identical, lofty, Victorian Gothic houses next door to it on William Street for his son and daughter. They dominated William Street and, for that matter, most of Yarmouth. The Shreves didn't even try to 'keep up with the Eakinses.' Few could.

Eakins built the house at 57 William Street in the 1870s for his daughter, Helen, and her husband, Job Hatfield (grandson of Jacob Lyon Hatfield of early Tusket). Beside it, at 55 William Street, stood its twin, built for his son, Arthur.

Arthur, born in Yarmouth in 1847, had been raised in Tusket where, at age twelve, he began his working career as a junior clerk for a shipbuilding firm. In his twenties he tried his luck in the United States, then married, and returned to Yarmouth in the early 1870s. In

Eakin/Hatfield house,
57 William Street

1874, he and Edward F. Parker established Parker Eakins & Co., a mercantile firm which, by the 1890s, had become one of the largest businesses in Nova Scotia. Their wholesale grocery company achieved considerable success in marketing boneless cod in 'Upper Canada' and elsewhere, calling it 'Nova Scotia Turkey.' Parker Eakins expanded and diversified, eventually owning sawmills and timberlands, exporting lumber, operating a fleet of schooners, and conducting trade with the West Indies, Spain, and Great Britain – a grand success story for two young partners who had started with no capital of their own. Eakins became one of Yarmouth's most famous sons. In his vigorous eighties he was described as a man with 'humorously twinkling eye and ruddy, smiling countenance' and as the 'doyen of Nova Scotia commercialdom, [the] exemplar of useful citizenship.' Arthur Eakins died in 1937 in his ninetieth year.

In January 1992 Arthur Eakins's home was destroyed in a disastrous fire. It was an irreplaceable loss for Yarmouth and the province. His sister's house now stands alone representing the pair, impressive but light-hearted, with soaring, pointed gables, finials, and decorative iron cresting, typical of the country villas found in architectural pattern books of the day. It was a style considered suitable for people of refinement and taste. The Eakins dwellings were the most striking houses in Yarmouth, a town where shipbuilders and shipowners had two homes – one on the oceans of the world and the other in the town where exuberance in architecture was the order of the day.

THE FRENCH SHORE,
THE ANNAPOLIS VALLEY,
TRURO

CHAPTER FIFTEEN

The French Shore and Digby

The expulsion of approximately 10,000 Acadians began in the summer of 1755 and continued for the next eight years. Ordered to the local British barracks, Acadian men and boys were told that they were prisoners and that they and their families would soon be deported. Their crime? They had refused to take an unqualified oath of allegiance to the British Crown and would not agree to participate in active military engagements against the French. They continued to claim neutrality in the French/English struggle for North America.

This struggle for Acadia, the lands now forming part of Quebec, eastern Maine, New Brunswick, Nova Scotia, and Prince Edward Island, had begun early in the seventeenth century. Acadians had seen their colony ruled, first, by one country, then, the other, during which time they tried to claim neutrality and farm their land. But it was not to be. The Acadians, predominantly French-speaking Catholics, were considered a threat to the security of the British cause. Colonel Charles Lawrence, lieutenant-governor of Nova Scotia, took action.

When the deportation began in September, the Acadians were forced onto waiting ships, and dispersed to various destinations, mainly in the other American colonies. Families were separated. Longfellow's Evangeline, in the poem so titled, written ninety-two years later, personified the expulsion and gained international recognition for the tragedy.

Although some Acadians fled and eluded capture, not all of them found a better fate. Many of those who had escaped the British in Nova Scotia, and had survived a winter in hiding, made their way to New Brunswick the following spring, walking through more than a hundred miles of wilderness. There they found pockets of Acadians at the Miramachi and elsewhere, all starving, all struggling to survive. Once safe in northern New Brunswick, Île Saint-Jean (now Prince Edward Island, but then a French possession), or one of the other pockets of refuge, they encountered several more winters of bitter cold and starvation. Some surrendered to the British as late as 1760. The dream, common to all, was to return home.

In September 1764, nearly ten years after the deportation began, the Acadians were allowed to return. But not to their homes. Those had long since been destroyed. Their land, much of it in the fruitful Annapolis Valley, had been taken over by New England Planters (settlers) who had come at the invitation of the government. In western Nova Scotia the Acadians settled instead at Eel Brook, near Yarmouth, and on land around St Mary's Bay. Others settled at Pubnico, on Cape Breton at Cheticamp and Isle Madame, in northern and eastern New Brunswick, along the Saint John River valley, and on Prince Edward Island at Malpeque.

And so, in 1766, Benoni d'Entremont, age twenty-one, left Massachusetts and returned to Pubnico. He had seen it last when, at age eleven, he watched as the village was burned by the British. The d'Entrement family were expelled from lands that had been theirs for more than a century – land granted in 1653 to their ancestor, Baron Philippe Mius d'Entremont, Baron of Pobomcoup (Pubnico), by Charles de Saint-Etienne La Tour, governor of Acadia. On his return, d'Entremont received land that had originally been part of the family barony. The government granted 5,000 acres on Pubnico harbour to eighteen Acadian families.

Five years later, in 1771, Benoni d'Entrement was able to build his frame house by the sea. It stood in Lower West Pubnico (not to be confused with neighbouring Pubnico, East Pubnico, West Pubnico, Middle West Pubnico, Middle East Pubnico, and Lower East Pubnico). A sea captain, Benoni was also a church leader and a justice of the peace. His son, Simon, became a member of the Legislative Assembly.

Most of the returned Acadians, however, settled by St Mary's Bay. Fifteen villages soon appeared scattered along the shore north of Yarmouth, between Beaver River and Weymouth. The seventeenth-century French spoken by the Acadians' ancestors survived the deportation and can be heard there today. The area was not historically French-speaking. It is believed that the only visits by Europeans to the St Mary's Bay area had been by Samuel de Champlain in 1604 and by parties of fugitive Acadians in the winter of 1755-6. Other than that, the sole occupants of this rugged, rocky, territory were the Mi'kmaq, who, by fishing and hunting, survived in one of the most inhospitable parts of the province. Thus, because the coast was so forbidding, the land was available for the returning Acadians.

Their communities were scattered deliberately. The government wanted no collective stronghold of Acadians threatening the peace. In fact, the first land grants to the returnees were called 'licences of occupation,' a tentative arrangement by the ever-cautious British. These were not succeeded by outright grants until the 1770s. Even then the land grants were contingent upon an oath of loyalty to the king. Most Acadians were ready to swear the oath. Above all, they wanted peace. They hoped to live quietly, attracting little notice. Their goals: to reunite their families; to build new homes; to adapt to this rugged coastline; and somehow to earn a livelihood. This they accomplished. Today more than 85 per cent of Clare Township's residents are descendants of those returned Acadians.

A house built in Comeauville by the Comeau family, shortly after they returned to Nova Scotia, has been moved to Meteghan. It stands on land granted to Bonaventure (Bonan) Robicheau, a descendant of Louis Robicheau, who settled in Port Royal in 1638. Today it is owned by La Société historique acadienne de la Baie Sainte-Marie.

The house has been restored to its original simplicity. Inside, massive beams and a large welcoming fireplace appear much as they did when it was built. Bright Acadian colours (white walls, yellow floors, blue woodwork) provide a cheerful note. Over the fireplace hangs a portrait of 'La Vieille Gigi,' an Acadian settler who sur-

Comeau house, moved and restored at Meteghan

vived the expulsion and returned to Nova Scotia to live out her 105 years. On the mantel beneath her portrait is written: 'Comme l'hirondelle rebâtit son nid après la tempête / Ainsi l'Acadien a rebâti sa demeure après l'exile. [Just as the swallow rebuilt its nest after the storm / So has the Acadian rebuilt his home after banishment.]'

François Lambert Bourneuf, a French prisoner of the British during the Napoleonic Wars, also found a haven on what is now called the French Shore. By 1813, when he came to Church Point, he had encountered adventures enough to last a lifetime.

From Regneville, in Normandy, Bourneuf had served as a sailor on a French frigate. Captured by the British in 1809, he was sent as a prisoner of war to Melville Prison, on the Northwest Arm, an inlet off Halifax harbour. In his journal, published as *Diary of a Frenchman*, edited by J. Alphonse Deveau, Bourneuf recorded that fellow prisoners earned money by 'knitting stockings, mitts, gloves, or purses, and some were spinning. Some were making model battleships rigged with silk and armed with cannons made from pennies. It took almost six months to make some of these models, and they sold for as much as twenty dollars.'

Twice Bourneuf escaped and was recaptured. His third try was successful. He then made his way to Shelburne, and finally to Pubnico, where he found himself among the Acadians. 'The first house I came to belonged to Simon d'Entrement [son of Benoni] but it was boarded up.' He found a place to live and remained there as a teacher until Benoni d'Entrement, then justice of the peace, warned him of trouble. D'Entrement had been challenged by a family in Shelburne for harbouring an escaped prisoner. He feared reprisals and advised Bourneuf to leave.

In May 1813, having just taken an oath of allegiance to the British Crown (the oath required of all returned Acadians), Bourneuf left Pubnico. He had been provided with a document proving his loyalty and allowing him a land grant. 'Never in all my life have I regretted leaving a place more,' he said. 'I had found myself in Heaven, among people so sweet and affable. All Acadians are good people, but the people of Pubnico more so than the others.'

Bourneuf headed to Church Point, where he met the remarkable Father Jean-Mandé Sigogne, a Catholic priest who had come to St Mary's Bay in 1799. Father Sigogne was the only priest serving the Catholics in Digby and Yarmouth counties, Acadians who lived along the lonely, lengthy stretch of coastline from St Mary's Bay to Cape Sable, the southwestern tip of Nova Scotia.

Father Signone faced challenges in abundance. He had found upon his arrival a combination of ignorance, illiteracy, and superstition, and so set out to baptize, conduct marriages, write wills and deeds, organize parish finances, compose learned sermons, take a census, build churches, and serve as justice of the peace. And he taught school, with subjects ranging from French, English, mathematics, history, and geography, to religion. Sigogne was dedicated to teaching his Acadian parishioners. Most were illiterate, as it was not yet legal to teach French in the schools, so Sigogne held classes in his church. When Bourneuf arrived on the scene, he began teaching with Father Sigogne.

After a time Bourneuf turned to the sea for his livelihood – possibly because he had, by then, acquired a wife, Marie Doucet. The family grew to include seven children. Three sons, François, Ambroise, and Philippe, together with their father, built a shipyard where thirty vessels were launched, ranging in size from 13 to 1,800 tons. Bourneuf represented Digby County in the Legislative Assembly for sixteen years, the first French-speaking representative for a mainly English-speaking county; he was also a justice of the peace. Although his shipbuilding enterprise went bankrupt in 1855, a Bourneuf retail merchandising business continued. Many years later, novelist Thomas Raddall immortalized François Lambert Bourneuf in *Hangman's Beach*, drawing upon his history for the character of Cascameau.

In 1859 Bourneuf faced an election in Digby County, the riding he had represented since 1843. In appealing to the voters for their renewed support, he asked them

The home of Ambroise Bourneuf, Little Brook

to overlook his business losses. He claimed to be writing his autobiography, a work which would explain that 'people have cheated me and stolen from me, and I hope that you will understand what I went through and that you will not blame me. I may have lost property but I have not lost my honour.' Bourneuf lost the election, however, but probably not because of his business failure: the election had been fought on religious grounds. Bourneuf and other Catholic members of the assembly had left the Liberal party when their leader, Joseph Howe, verbally attacked Catholics for allegedly failing to support the British in the Crimean War. Howe argued that he had the right to ridicule any doctrine he found absurd. It was not the finest hour for the man who brought responsible government to Nova Scotia.

Bourneuf was in his eighties when he died in 1871. His second son, Ambroise, born in 1821, worked in the

Église Ste-Marie, Church
Point

family business for a while and then became Clare Township's customs officer – in those days a prestigious and powerful position. In 1840, while still a young man, he had built a house at Little Brook. It overlooked one of the many coves along St Mary's Bay, which, after the expulsion, had sheltered the returning Acadians. As a shipbuilder, he brought to the task his familiarity with construction techniques, for every detail of his home evinces painstaking care. Today this storey-and-a-half house and a three-gabled barn, both painted a deep burgundy, are owned by his great-grandson. A grandson, Joseph Willie Comeau, represented Digby County in the legislature for most of the years between 1907 and 1948, when he was appointed to the Senate. A granddaughter, Alice Bourneuf, was the first woman to be appointed to the Faculty of Arts and Science at Boston College, a Jesuit academy.

In nearby Church Point, a magnificent architectural feat was accomplished in 1905. Église Ste-Marie was built by an illiterate Acadian, Leo Melanson, following plans drawn by Auguste Regeneault, a French architect. It is, according to Professor Neil Boucher of Université Sainte-Anne, Point-de-l'Église, the largest wooden church in North America.

There had been three other churches on St Mary's Bay – the first was built at Church Point by an itinerant missionary in 1774, and used by Father Sigogne on his arrival in 1799. Sigogne called it Sainte-Marie. The second, opened in 1808, was destroyed by fire in 1820.

Interior, Église Ste-Marie

The third, completed in 1829, was torn down in 1905 when the present church was built.

The breathtaking new Église Ste-Marie dwarfed its predecessors. Melanson's original steeple, built with forty tons of rock inside to serve as ballast, originally soared more than 200 feet into the air. Lightning struck it one day, however, and flames engulfed the upper section. The church was saved (by heavenly intervention, it was said) when a timely downpour extinguished the fire. Only a small portion of the steeple was lost.

Inspiration for the church came from its priest, Father Pierre-Marie Dagnaud, a talented mathematician and head of the adjacent Université Sainte-Anne. The contributions of these three men – priest, architect, and builder – combined to produce a stately symbol of their faith. It stands with serene confidence, dominating the landscape, its spire visible for miles in every direction, proclaiming dramatically the Acadian presence today.

In spite of the furore caused when he antagonized Bourneuf and the rest of Nova Scotia's Catholics, Joseph Howe was under full sail when he visited Digby in June 1859.

Mr Howe In Digby – Meeting At Bear River
The day after the festival at Bridgetown, Mr Howe went down in the steamer to Digby and passed a few days with his only sister, who resides there. He rode down the shore as far as Weymouth, being everywhere cordially received by his old friends and supporters ... Returning up the south side of the Basin of Annapolis, he was followed out of Digby by five and twenty waggons ... at the head of Navigation and Bear River, 250 men were assembled to meet him, and nearly all the

Edwin Randolph Oakes
house, Montague Row,
Digby

women in the place, dressed in their holiday attire, crowded the gallery of an old meeting house, in which he addressed the people for several hours. A public dinner was given to him, got up in capital style, the room being tastefully decorated with oak leaves. (*The Novascotian*, 27 June 1859)

Howe's triumphal parade on that June day might well have been watched by the merchant Edwin Randolph Oakes from his newly completed home on Montague Row in Digby. From the graceful window beneath the central gable, Oakes enjoyed an unrestricted view of the entire harbour and the main street.

Edwin R. Oakes was a grandson of pioneer Jesse Oakes, who had arrived in Digby with the Loyalists in 1783. Jesse's son, Henry, married Mary Fitzrandolph and settled in Grand Joggin, in the Acacia Valley near Digby, on the old post road which wound its way through the Annapolis Valley between Digby and Ha-

The home of Edwin's parents, Henry and Mary Oakes, Grand Joggin, the Acacia Valley, near Digby

A view of Digby in 1835, hand-coloured lithograph by Mary G. Hall

lifax. The lovely frame house still stands there, on what is now a secluded road by the Annapolis River near Digby. Edwin was born there in 1816.

Edwin married Georgina Jane Bragg. In 1839 he bought a small cottage in Digby, where they could live while keeping daily watch on the construction of their grand house, which was being built on a rise overlooking the harbour. The cottage was then fifty-six years old. It had been built in 1783 by a Loyalist, James Holdsworth, who founded a distinguished family, members of which became, variously, a member of the Legislative Assembly, warden of the municipality, justice of the peace, and judge. The cottage was built the same year that the first Loyalists sailed into Digby (then called Conway) under the command of Admiral Sir Robert Digby, Rear Admiral of the British Fleet, who supervised the settlement, provided for distribution of the King's Bounty (rations), and gave the town his name.

The old cottage had seen its share of excitement. In early years it had served as a tavern, where matters ranging from land transactions to news of the day were discussed. When the realities of local life became unbearable, transport to New England could be arranged there and provided by one of the young Holdsworths. The militia (often the butt of local humour) met at the tavern. Rumours of imminent attacks by American privateers were rampant during the late eighteenth and early nineteenth centuries, when England and the United States were frequently in conflict, and the militia reportedly made the tavern its first port of call before rushing to any defence of the town.

Legend has it that, on one occasion, after reports that a raider had been sighted off Weymouth, the militia (well fortified with liquid courage) marched through the night all the way to Weymouth North. Dawn brought fog. One Major Tiffany, in command, marched his troops to the shore. Rustling was heard in the bush. The major barked: 'Who goes there?' No reply. 'Fire!' cried Tiffany. In the accepted fashion, the front rank knelt so that the rear rank could fire over their heads. Volleys went off. The rustling ceased. Then, in a scenario not unknown today, the fearless troops discovered their 'invader' – a cow. Major Tiffany, then in his late twenties, was subsequently retired on full pay. He lived to be ninety-two. Unfortunately this historic tavern, the scene of so much local lore, no longer exists.

Life was quieter when Oakes bought the property.

Along with the land, he had purchased half of a barn which straddled two lots. This curious purchase was completed a few years later, when he bought the remaining half of the barn and the adjoining property. The barn, therefore, predates the Oakes house. It remains facing First Avenue.

Oakes took three years to complete his house. It overlooks the harbour, a commanding and dignified structure. Tall windows, classical mouldings, a gable graced with finely wrought bargeboard – throughout the house no detail escaped the builder's devoted attention. It was a fitting home for this successful merchant who was elected to the House of Commons in 1874 and later became a member of the Council in Nova Scotia. His portrait, on the wall of his Montague Street house, shows him in the Upper Chamber (now the Red Room) of Province House. When Oakes died in 1889, *The Digby Weekly Courier* noted: 'Ever genial and unassuming, there was in his heart a spring of kindness which never failed to respond when appealed to by a struggling friend, young or old, and many a young man when struggling to hold on in the world has been taken by the hand by the late Mr Oakes.' His fine house is occupied today by a descendant.

In the early 1800s Joshua Marsden, a Methodist missionary, had a few words to say on the subject of taverns (such as Holdsworth's in Digby) and the general morals of the community. 'Jesus Christ,' he lamented, 'did not appear to have one foot of ground in all Digby.'

Preacher Marsden, however, would not likely have uttered such a dogmatic remark in the presence of Bishop Charles Inglis, the first Nova Scotian to be consecrated as bishop of the province. He knew Digby well, and his influence had been felt there for some years before Marsden appeared. In fact Inglis had laid the cornerstone for Digby's Trinity Church in September 1791. Its rector was one of his most devoted clergymen, the Rev. Roger Viets, originally of Simsbury, Connecticut. A Loyalist, as were most of his parishioners, Roger Viets had been imprisoned and fined during the American Revolution for supplying food to other Loyalists.

Viets never lacked for challenges. In order to support his family he ran a farm as well as his parish, and spent much of his tenure in Digby battling against the 'enthusiasm' of evangelist Henry Alline, whose spellbinding sermons were drawing huge crowds in the Planter settlements along the Annapolis Valley and in south-

The Oakes barn, First Avenue

western Nova Scotia. Alline was successfully enticing the faithful away from the established church.

Trinity Church was built with the help of Admiral Digby. He had offered a generous £150 to the Loyalist community, contingent upon the church being built of stone or brick. The parishioners, no doubt from necessity, built their church of wood. So Digby donated only £100 and a bell.

By 1876 it was apparent that the church, then nearly a hundred years old, needed to be enlarged. Reverend Ambrose, rector at the time, began to consider the matter of an architect. He wrote for suggestions to Andrew Gray, a former rector of Trinity but then pastor of Grace Church, Boston. Gray's reply was emphatic. The best possible choice would be Stephen C. Earle, a New England architect who, though formerly a Quaker, was now, fittingly, an Episcopalian. The talented Mr Earle was also a bank president, a musician, and the designer of more than forty New England churches. The local builder would be M.L. Oliver, a contractor who had already bought the original church for $70 after some discussion as to whether it should be made into a court-house.

One can tell at a glance that the architect of Trinity Church was acquainted with ships and familiar with their construction – not surprising in a New Englander. Curved trusses supporting the roof make it resemble a ship's hull upside down. The new church was consecrated on 15 October 1880 by Bishop Hibbert Binney. Its architect's reputation soon spread as other Anglicans saw his work. Just two years later, at the other end of the Annapolis Valley, Christ Church, Windsor, also designed by Stephen Earle, opened its doors.

Trinity Church, Digby

CHAPTER SIXTEEN

Annapolis Royal

In 1744, Captain Michel de Gannes de Falaise of the French forces at Louisbourg was ordered to attack and recapture the town of his birth, Annapolis Royal (originally Port-Royal). De Gannes was wealthy and socially adept, but with a military career yet to show any signs of distinction, and on this occasion he was unsuccessful. When expected reinforcements failed to show up, he called off the attack and retreated to Louisbourg. Fortunately so, for as a result, his family home, now 477 St George Street, was spared. The house had served as a rendezvous for families and officers, both French and English, and the home of two astute and powerful women.

Had Michel de Gannes's proposed attack succeeded, he would have raised the French flag in Annapolis for the fifth time in an area over which the French and English had been fighting like dogs with a bone since its founding by the French in 1605. It changed hands seven times before the final British attack of 1710 when the French general Daniel d'Auger de Subercase handed the keys of the fort to a triumphant General Francis Nicholson. 'Sir,' said Subercase, 'I'm very sorry for the misfortune of the King my master in losing such a brave Fort, and the territories adjoining, but count myself happy in falling into the hands of so noble and generous a General, and now deliver up the Keys of the Fort and magazines into your hands, hoping to give you a visit next Spring.' Subercase did not return in the spring. The town remained British and was given its present name.

Michel de Gannes's family was part of Acadian aristocracy. His great-grandfather, Nicolas Denys (known to the Mi'kmaq as La Grande Barbe for his white beard), had been sent by the Compagnie de la Nouvelle-

France in 1632 to establish a colony in the new world. At one time he had rights to a substantial part of the Gulf of St Lawrence, including Cape Breton and Ile Saint-Jean (Prince Edward Island). He assisted groups of settlers and operated as merchant, lumberman, fisherman, and businessman. In his seventies he wrote a book on seventeenth-century Acadia.

Michel's maternal grandfather was Michel Leneuf de La Vallière et de Beaubassin, favourite of Frontenac and commandant and governor of Acadia. Michel's father was Louis de Gannes de Falaise, a knight of the Order of Saint-Louis, who came to Port-Royal as a captain in 1696, married Marguerite Leneuf de La Vallière et de Beaubassin, and was appointed town major in 1704. It was he who, in 1708, built the frame house on St George Street, replacing an earlier one that had been burned by the English forces the previous year. The house, one of the oldest in Canada, has 'wattle and daub' walls. This ancient European building technique, which was popular in seventeenth-century Acadia, uses clay and straw infill in the wall cavity.

The military career of young Michel gathered momentum in later years, and he became a credit to his illustrious ancestors. In 1745, at the siege of Louisbourg, his home since 1722, he fought courageously and, like his father, was created a knight of the Order of Saint-Louis.

De Gannes at one point in his colourful life encountered a vexing domestic problem. His mistress had recently given birth to a child who, he admitted, might be 'of his doing.' When she heard of his impending marriage to Élisabeth de Catalogne, she made a public objection. De Gannes managed to marry the lady of his choice none the less, postponing the wedding by just one week.

Some years after the 1710 conquest, the predominant voices in the St George Street house became English. By 1727 the new owner was a highly controversial Irishman, Alexander Cosby.

Cosby's career was fraught with quarrels as he dealt with rivals for the various positions he held or hoped to hold. His brother-in-law, Richard Philipps, then governor of Nova Scotia, was an immense help, naming Cosby lieutenant-governor of the town and fort of Annapolis Royal, and member, later president, of Nova Scotia's governing council. Such help did not, of course, endear Cosby to his rivals. Personality clashes and animosity were a feature of a career that ended with Cosby's sudden and unexplained death at age fifty-seven in his Annapolis home, on 27 December 1742.

If Cosby was irascible, his young wife, Anne, and her mother, the beautiful and ambitious Marie-Madeleine Winniett (née Maisonnat), were women worth knowing. Marie-Madeleine was the daughter of a French privateer captain, Pierre Maisonnat (called Baptiste), who successfully harassed English shipping on the Atlantic coast. He seized prizes in the waters off Boston, where he was twice imprisoned. Baptiste had also managed to acquire several wives simultaneously, some in France, some in Holland – distance providing a useful barrier between them. Marie-Madeleine's mother, Madeleine Bourg, was listed as Baptiste's wife when the 1693 census was taken in Port-Royal. She was then sixteen, and living in a house that contained numerous cattle and fifteen guns.

When she reached age sixteen, Marie-Madeleine married an English lieutenant, William Winniett. He was a Boston merchant who had served on one of the thirty-six ships that had taken part in the successful British attack on Port-Royal in 1710. Winniett later established a profitable trading business in town. Theirs was one of the few Acadian–English marriages before the expulsion of the Acadians in 1755. The Winnietts, who became parents of thirteen children, are considered to be among the oldest English families resident in the Maritime provinces.

Marie-Madeleine became a power in the colony. After her husband's sudden death (he drowned in Boston harbour) she was left impoverished but resolutely carried on his mercantile business for another thirty years. Over the years her three daughters married prominent British men and, through these family connections and her business acumen, she became an influential senior member of the community, respected, and included in the important decisions of the day.

(A footnote to history: Of the Winnietts' many descendants, a great-grandson was Sir William Robert Wolseley Winniett, knighted for his services to the British colonies in Africa. He married Augusta Julia Fenwick, a goddaughter of Edward Augustus, Duke of Kent, and named, one would assume, after the Prince and Julie. Julia's father, William Fenwick, was the Commanding Royal Engineer responsible for building the commanding officer's residence in Royal Artillery Park, Halifax.)

When she died, Marie-Madeleine bequeathed to her daughter Anne all her wearing apparel and her 'new Silver Porringer.' The remainder of her possessions were divided among the other twelve children. Anne, one of the six Winniett daughters, had married Alexander Cosby in 1726, when she was fourteen and he forty-one. The marriage pleased Marie-Madeleine because it brought powerful connections and security. Just a year after the marriage, Cosby became a member of the colony's governing council.

When Cosby died, Anne held the St George Street property until her death in 1788 at the age of seventy-six. The house was inherited by her son, Philipps Cosby (later Admiral of the White in the British navy); a daughter, Anne (who married William Wolseley, also a British admiral); and a grandchild, Mary Buchanan. Philipps Cosby succeeded to his father's family estates at Stradbally Hall in Ireland. In her will, Anne Cosby freed her three slaves: 'I do also give and devise unto my black Woman named Rose, a Molotto Girl name Agatha and my black Man named John Bulkley to each and every of them their full Freedom and discharge from all Servitude as Slaves from the day of my decease forever.'

For the next twenty-one years, the Cosby estate was administered for the heirs by Thomas Henry Barclay, a lawyer and a prominent Loyalist who had settled in Annapolis Royal in the late 1870s. During this time the old house was rented. Barclay himself, then in his fifties,

De Gannes/Cosby house,
477 St George Street

may have lived there with his wife, Susan, and some of their twelve children. Indeed, Thomas or some Barclay offspring scratched his or her name into the glass in the front-bedroom window, where it remains today. A lawyer and a gifted orator, Barclay represented Annapolis in the provincial legislature, was Speaker of the House of Assembly, and later British Consul in New York.

When Anne Cosby's heirs sold the house in 1809 to the Rev. Cyrus Perkins, assistant at St Luke's Anglican Church, the building was within a year of reaching the venerable age of 100. Now it is nearly 300 years old. It stands as a symbol of the French/English struggle in Canada – a struggle with echoes heard to this day.

The finest house in town for many years belonged to John Adams, a Boston merchant and sea captain who came to Annapolis Royal as part of the victorious British forces in 1710. He saw opportunities and stayed. Working with Acadians and Natives, he became a land agent, contractor, and trader, and the first prominent merchant in English Canada. As deputy collector of customs, he locked horns with William Winniett and his bristly son-in-law, Alexander Cosby.

Within two or three years of his arrival, Adams was able to build himself a large one-storey frame building on Lower St George Street. It was constructed with Acadian labour and building techniques, in particular the use of wattle and daub. Thirty years later the house was worth £250, while the smaller houses in town could be picked up for a mere £30. During Adams's twenty-year term on the colony's governing council, meetings were held in his house – the oldest surviving building to be associated with the saga of English rule in Canada.

For four months in 1739–40 Adams was president of the council until another claimant to the position, Major Paul Mascarene, wrested the title from him after a stormy meeting. Adams left for Boston a bitter man, unable even to get a pension from the British in spite of his claim that he had suffered eye damage during an Indian attack on Annapolis Royal in 1724 in which he had to fight without 'hatt or wigg.'

In 1745 the Adams house was damaged in yet another Indian attack. It was sold that year to a military man, Lieutenant John Hamilton. Twenty years later, Thomas Williams, Commissary and Ordnance Storekeeper at Fort Anne, bought the property. (Sir William Fenwick Williams, a hero in the Crimean War and later

Sen. John W. Ritchie

lieutenant-governor of Nova Scotia, was his grandson – or perhaps not, if rumours of the day could be credited. Sir William was said to be an illegitimate son of the Duke of Kent, then living in Halifax. This would have made him a half-brother of Queen Victoria, and probably accounts for the fact that he was not in a hurry to discount the rumours.) By 1780 the house had seen other occupants and other uses. For a time it served as an inn run by Frederick Sinclair, who later relocated next door.

In 1781, more than forty years after John Adams's unhappy departure, his handsome house became home to the Ritchies, one of Canada's most significant legislative and judicial families. It remained in that family for the next ninety years, during which time the second storey was added, the interior plastered, and some ornamental trim added to the doors.

John Ritchie, who bought the Adams house, was a Scot. At age twenty-five, in 1770, he had sailed from Edinburgh with his wife, Janet, to Boston, where his uncle ran a mercantile business. Five years later the Ritchies moved to Annapolis Royal. That year a son was born and Janet died. Within a year John had remarried; he and his new wife, Alicia Maria Le Quesne, in July 1781, moved into the newly purchased Adams house. Six weeks later Annapolis Royal was attacked by two American ships, and Ritchie was taken hostage. Although he was later released he was forced to forswear any further action against the American rebels. So Ritchie settled down to practise law and raise lawyers, with whom the family tree is laden. He himself was a justice

Adams/Ritchie house,
Lower St George Street

of the peace and judge of the Court of Common Pleas, as well as owning a mercantile business. His descendants included four judges. One grandson became Chief Justice of the Supreme Court of Canada in 1879.

John Ritchie died in 1790, leaving Alicia with four children aged five to fifteen, but little else. Perhaps the work on the house had cost more than was expected. The inventory of his effects had a total value of only £159, including goods from his mercantile business – almost 150 yards of materials such as silk, gauze, and broadcloth; soldiers' coats; 25 hammers; and various other tools and hardware; plus 3 'teeth brushes'; a large double sleigh on springs; and a cow.

John Ritchie's first son, Thomas, inherited the homestead. He became a lawyer like his father, but unlike his father he was financially successful. In one year alone more than three-quarters of the cases in Annapolis County had the Ritchie name on them. From 1806 to 1824 he represented Annapolis County in the provincial legislature, without ever needing to campaign, for he was never opposed. It was said locally that Annapolis 'belongs to the Devil, the Church, and Judge Ritchie.'

Unfortunately, Ritchie's personal life did not run quite so smoothly. His first wife, Elizabeth Wildman Johnston, the mother of five sons and two daughters, died in a house fire shortly after the birth of their last son; his second wife, Elizabeth Best, died two years after their 1823 marriage, when she was thrown from a horse. With his third wife, Anne, one of the seventeen children of Yarmouth physician and judge Joseph Norman Bond, he had one son and one daughter.

Sir William Johnstone Ritchie, Chief Justice of Canada, 1891

Five of Thomas Ritchie's sons became lawyers and three received judicial appointments – John William Ritchie, and J. Norman Ritchie of the Supreme Court of Nova Scotia and the brilliant Sir William Johnston Ritchie, Chief Justice of the Supreme Court of Canada. Ten of Thomas Ritchie's grandsons were lawyers.

Born in the Adams/Ritchie house in 1808, John William became a prominent lawyer and politician in the family tradition, and eventually solicitor general in the provincial government of J.W. Johnston (his uncle) and Charles Tupper. He steered the Confederation legislation through the Nova Scotia legislature, no easy task as the prospect of union was anything but popular. Ritchie became a senator in 1867, and a justice in the Supreme Court of Nova Scotia in 1870. In 1967 the federal government officially designated him a Father of Confederation.

His younger brother, William, was remembered in Annapolis as a 'rollicking, rosy-cheeked, bright-eyed boy, full of fun and animal spirits.' He studied at the Pictou Academy under Thomas McCulloch and, while still a young man, moved to New Brunswick, where he was admitted to the bar in 1838. He rose to be a puisne judge of the Supreme Court of that province and, later, served as Chief Justice of Canada from 1879 to 1892. He was knighted in 1881 and acted as deputy to Governor General Lord Lansdowne.

The last word in the success saga of the Ritchies should go to a woman. Eliza, John William Ritchie's daughter, graduated with honours from Dalhousie in 1887, the first woman to earn a degree of bachelor of letters at that university. She went on to earn a PhD at Cornell University – and became the first Canadian woman to secure a doctorate. After further study in Leipzig and Oxford, Eliza became associate professor at Wellesley College, Massachusetts, then returned to her beloved Nova Scotia to teach philosophy at Dalhousie. A strong suffragist, Dr Ritchie was in the forefront of the feminist movement in Halifax until the end of the First World War. In 1919 she was appointed to the Dalhousie board of governors – the first woman in Canada to be so honoured.

Next door to the Ritchie house on Lower St George Street stands an equally historic building, this one an inn. Like the Ritchie house, it has been a part of Annapolis Royal since the first years of the eighteenth century.

The land on which the inn stood had belonged at one time to descendants of the notable Charles de Saint-Étienne de La Tour, a trader, soldier, and colonizer, born in the 1660s at Cape Sable. He and his family were successful in winning a long-standing dispute with the Le Bourgne family about inherited lands, which gave the La Tours rights over extensive tracts in various parts of the province, including Port-Royal. Severely wounded during the attack on that town in 1710, La Tour recovered to work as an interpreter with the Indians on Île Royale. He died in the garrison at Louisburg in 1731.

In 1710 La Tour's granddaughter, Jeanne, and her husband, David du Pontiff, had sold the Port-Royal property to a Quebec silversmith, Jean-Baptiste Soullard, and his Acadian wife, Louise Comeau. Soullard had left Quebec for Port-Royal after a self-confessed theft from his father, a well-known Quebec goldsmith and gunsmith. It is believed that the Soullards built the house in early 1710, shortly before the British attacked and took the town from the French for the last time. After the conquest, the Soullards sold to their neighbour, the prosperous John Adams.

Adams found a tenant for the Soullard house, then sold it in 1713 to Sir Charles Hobby, lieutenant-governor of the colony, for whom Adams was acting as agent. From this transaction in 1713 a treasured document exists. The deed of sale not only mentions the house, an unusual occurrence in itself, but details the entire history of the property. For the next twenty years it was leased, the most interesting of the tenants being Captain John Alden, a merchant from the Plymouth colony. He was a trader with Acadia and a grandson of the *Mayflower* pilgrim John Alden – the man who gained immortality through his marriage proposal to Priscilla Mullens. Made on behalf of another man, it elicited the reply, 'Speak for yourself, John.'

During the 1740s Annapolis Royal sustained several attacks (none successful) by Natives and the French. By this time the house was owned by Corporal William Sanders, who sold it in 1747 to James Whitechurch, also of the British army. His wife, Rebecca, had been licensed the previous year to sell 'strong drink' to the thirsty locals. So successful was this venture that the building remained an inn for the next 200 years.

Sinclair Inn, Lower St
George Street

The innkeeper whose name is most frequently associated with the hostel is Frederick Sinclair, who bought
the property in 1781. He had been renting the Adams/
Ritchie house next door and operating an inn there.
Business was given a boost two years after he took over
when 2,500 Loyalists arrived in town. Expansion was
in order. Records suggest that Sinclair enlarged the
property by attaching an existing structure to it.

Sinclair, like many of his neighbours, owned slaves.
In 1787 he purchased 'a negro wench ... from Richard
Betts of New York ... for the sum of twenty-one pounds,
current money of the Province of Nova Scotia.' On his
death in 1800 Sinclair left an estate of more than £873
to be invested for his wife, Mary, or, in the event of
her death, his daughter, Hannah. The inventory of his
estate included a house with nine principal rooms, eight
bedsteads and bedding, various pieces of silver, furniture, and paintings, all of which indicated a sizeable establishment. After his death Mary Sinclair ran the inn
for another twenty years.

Meanwhile, the Sinclairs' daughter, Hannah, had
married Peter Balser. They subsequently separated. Even
after Mary Sinclair died she managed to keep a tight
rein on her daughter from the grave. She left her estate
to Hannah 'so long as she lives separate and apart from
her present husband Peter Balser and so long as she
lives separate and apart and unconnected with any man,
and no longer.'

In 1852 the establishment was still popular. One trav-
eller, a Colonel Sleigh, visited Annapolis that year and
made a brief and unpleasant stay at another inn before
switching to the competition, presumably Sinclair's. He
recorded the events in his diary:

We had our luggage transferred to the hall of the small hotel
where the coach stopped ... a hostelry patronized by the present contractors for the mail service, in opposition to a larger
and far more commodious one adjoining it. To my inquiry for
various wants, the reply was invariably, 'Not to begot', 'Not
market day', 'All eaten', 'Can give you fried pork and tea'. This
last notification sufficed. I at once ordered all my trunks to be
taken into the road, while I sought for more hospitable quarters. During the bustle attendant upon this rapid proceeding,
I was aided in my hasty efforts to quit the abominable inn, by
a curious old Negro woman, rather stunted in growth, as
black as the ace of spades, and dressed in a man's coat and felt
hat; she had a small stick in her hand which she applied lustily

to the backs of all who did not jump instantly out of her way. Poor old dame! She was evidently a privileged character.

This woman was Rose Fortune, a fixture in town. She wore a man's coat and a white cap, topped by a man's hat. She was seen with her wheelbarrow transporting baggage from incoming boats to any destination around town.

The apartments we were ushered into consisted of a delightful, well-furnished drawing-room, looking out upon the Annapolis river and the hills beyond, a bedroom, equally pleasantly situated. The walls of both were covered by a painting representing Indian scenery, most admirably executed by an itinerant artist who some years ago paid for his board by the exercise of his brush and pallet.

That painting can still be seen on the walls of the large front room, although much of it is covered by wallpaper.

Back in 1791, when Sinclair had been operating from these premises for ten years, he offered his hostel to the Supreme Court to use as a court-house. He hoped to lure the business away from Mr Winniett's house, where the court was holding its sessions, offering his 'large room below stairs.' Court proceedings usually took place in inns. The only public buildings available in many communities, they served as everything from court-house to Sunday school. (The first court of common law in Canada had been established in Annapolis in 1721. Justice in those early days of settlement was not always apparent, and punishment could be swift and

Annapolis County Court House, St George Street and Highway 1

brutal. The case of one George Armstrong was typical. In 1725 he was convicted of insulting his master and sentenced to stand on a gallows with a rope around his neck and a sign, 'Audacious Villain', attached to the rope, this to be followed by the lash.)

Sinclair's offer of 1791 was not accepted because that year the government decided to build a new court-house and jail. Both were destroyed by fire in 1835. The present court-house was built two years later. The Annapolis County Court House, at the junction of Highway 1 and St George Street, is now the oldest court-house still in use in the province. Designed by Francis Le Cain, the son of nearby Fort Anne's master artificer, the building is similar in plan to the original court-house, which was a two-storey, hip-roofed building. Added authority was given the 1837 court-house by introducing a pedimented portico, a large door with fan transom, two flights of stone steps, and distinctive chimneys. The chimneys were removed during a 1922 enlargement, at which time a cupola was added to the roof.

Of the many trials that took place in the old court-house, the 1880 murder trial of Joseph Thibault ranks as one of the most horrible and sensational ever heard in the province. In September of that year, the body of Christine Hill, inmate of a poorhouse near Digby, was found burning in a field near Milford, a village inland from Annapolis Royal. Thibault, keeper of the poorhouse, was accused of her murder. The prosecution was directed by the attorney general himself, later the Rt Hon. Sir John Thompson, premier of the province, justice in the Supreme Court of Nova Scotia, federal minister of justice, and prime minister. Thompson, one of the greatest lawyers of his time, with a brilliant legal mind, was known to emerge from most of his cases victorious.

Evidence established that Thibault had been seen driving Christine Hill away in his wagon in broad daylight and returning in haste alone. The packed court-house heard the prosecution suggest that Hill, 'a woman in her mid-thirties hardened in appearance by a life of poverty – short with stooped shoulders, a thin face and several front missing teeth,' had been hit on the head, then burned while still alive. She was pregnant. When the defence suggested that Thibault would never have been so unwise as to be seen in broad daylight in a wagon with a woman he intended to murder, Thompson replied sternly, 'Men are never wise when they resort to crime. Innocence is the only wisdom.' During the

Sir John Thompson

trial, when an official of the poorhouse district could not recall how many inmates there were at the Digby institution, Mr Justice Weatherbe interceded. 'If they had been sheep or cattle,' he remarked, 'you would have had an accurate list.' Thompson reviewed the law and testimony for four hours, but it took the jury only an hour and a half to come back with a guilty verdict.

Thibault was hanged on 8 February 1881. A crowd of 800 had gathered to watch and, in their eagerness to see the spectacle, tore down a twenty-foot fence that obstructed their view of the gallows. It took the convicted man fourteen minutes to die.

Joseph Thibault may or may not have been ready to

St Luke's Anglican Church

meet his Maker on that February day, but there was little doubt about the Rev. John Millidge. He died in 1830 while serving communion at Clementsport, across the bay from Annapolis Royal. He was buried under the chancel of St Luke's Anglican Church on St George Street in Annapolis Royal, a beautiful frame building which was erected during his incumbency there (1817–30). According to local legend, when a new chancel was built in later years it was discovered that the good rector's Irish servant had provided Millidge with two clean white frilled shirts, initialled 'J.M.,' that were buried with him, one at his head and one at his feet, presumably in the belief that cleanliness, even in shirts, was next to godliness – and de rigueur when meeting one's Maker.

Of Loyalist stock, John Millidge came from a family that suffered the enduring splits that were a result of the American Revolution. Family members sometimes chose opposing sides and never met again. Millidge, born in New Jersey in 1771, was one of the three sons of Colonel Thomas Millidge of the New Jersey Volunteers and his wife, Mercy Baker. The family left for Nova Scotia in 1783. Son Stephen settled in Shelburne; Thomas became a merchant in Saint John, New Brunswick; John was educated at King's College and became an Anglican clergyman in Annapolis Royal.

The Rev. John Millidge was the namesake of a John Millidge who had fought with the rebels in the American Revolution and became governor of Georgia at war's end. Thirty years later, in 1805, Governor Millidge wrote to the Rev. John Millidge in Nova Scotia, asking after the Loyalist branch of the family. In particular he asked if there were any male descendants. The letter, with some conditions, contained an offer to have one boy come to visit him in Georgia. This letter prompted an immediate reply from John Millidge, but he heard nothing more. After four years, Millidge wrote again to his American relative in an effort to understand the lack of a reply. He wondered if there were still 'feelings' over the fact that his branch of the family had supported the British, but hoped that those feelings would be quickly forgotten. He continued:

I feel at a loss to ascertain the cause of your long silence ... I am sometimes induced to imagine that my letter has never reached you, and this might account for your silence; at other times I am led to suppose that the difficulties of our intercourse, arising out of the extraordinary situation in which our countries have been placed for so long a time, might be the reason why you have not given me the favour of an answer.

John Millidge was married twice, first to Ann Botsford, by whom he had a son, Thomas Botsford Millidge, and then to Hannah Simonds, by whom he had another son, John J. Millidge. In his letter to Governor Millidge, John momentarily forgot his second son (then a baby): 'at the time I wrote [the first 1805 letter] I mentioned there were but two boys in our family, since then there remains but one, my own son about 12 years of age, the son left by my brother Stephen being unfortunately drowned with his mother about two years since.' But he belatedly recalled his other son and added a postscript to make amends: 'I find I have made a mistake, there are yet two boys, I forgot to mention an infant son of mine ... ' There is no record of a reply from Georgia.

Millidge built his home, Girvan Bank, at 478 St George Street, just up from the church, in 1817, choosing the romantic Regency style popular during the reign of George IV. The house contained nine fireplaces and numerous Adam mantelpieces. Bought in 1842 by George Runciman, the building was then enlarged to its present size. Over the years further alterations were made, including the addition of the verandah in the 1920s.

George Runciman was a merchant and a successful one. When he died he left his 'Shop and Dwelling house above, also the Store adjoining and premises attached ... also the stock and outstanding notes,' to his

Millidge/Runciman house, Girvan Bank, 478 St George Street

son, John Henry Runciman. To his daughters, Isabella and Eliza, he left his Regency cottage, and a 200-acre farm 'on the New Lunenburgh Road,' 250 acres in Dalhousie Township, a house in Clements, and 'other Marsh land.'

In Granville Ferry, across from Annapolis Royal, on the north shore of the basin that Champlain, in 1604, called the Royal Harbour, stands a one-and-half-storey 'salt box.' (This term describes a house whose roof slopes from the front to cover a lower addition at the rear, the whole taking on a shape that resembles an eighteenth-century salt box.) The house, called North Hills, has a hand-hewn timber frame covered by weathered cedar shakes.

The land on which it stands was first granted to Benjamin Rumsey in 1764, nine years after the Acadian expulsion. This grant was for 1,000 acres, measured from high tide on the Annapolis River to low tide on the Bay of Fundy shore.

In 1798 the land passed to Paul Amberman, whose name is on the muster rolls of discharged officers and disbanded soldiers taken in the County of Annapolis between 18 and 24 June 1784. Amberman, born in New York of Dutch descent, had arrived with the Loyalists the previous year when he was thirty-nine years old. He had been married to Mary Ditmares for twelve years and they had three children – Mary; Paul, Jr; and Dowe – and a slave, Jane. Amberman came with the money to buy land, and over the next few years acquired almost 1,500 acres in the vicinity of Granville and Annapolis. He bought a 500-acre farm from Benjamin Rumsey plus

Paul Amberman house,
Granville Ferry

another 64 acres, orchards, and cattle from Anne Williams, a widow.

Amberman ran the large farm and a cider mill, and
enlarged his house with a summer kitchen on the west
side and a storey-and-a-half addition on the east. The
building then could house two families. On his death
in 1811, Amberman left his daughter, Mary Frome, £75.
To his son Paul, 'should be return to this place,' he left
£50, and to his son Dowe, the east half of the farm
and his personal estate. The west half went to Dowe's
children. The house remained in the Amberman family
until 1964. It is now open to the public, operated jointly
by the Nova Scotia Museum and the Historic Restoration Society of Annapolis County.

Port-Royal had prospered from the day in 1605 when
the first French colonists under Samuel de Champlain
sailed into the sheltered body of water they had named
Royal Harbour. (They had first seen it in the spring
of 1604 but had spent the winter in what is now the
state of Maine.) Port-Royal became the garrison town
and capital of French Nova Scotia. The forest was cleared
and crops flourished in the good soil. Its buildings were
standing three years before Quebec was founded. The
first fur-trading post was built on the north side of the
river by 1605. A social order, the Ordre du Bon Temps,
was founded to keep spirits up during the winter of
1606-7. The last French fort, Fort Anne, now a national
park, was built beginning in 1702. It withstood an assault two years later. The town survived long years of
siege from 1605 until the final British capture in 1710,
and witnessed the tragic deportation of 1,600 Acadians
who were forced onto vessels in the harbour in 1755.

Annapolis Royal occupied a position of prominence
until 1749. That year, the British government decided
that, to counteract French strength, an English capital
should be founded on the south shore of Nova Scotia.
Halifax replaced Annapolis Royal. Gradually the garrisons left the town and its influence waned.

But a significant event was still to come before the
turn of the century, one that eclipsed all others in splendour, romance, and significance. No matter that the
troops had departed, with a consequent dimming of the
town's social life. All this was forgotten with the arrival
in 1794, for a visit of some weeks, of Prince Edward
Augustus, fourth son of George III, the future Duke
of Kent and, later, the father of Queen Victoria. His
mistress, Thérèse-Bernardine, Comtesse de Montgenet,

thirty-four, known as Mme de Saint-Laurent (or Julie as he called her), joined him on a subsequent visit.

Julie charmed her way around the world with the duke. She was accepted in most social circles, and some people assumed that a morganatic marriage existed. Theories abounded about children supposedly born to Julie and Edward (or to Edward and various other women). These offspring, it was said, were raised by local families. In several cases the couple acted as godparents for a newborn, raising suspicions that the candidate was more than a godchild to them. Annapolis had its share of these rumours. Sir William Fenwick Williams was one such, and at least two other children were rumoured to have been born to the couple and raised by Annapolis Royal families. (Annapolis did not have exclusive right to these rumours: two Quebec children are credited to the couple, two in Halifax, and four at other locations.) Such stories, of course, lost nothing in the telling.

Julie and Edward were said to have been entertained in the de Gannes/Cosby house. Perhaps they were. Only the legends live on.

CHAPTER SEVENTEEN

Belleisle

Acadia was courted, captured, and recaptured for nearly a century. Powerful nations sought control over Acadia's vast resources, and so did powerful overlords, such as Nicolas Denys and Charles de Saint-Etienne de La Tour, both of whom, under the Compagnie de la Nouvelle-France, sought to colonize its vast area. Seigneuries (large land grants) were awarded to prominent men as a feudal tenure so that they could trade and establish permanent settlements in the New World, although the complex seigneurial system, with its duties and obligations, was not followed as in Quebec. Philippe Mius d'Entremont, Baron de Pobomcoup, was seigneur of Cape Sable. Michel Leneuf de la Vallière et de Beaubassin 'owned' Chignecto.

The Acadians were sailors, soldiers, and fishermen, but most were farmers. They had one valuable asset: they knew of diking procedures. Industrious, prolific, and mainly illiterate, they made up the vast empire called Acadia that included the three present Maritime provinces and parts of Maine and Quebec.

While the tumultuous events of the seventeenth and eighteenth centuries swirled round them, Acadians living by the salt marshes along the Bay of Fundy focused on what really mattered: supporting their growing families and building dikes – raised ridges built with sod and augmented with logs. Dikes were a remarkable achievement. They turned marshland into viable farmland that produced grains and vegetables and supported cattle and sheep. At low tide a valve, called an *aboiteau*, opened and the marsh drained. At high tide the valve closed to keep the high Fundy waters out. Rain naturally 'washed' the marshes of their salt content once the ocean was prevented from coming in.

Next to the regime at Port-Royal, Belleisle, eight kilometres to the east, on the north shore of the Annapolis River, was the largest Acadian settlement. As early as 1688 it boasted a population of seventy-four, eighteen more than the capital. All its houses were built on the Belleisle Marsh, the largest marsh on the river. Dikes had made this possible.

No Acadian houses remain standing. They were burned by government order. Recent archaeological evidence from Belleisle, however, gives some idea of their construction in this area. A typical house consisted of one large all-purpose room with a loft above. It had a large interior fireplace, lined with local brick and slate, with an opening to a clay oven base on the exterior. Marsh grass formed the thatched roof. When mixed with local clay, the same grass made a plaster-like substance which formed the walls. On the interior it was given a finishing coat of white clay. (In other areas Acadian houses were built of logs caulked with moss, clay, or wattle and daub – a mixture of straw and mud.) Foundations were of fieldstone and survived when the houses were burned in 1755, when the British government deported the population. On these foundations new houses were built a few years later, most by New England Planters.

The Planters came from Massachusetts, Rhode Island, and, the largest contingent, from Connecticut. They came by invitation, some 2,000 households, 8,000 settlers in number, between 1760 and 1768.

Governor Charles Lawrence had been making efforts

Acadian house, Belleisle, about 1720, a conception by Azor Vienneau based on archaeological and historical evidence

to persuade New Englanders to come to the British colony ever since the Acadians were deported. He wanted men and women loyal to the British Crown and experienced in wilderness farming. The prospective settlers were wary, however, fearful of renewed attacks by French and Mi'kmaqs and uneasy with Nova Scotia's military government. Finally, Lawrence called an assembly, the first representative government in what is now Canada. Then he issued a proclamation in *The Boston Gazette* in 1758, announcing that free land was available. There was immediate interest. A second proclamation followed a few months later. Agents came. A vessel took them around Yarmouth and up to the Bay of Fundy where they saw the Annapolis River and Minas Basin. They disembarked, saw the rich land, and immediately committed their people to settlement.

Most of the Massachusetts Planters settled in the Annapolis or Granville area. Among them was Abijah Parker, age thirty-eight, from Groton, Massachusetts. His great-grandfather, Thomas Parker, had sailed from England to Massachusetts on the *Susan and Ellen* in 1635. His grant in Belleisle, made in 1765, was a generous 500 acres, a typical long strip, partly marsh, partly flat land, partly mountain, ending at the Bay of Fundy. Abijah erected a frame house there, on foundations built by Acadians. In April 1764 he married Miriam Johnson Ricketson, the widow of Timothy Ricketson, a victim of smallpox. They had seven children. Abijah died in 1780.

In later years Obadiah Parker, Abijah and Miriam's fifth child, replaced the frame house with what is

Obadiah Parker house

thought to be the first brick house in the county. Obadiah had spent some time in Boston as a young man learning the skills of the building trade, so his house was better than many. The building is one and a half storeys. It has double brick exterior walls, separated by an air space which provided insulation. Its summer kitchen may have been part of Abijah's frame homestead. The present front of the house, which faces the road, was originally the back, because the building overlooked the marsh on its south side. In the 1830s the original windows and doors were bricked over and a new front door, deeply recessed because of the double-wall construction, was cut through on the road side. The present six-over-six windows beside it were set in at that time. In the basement, the remains of Acadian fireplaces are evidence of the building's historic origins.

CHAPTER EIGHTEEN

Wolfville and Starr's Point

The first name Wolfville bore was ignominious. It was called Mud Creek. It could equally well have been called Connecticut North. In June 1760, five years after the Acadians had been shipped out of the Annapolis Valley, twenty-two ships carrying Connecticut settlers and their cattle and farm equipment sailed up the Bay of Fundy through the Minas Channel, then swung around Cape Blomidon and landed in the sheltered Minas Basin. There were 1,100 passengers on board.

The New Englanders had not undertaken this trip unprepared. Emissaries had been to Halifax to discuss the terms of the land grants that the British colonial government had advertised in 1758. The offer was attractive: 100 acres for the family head and 50 acres for each member of the household; no taxes until ten years had passed and then a tax of only one shilling for each 50 acres; a combination of upland, meadow, and marsh for each family head; a bushel of grain each month for a year if needed; religious freedom; and a New England form of government, an assembly to which each township that had fifty settlers could elect two of their number. Each grantee was to cultivate or improve one-third of his land every ten years for thirty years.

It was love at first sight. The agents immediately arranged to settle four townships near the Minas Basin – Horton, Cornwallis, Falmouth, and Newport. Word of these prime lands quickly spread, and that year eager agents received grants for Onslow, Granville, Annapolis, Cumberland, Amherst, Sackville, Tinmouth (New Dublin), Liverpool, Barrington, and Yarmouth townships.

The terms were good because the government was more than anxious to fill the lands vacated by the Acadians, lands on which the remains of charred houses still lay. The Planters had every reason to take up the offer. Descendants of early settlers in the New England colonies, they were seeking new frontiers, since prime land in New England had become costly and now was mostly occupied. They were used to moving on to new land, and here was the promise of a large farm with more available for their sons. And so, from 1760 to 1768, approximately 2,000 heads of household (8,000 settlers) 'planted' themselves in Nova Scotia and became the largest single component of the colony's population. This large anglophone immigration, the first of its size in Canada, has until recently been virtually ignored as a significant event in Canadian history. In recent years a group of dedicated scholars, centred in Acadia University, has undertaken to remedy the oversight.

Among the Planters who arrived in 1761 was a cabinetmaker, John Atwell; his wife, Ruth; and their children, Holthun, Nancy, Ester, and Richard. Another son and daughter were born by the time of the 1770 census. Their small frame house, built in the 1760s, stands today at 450 Main Street, on the northeast corner of the old Acadian road between Annapolis and Grand Pré and the road which leads to the Cornwallis ferry. It grew in the hands of various owners over the years, but remains as the oldest house in Wolfville.

Atwell sold his house and barn in 1774 to two farmers from Yorkshire for £99. Records show that he had prospered: he then owned 500 acres, including marsh land, dike land, and upland, cleared and uncleared. Three years later the Yorkshiremen sold it to Edward DeWolf, who enlarged the house and sold it three years later to his younger brother, the distinguished Elisha DeWolf. He and his family lived in it for more than half a century.

The DeWolfs were Planters, descendants of Balthasar DeWolf, who had come to the New World when New York was still called New Amsterdam. Three of them, Simeon, Jehiel, and Nathan – all cousins – had left Connecticut with their families in 1761 to settle in Nova Scotia. Edward and Elisha were sons of Nathan DeWolf, one of those three cousins.

During a long and productive life, Elisha DeWolf became high sheriff of King's County, a member of the provincial legislature, assistant judge of Common Pleas, postmaster, collector of customs, and justice of the peace. While working his way through all these appointments, he was busy at home as well. He and his wife, Margaret Ratchford, produced thirteen children in twenty-three years. Their home grew along with the family. The two-storey clapboard building was altered in the late nineteenth century but has recently been restored to its original character. The five-bay façade with simple entrance, small-paned windows, and balanced chimneys is an example of the sheer beauty of balance and symmetry.

The DeWolfs' social position, coupled with the amenities of their home, gave them the opportunity to act as hosts to the Duke of Kent and his entourage when they arrived in Wolfville in 1794. The king's son, recently arrived in Nova Scotia, was travelling from Halifax through the Annapolis Valley on his way to New Brunswick. At every outpost along the way he was greeted by the leading dignitaries of the day and by an adoring public. The Duke left the DeWolfs a gift of tapestries. When Thomas Andrew Strange DeWolf, Elisha's son, was married to Nancy Crane in 1817, the Duke sent some cherished wallpaper showing a classical garden landscape. To honour the Duke's visit, Elisha's house was later named Kent Lodge.

In his will, Elisha DeWolf left Margaret £150, the use of his chairs, tables, a horse, sleigh, chaise, and harness, the use of 'two good milch cows ... also sufficient fire wood to be cut up at the door of her dwelling house,' and the household furniture. He left land to eight children: William, Sophia Henrietta, James Ratchford, Olivia, Margaret Maria, Mary Lucilla, Thomas Andrew Strange, and Elisha, Jr. The others presumably had either died or had been otherwise looked after.

Elisha, Jr, the eleventh child, was, like his father, a

Elisha DeWolf house,
450 Main Street, Wolfville

member of the legislature. Young Elisha, however, had the misfortune of being in the House of Assembly at the same time as Joseph Howe, and so sometimes became a target for Howe's barbed remarks. When Elisha criticized Howe for his intemperate tongue, the great man replied:

That Hon. gentleman, Sir, regrets the use of strong language, – would he desire to cure a violent disease by means of water gruel? I am glad to see him, Sir, in such a high state of health, but if his physician last winter, treated him as mildly as he wishes the diseases of the Country to be treated, he never would have sat here again. (*The Novascotian*, 14 February 1839)

Main Street today is dotted with the homes of De-Wolf descendants. Dr Watson Kirkconnell, retired president of Acadia University, identified several: the home of Thomas Andrew Strange DeWolf (Front and Gaspereaux, built in 1817), the home of Elisha DeWolf, Jr (369 Main Street, built in 1835), the Charles DeWolf house (95 Main Street, built in 1839), the Andrew De-Wolf Barss house (106 Main Street, built in 1864), the Margaret Maria DeWolf Starr house (94 Main Street, built in 1855), the Daniel DeWolf house (126 Main Street, built in 1802), the Abigail DeWolf house (113 Main Street, built in 1854), the Lucilla DeWolf Clarke house (89 Main Street, built in 1831), and his own home, built in 1801 by Stephen DeWolf, son of Edward DeWolf.

Charles DeWolf house,
95 Main Street

The DeWolf name was well respected in the community. In 1828 the citizens of Mud Creek happily changed the name of their community to Wolfville.

John Burbidge was, like Elisha DeWolf, an important man in his home town at Starr's Point in Cornwallis Township. A commander of the militia, he too entertained the Duke of Kent on his 1794 trip along the Annapolis Valley.

Burbidge was one of the original Haligonians. Although English-born, he arrived there from Louisbourg in 1749, the year that Halifax was founded. He was said to have built the first frame house in the new town. In 1764 he moved to Cornwallis Township. By the time of the Duke of Kent's visit thirty years later, he was colonel of the King's County militia and judge of the Inferior Court of Common Pleas. He had been Collector of Customs and had represented both Halifax and Cornwallis townships in the legislature.

A devout member of the Church of England, Burbidge drew up a memorandum in 1790 freeing his slaves, a practice becoming common among some slave-owners in Nova Scotia. He ordered that they be taught to read, and he also provided for the purchase of two outfits for each of them, one to be designated for Sunday best. Burbidge died in 1812 at the age of ninety-four.

It was Burbidge who in 1778 persuaded authorities to build a barracks and station troops in Cornwallis Township, at Starr's Point, just north of Wolfville. The township had been laid out in 1760 by Samuel Starr, who had come from Norwich, Connecticut, where his family had lived for more than a century. He had been one of an advance party of Planters who came to check out the land and the terms under which it would be granted. Starr explored the Minas Basin. When he came to what was to become Cornwallis Township he looked no farther, returning a year later as a grantee.

Starr was appointed the 'lot-layer,' and as such was responsible for laying out the town site. He followed the New England practice. Each settler's allotment included a garden lot, farm lot, dike lot, and town lot. There was a central parade (or common ground) within the town. Space was allowed for a church, minister's house, and school.

Although Starr and the other Planters at Cornwallis were tucked, presumably safely, in a bay near Cape Blomidon, they were well aware of the danger posed by American privateers during the Revolution in the south-

Andrew DeWolf Barss house, 106 Main Street

ern colonies. The government had been petitioned to send ships to police the vulnerable Bay of Fundy and provide protection for the New Englanders who were establishing themselves on the recently vacated Acadian lands. But no one in Halifax appeared concerned, although a fort in each township had been part of the bargain made with the Planters. Then one summer day in 1777, thirty or forty armed men arrived in whaling boats and landed on the shore of the Minas Basin. One settler, William Best of Cornwallis, lost £1,000 worth of property in the raid. Finally, Halifax took notice. John Burbidge had been trying to persuade the authorities that a barracks should be built in Cornwallis; he argued that Halifax was dependent upon the Annapolis Valley for farm produce and that the security of the area was therefore of prime importance. The attack spoke more clearly than his arguments. He quickly wrote to Lieutenant-Governor Sir Richard Hughes: 'From which violent and Audacious Robery your Memorialist and many of the principal Inhabitants do Apprehend themselves, both lives and property, in Eminent Danger, and will be induced to remove with their familys from their Settlements unless some protection can be had for their future Security.'

Burbidge's letter was written on 20 August 1778. Just three weeks later he wrote to announce that the barracks had been erected. One can only conclude that he did not wait for permission or that mail delivery was instantaneous.

Acacia Croft, originally a barracks, Starr's Point, RR 1, Port Williams

Burbidge noted that the barracks, built on land owned by Samuel Starr, had two rooms below with berths in each room for twenty men, a good fireplace in each, and eight cradles in the loft that would hold sixteen more men. Officers could be provided with quarters at a house about ten rods from the barracks.

It cost £70 to build the original barracks. Within six weeks, however, Burbidge was writing to say that the barracks needed to be refitted as officers' quarters and a new, larger, barracks constructed. A two-storey frame house was purchased for £16, moved to the site, and attached to the east end of the barracks. A second storey was added to that building as well. When finished, the cost was assessed. An original estimate of just over £200 for the addition had spiralled to £700, owing in part to spontaneous 'extras' such as the pickets around the building that caused it to be called, perhaps facetiously, Fort Hughes. The Legislative Assembly, which was responsible for the bills, decided that the building should be put up for sale.

In 1782 Samuel Starr, who had kept title to the property, sold the land and the barracks and they became a private residence called Acacia Croft – named for the acacia (black locust) trees found on the property. The new owner, John Whidden, was a judge, militia officer, and customs officer. It is believed that he used the house for his customs duties. After his death in 1794 the house was inherited by his son and daughter, David and Hannah. David purchased his sister's interest and made Acacia Croft his home. David Whidden served as high sheriff and, like his father, was a judge and customs officer. David's son, John, bought the property at public auction when David died, and Acacia Croft stayed in the Whidden family until his own death in 1849. One year later the house was bought by James Heales of Saint John. Acacia Croft remained in the Heales family until 1921. Thus only two families had owned it in the 139 years since John Whidden's purchase.

Years of neglect followed, but today Acacia Croft, beautifully restored, attracts visitors as a bed-and-breakfast establishment. It is called The Planters' Barracks.

From Acacia Croft, John Whidden could have watched as an elegant brick house took shape across the field. It was to be his daughter's home. Hannah Whidden had married Charles Ramage Prescott, a Halifax merchant, in 1796 and had gone to live with him

Hannah Prescott

in the capital. In 1812 they left Halifax and settled at Cornwallis. The couple and their six children (a seventh had died in infancy) moved in with the Whiddens while work was progressing on Acacia Grove, the Georgian house they had commissioned before leaving Halifax. But Hannah died the following year and it is unlikely that she ever lived in her new home.

Charles Prescott was an immigrant whose roots in Nova Scotia predated the arrival of the Planters. He was the son of Jonathan Prescott, a doctor and engineer who had established his name during the siege of Louisbourg in 1745, and had later acted bravely to defend Chester against American privateers. From 1800 to 1811 Charles Prescott was the senior partner in Prescott, Lawson and Company, a firm that was part of the vibrant mercantile life of Halifax, trading around the world and privateering during the Napoleonic era.

All this ended when, as a result of failing health, Prescott decided to leave Halifax and settle in the drier, sunnier climate of the Annapolis Valley. There he began a second career. In time, and thanks largely to his efforts, the valley grew bright with apple blossoms every spring. The climate and the less pressured life did wonders for his health.

A year after Hannah's death he married Mariah Hammill and fathered another five children. (Of his first family, Charles died at twenty, John at thirty-six, and Mary at sixteen.) In his new life he became a magistrate, member of the legislature, president of the agricultural society, and an appointee to the Legislative Council, on which he served for thirteen years.

Built of locally made bricks, Acacia Grove epitomized

The Prescott house, Acacia Grove, Starr's Point

the elegance of the Georgian style, proportion and symmetry its hallmark. It was commodious and comfortable, and reflected its owner's refinement, wealth, and importance in the community. An ample entrance hall, flanked by large rooms for conversation and dining, signified the open-handed, generous hospitality that visitors could expect. Bedrooms, too, were sizeable. Servants slept on the third floor.

The garden at Acacia Grove was Charles Prescott's consuming interest. As well as the acacias, a wide variety of other trees surrounded the house. He planted an orchard, extensive vegetable gardens, and, separated and protected by a stone wall and divided by paths, a rockery, and flower beds. Prescott was a horticultural artist. Joseph Howe, in *Western and Eastern Rambles*, enthused that 'it would take a day to examine Mr Prescott's beautiful and extensive gardens, where every variety of fruit which the country will produce is blended with every flower, and where the perfection of modern Horticulture may be viewed in successful operation.' In the rock garden at Acacia Grove are two Gravenstein apple trees. They are tangible reminders that Prescott is best remembered today as the man who introduced the Gravenstein and Ribston Pippin apples, and a host of other fruits and vegetables, to the Annapolis Valley.

Acacia Grove had numerous outbuildings, including a hothouse. Here, Prescott experimented with grafting fruit trees. He imported trees and vegetables from around the world in order to find those that were suitable to Nova Scotia's climate. In time the orchards and gardens at Acacia Grove overflowed with an abundance of melons, peaches, grapes, plums, apples, strawberries, raspberries, and nectarines. Prescott gladly gave away buds for grafting. He started the Fruit Growers Association and was a member of the horticultural societies of King's County and Nova Scotia, and an honorary member of the horticultural societies of New York, Boston, and London.

Charles Ramage Prescott died at eighty-seven, after forty-seven productive years in the Annapolis Valley. Acacia Grove remained in the family, but over time it deteriorated. Then, in the 1930s, this wonderful house was rescued by his great-granddaughter. With determination and devotion she restored it to its original splendour. The gardens, too, were given a new lease on life. Acacia Grove, now a National Historic Site, is open to the public from May to October.

CHAPTER NINETEEN

Grand Pré

On 2 September 1755, Lieutenant-Colonel John Winslow, on orders from Lieutenant-Governor Charles Lawrence, summoned 'both old men and young men, as well as all the lads of ten years of age' to his headquarters in the small church at Grand Pré. When all 400 were assembled, Winslow made his announcement:

The part of duty I am now upon, though necessary, is very disagreeable to my natural make and temper, as I know it must be grievous to you, who are of the same species; but it is not my business to animadvert but to obey such orders as I receive, and therefore, without hesitation, shall deliver you his Majesty's orders and instructions, namely – that your lands and tenements, cattle of all kinds and live stock of all sorts, are forfeited to the Crown; with all other your effects, saving your money and household goods, and you yourselves to be removed from this his Province.

Accordingly, 1,923 Acadian men, women, and children became His Majesty's prisoners awaiting deportation. Winslow knew that his prisoners vastly outnumbered his troops. To be safe, he placed 200 of the men he was holding on five vessels waiting in the harbour. Those few who escaped his troops were hunted down, shot, or forced to watch their home and possessions being burned. The rebellion subsided. After twenty-one days of imprisonment, the embarkation began. The last vessel embarked from Grand Pré on 18 December. Families were separated. Young men were deported first, then old men, then women and children. In Minas District, 255 houses, 276 barns, 155 outbuildings, 11 mills, and 1 church were burned.

Grand Pré became a symbol of their exile when Henry Wadsworth Longfellow chose it as the setting for his poem *Evangeline*. Today the Memorial Chapel in Grand Pré National Historic Park commemorates the little church in which the Acadians of Grand Pré heard the news of their expulsion.

The Acadians' exile was followed by the immigration of New Englanders to take up free land. One of these Planters was Jeremiah Calkin, of Lebanon, Connecticut. He came in 1765 with his wife, Mary, and their two sons, one of 200 families to settle in Horton Township. Four more sons and three daughters were born to Jeremiah and Mary in their new home.

Between 1765 and 1777 Calkin bought more land – nine good parcels. The house he built is one of the oldest surviving Planter houses. It has recently been moved from Wallbrook, its original site, to the Mitchell Road Hill in nearby Grand Pré. That move allowed a detailed structural study of a typical Planter house and made clear the link between the Planters' buildings and those of the Acadians.

Built in 1768, the Calkin house was erected on existing Acadian foundations. Those rough fieldstone walls support the west half of the house. The other half, the later eighteenth-century addition, stands on foundation walls of finished stone. In the Acadian section of the cellar, foundations for a chimney indicate that a large open cooking fireplace was originally centred on the wall at the west end. Structural details suggest that the first floor consisted of one large open room with narrow stairs leading to a loft above.

Some time before the end of the eighteenth century, Calkin began work on an addition. He extended the

The exile of the Acadians from Grand Pré; wood engraving from The Conquest of Canada *by G.D. Warburton, published in 1850*

chimney from the base of the west wall of the Acadian section to the first and second floors. As the family prospered, rooms were partitioned on the first floor and more elaborate details such as a corner chimney and mantel were added. There were four bedrooms on the second floor of the addition, and the loft, which originally housed all the children, was divided into two separate bedrooms. The gambrel roof, a popular feature, allowed for extra headroom on the upper level. The Calkin house reflects the New England influence, use of local materials, and availability of craftsmen with New England roots.

In 1769, while Jeremiah Calkin was completing work on his Nova Scotia home, George Gillmore, age forty-nine, emigrated from Scotland to the American colonies. Twenty-two years later, at age seventy-one, after many moves, and periods when he lacked adequate food and clothing for himself and his family, he made his final and most successful move – to Grand Pré. Here he was responsible for building what is now the oldest Presbyterian church in Canada, a graceful frame building sheltered by a grove of trees.

Gillmore's studies in Scotland included logic, metaphysics, and natural philosophy. But this esoteric education did little to prepare him for life in the American colonies, where he intended to teach and preach. The first rude awakening for this gentle soul came during the crossing when, for eleven weeks, he was forced to endure the coarse manners of his fellow passengers and the crew. In retrospect, the voyage may have been a high point in what was a stressful, difficult life.

Settling first in Massachusetts and then in Connec-

Jeremiah Calkin house

ticut, Gillmore began teaching and preaching as planned. But his arrival coincided with the rise of rebellious sentiments in the colonies – traitorous ideas for which he had no sympathy. He earnestly made his Loyalist viewpoint known and was soon forced to give up preaching altogether and take up farming instead. This did little to stop the persecution. He moved to New York and resumed preaching. The result was the same. Gillmore was once again forced to leave his parish.

After the defeat of the British, George Gillmore left for Quebec. Here too he fared poorly. People in Quebec, he said, had closed minds and closed purses. He turned to the good British colony of 'New Scotland' and took passage for Halifax, hoping for a new and better life. But this better life was not to be. Not yet. His next stop was Windsor, where he found the Presbyterians unenthusiastic and unable to provide him with a living. When he was sixty-eight, he returned to Scotland to plead with the authorities for a pension. He was desperate, he said, after a life of peril and poverty. They granted him a meagre pension of £20 yearly.

In 1791 Gillmore was sent to Grand Pré. He was still a fighter and a devout 'Covenantor' who had no use for Nova Scotia's Bishop Charles Inglis or for the Church of England. Nor was he afraid to speak out. Gillmore's parishioners were mostly Planters, dissenters who were Congregationalists, as they had been in New England. The American Revolution had strained their relationship with the churches they had left behind, some of which had been supporting them financially. The rift became a break. Many Congregationalists became supporters of the dynamic Henry Alline and his New Light ministry with its loosely knit organization, its message of new birth, and Alline's emotionally charged services full of song and the rapturous shouts of the newly converted. Eventually many other Congregationalists merged with the Baptist Church. In Gillmore's parish it was the Presbyterian tradition that grew stronger.

After preaching for thirteen years in the congregation's small meeting-house, built in the 1770s, Gillmore made plans for a larger church. In 1804 the present frame building was started under his direction. The Covenantors' church was completed in 1811. It was similar to a New England meeting-house with high pews and a pulpit that reached halfway to the ceiling, and from which Gillmore could send down on the heads of his parishioners words of damnation and salvation. Not for long, however. The dauntless George Gillmore died that fall.

In 1818 a tower, belfry, and steeple were added to one end of the building. Later the church became part of the Reformed Presbyterian Church of Ireland. Time passed and, for eighteen years or so, it stood deserted, falling into disrepair. Finally it was bought by the Presbyterian Church of Canada, which in 1925 became part of the United Church of Canada. Today the church, a member of the Wolfville United Church Charge, is open for services during the summer.

The small meeting-house that was removed to make room for Gillmore's church was acquired by an Irish Presbyterian, Robert Laird. He had arrived in Nova Sco-

The Covenantors' Church

tia from Ireland in 1770, settling first in Windsor, where he married Jane Palmer. The couple bought land in Grand Pré on a hill overlooking the marshlands, and they moved the old meeting-house to the site. It became their home while a new house, a dignified two-storey Georgian, was built as an addition to the simple meeting-house.

The house was eventually inherited by Robert and Jane's three daughters, as their sons had already been provided for. The only daughter to marry was Elizabeth, who became the wife of John McNeil Stewart.

Stewart had come to North America as an impressed sailor in the British navy. He had jumped ship near Pictou in 1810, and successfully eluded capture. Little is known about his later life, but, after his death in 1828, Elizabeth lived on in the house with her two unmarried sisters, Catherine and Eleanor. The house then passed to her sons. It was still in the same family more than 180 years later. The name of its builder, Robert Laird, stayed in the family as well. His great-grandson, Sir Robert Laird Borden, was born in Grand Pré in 1854. He became head of a prestigious Halifax law firm, a member of Parliament, and the eighth prime minister of Canada. Borden led the country during the First World War. It was he who insisted that Canadian soldiers fight together, so that Vimy Ridge fell to a purely Canadian unit. And it was his government that introduced the first direct taxation by Ottawa – an income tax put into effect in 1917 as a 'temporary' measure.

Robert Laird house

CHAPTER TWENTY

Newport Landing and Windsor

High on a bank above the Ste-Croix River stands the Old Stone House, a venerable building of indeterminate age. No one knows just how old it is, although theories abound. The house was built, some believe, to serve as a mass house or religious centre, and a construction date of 1699 has been suggested as a possibility.

There are intriguing pieces of information concerning the mystery of the house: a manuscript map of 1738–48 in the National Maritime Museum in Greenwich, England, indicates a path or portage from Chebucto Bay (Bedford Basin) to the bank of the Ste-Croix River very near the Old Stone House. Marked on the map is 'mission Sauvages chebanacady,' with the name of 'Labbe de Loutre,' the dreaded missionary who became the terror of the Acadians as well as the British, encouraging the Mi'kmaqs to seek British scalps in Halifax and threatening Acadians with a similar fate if they did not follow his orders.

The construction of the basement adds to the mystery. No ordinary cellar this – vaulted ceilings and stone archways suggest that, just possibly, it was used by a religious order, one such as that noted by an American surveyor who, on a 1731 voyage to Nova Scotia, mentioned seeing 'Mass House[s] ... on one of which they hang a Flagg Morning and Evening for Prayers, to the other the Priest goes once a day only, Habited like a Fool in Petticoats, with a Man after him with a Bell in one Hand ringing at every door and a lighted candle and Lanthorn in the other.'

The mystery surrounding this stone house has intrigued the Jesuit Fathers, whose archivist, Father Edward Dowling, has commented that if the house had such antecedents it would have been built with religious or political money from France.

Whatever the background of the Old Stone House, there is no doubt that the French had settled on the eastern side of the Piziquid (Avon) River as early as 1685. When the vessel *Envieux* arrived in Rochelle, France, in 1698, it carried a message from the priest de Thury asking to be stationed at the fork of two rivers, which he called Aquixadi and Pegitegiak, that is, the Ste-Croix and the Piziquid (Avon). He asked for a grant of land there, another fact that fuels speculation about the origin of the Old Stone House. The census of 1701 establishes that eight Acadian families were then living near the site, along the Ste-Croix, a meandering offshoot of the Piziquid, in the small area between what is now Newport Landing and Newport Station. There were in total forty-five children and ninety-one cattle. Each family owned one or two muskets.

This community was swept away in the expulsion of the Acadians in 1755. Although the British did not destroy the houses in this area, as happened elsewhere, some buildings were burned after the deportation, during the Seven Years War between England and France; the fate of the Old Stone House at that time is unknown. Since the first floor was gutted by fire at a later date, construction details do not exist to assist the search. Perhaps one of its subsequent owners built the house on those early foundations.

Beginning in 1760 an influx of New England Planters who received grants and settled on the abandoned Acadian farms occurred. In this region, many came from Rhode Island.

Two of them, bachelors, jointly drew the farm lot on which the Old Stone House stands. They were Aaron

Old Stone House, Newport
Landing

Butts, a Rhode Islander, and George Brightman, who came from Dartmouth, Massachusetts. Details in the inventory of his estate indicate that Brightman was a well-turned-out gentleman in silver knee buckles and a silver sword and carrying a walking stick.

In April 1763 Butts and Brightman sold to John Chambers, another Rhode Island Planter. Chambers, also a bachelor, had arrived on the sloop *Sally* along with thirty-five other men and their families who had left Newport, Rhode Island, for the 'Newport of the North.' John Chambers became a 'surveyor to make proper allowance for broken and unprofitable land' and chairman of the township's survey committee. One of his bills for services rendered included charges for a gallon of rum.

The man who bought the stone house from Chambers in 1818 was a lawyer, politician, judge, and author. He created an unforgettable character, Sam Slick, who became well known on both sides of the Atlantic and on both sides of the Canada–U.S. border.

Sam Slick was a Yankee clockmaker. He travelled Nova Scotia selling clocks, and dispensing gratuitous advice ('give and take, live and let live') and caustic commentary ('this country is going to the dogs.') His creator was Thomas Chandler Haliburton. As a judge, Haliburton also travelled the province, dispensing his own words of wisdom and caustic comment, often to a captive audience.

Haliburton was the son of William Hersey Otis Haliburton and Lucy Chandler Grant, and the grandson of William Haliburton, who had who emigrated to Nova Scotia in 1761, boasting a family connection with Sir Walter Scott. Lucy Haliburton had lost both her parents, dedicated Loyalists, in a shipwreck on the Bay of Fundy. She died at the age of twenty-three, in 1797, in her Windsor home, when Thomas was only a few months old. The boy was raised by William's second wife, Susanna Boutineau (Francklin) Davis, the daughter of a former lieutenant-governor, Michael Francklin. Thomas Haliburton grew up in Windsor, a garrison town that was the summer retreat for many Haligonians of political, social, and mercantile prominence.

By 1810 Haliburton had graduated from Windsor's prestigious King's College School with a healthy quota of Latin, Greek, Anglicanism, and confidence, thanks to his attendance at what was the oldest school in the British Commonwealth outside Britain. In 1815 he received his B.A. from King's College, then also in Windsor. His next year was eventful. On a trip to England, he visited a relative, met that man's young ward, Louisa Neville, married her, and took her back to Windsor. She was the only daughter of Captain Laurence Neville of the 19th Light Dragoons. Louisa Neville had, upon her mother's death, been placed in the care of a friendly widow who subsequently married an adventurer, and accompanied him to France, with Louisa in tow. When her father eventually located her, Louisa was promptly placed in the care of Haliburton's relative, where, in 1816, young Thomas found her.

Two years later Haliburton, then a law student, bought the Old Stone House in Newport Landing and called it Henley Farm, after Louisa's English home, Henley-on-Thames. The Haliburtons eventually became parents of eleven children, three of whom died in infancy.

Haliburton was admitted to the bar in 1820, and the family moved to Annapolis Royal, where he established a law practice and began his political career. As a member of the legislature for Annapolis from 1826 to 1829, he variously titillated and outraged his fellow members by giving vent to the acerbic humour that later became part of the wit and wisdom of Sam Slick. Once, when a bill with many amendments was introduced into the House, Haliburton claimed that it was 'prepared in such a shape that it seemed as if the author had been desirous that its importance, like that of a comet, should be measured by the length of its tail.' Nor was Haliburton above punning, noting that in his county 'they had a Judge for a Colonel,' a fitting choice, he said 'for he is well accustomed to make a charge!'

Not all members of the House were as amused by such quips as was their author. In 1829 Haliburton applied for the vacancy which had occurred in the Inferior Court of Common Pleas on his father's death. His appointment, it was said, had as much to do with getting him out of the House as it had in getting him onto the Bench. He took his sense of humour with him, however, and became known as the punning judge. During a trial for the recovery of insurance on some drums of codfish, before calling the next witness, a Mr Fife, Judge Haliburton solemnly intoned: 'Now that we have got through the drums lets have the fifes.' An Orier, calling the jurymen, was lustily repeating the name of Nicholas Sarre, when the irrepressible Haliburton called out

Thomas Chandler Haliburton, creator of Sam Slick

'Hold! He has been dead for six months.' (Nicholas, Czar of Russia, had died the previous March.)

Haliburton owned the Old Stone House in Newport Landing for sixteen years, although his time was spent mainly in Annapolis. During that period he began his career as a writer, prompting *The Colonial Patriot*, 22 February 1828, to report glowingly of this 'patriotic attempt, by a Nova-Scotian of such brilliant talents as Mr. Haliburton is allowed to possess, to raise his country from its present depressed position in the scale of literary fame.'

In 1829 his *History of Nova Scotia, An Historical and Statistical Account of the Province* was published. *The Clockmaker; or, The Sayings and Doings of Samuel Slick, of Slickville* made its first appearance in 1835.

The Old Stone House had been sold the year before Sam Slick first strode onto the scene, this time to James Sprott. Four years later it passed into the Allison family – John, then Robert and his son, Joseph P. Allison, where it remained until 1910.

By the time the Haliburtons sold the stone house, they were immersed in plans for a move to Windsor and the construction of their new home, Clifton. The new house was small, of one storey only, but the ambitions of its owner were grand, and so what the building lacked in size it is said to have gained in refinement, the Haliburtons being intent on maintaining a social presence. Clifton was a frame building, set on Ferry Hill, overlooking the town of Windsor. Louisa created fanciful gardens, efforts described in *Canadian Scenery*, published in London in 1842, the year following her death.

This charming retreat is surrounded by thriving plantations of beech, white maple, poplar, juniper, and other ornamental trees. Fruits of the most delicate kinds are produced in the garden; indeed, the sheltered situation of Windsor is peculiarly favourable for raising the tender produce of more genial climates. Mr Haliburton remarks, that 'peaches, though subject, from the early blossoms they put forth, to be injured by frosts, have been known to ripen without artificial aid or even common shelter; and grapes, pears and quinces, and a great variety of summer and autumnal plums, arrive at perfection in all ordinary seasons.'

Perhaps Louisa derived inspiration from reports of the exotic plantings – flowers, trees, and shrubs – that made Charles Prescott's gardens at Acacia Grove, Starr's Point, the talk of the Annapolis Valley.

Louisa's creative imagination was passed on to two of her daughters. Amelia, wife of the Rev. Edwin Gilpin, was a talented artist, noted for her landscapes. Laura exhibited in London with the Royal Academy. She married William Cunard, son of their friend, the shipping magnate Samuel Cunard, a match that no doubt warmed her father's heart.

Clifton has been changed dramatically since it was built. The original house was on two levels, with the front entrance (now on the rear façade) facing a side hill. Two principal rooms were flanked by wings, with a hall behind, a cellar kitchen below, and a loft above. The space included a butler's pantry, a smoking room, and an oak-panelled hall. The present library (where it has been incorrectly assumed that *The Clockmaker* was written) was not part of the original house, nor was the present dining-room with its vaulted ceiling. Both were added, along with dormer windows, a porch, a belvedere, a second roof over the original, and a *porte-cochère*.

Haliburton did create Sam Slick at Clifton, even if not in the present library. Slick was a brash, know-it-all Yankee whose down-home colloquialisms became familiar throughout the English-speaking world. The British public was so fascinated with his 'transatlantic slang' that Haliburton's popularity rivalled, for a time, that of Charles Dickens. The dialect in *The Clockmaker* made a fascinating study for linguists. Expressions such as

The residence of Judge Haliburton, about 1842; engraving, after a work by William Henry Bartlett

'quick as a wink' and 'barking up the wrong tree' became part of our language. Sam was a vehicle through which Haliburton could express his opinions – on everything from the Yankee work ethic to British conceit and the failings of his own countrymen. Nova Scotians were lazy, he chided, and they talked too much. But, had the Yankees been running this country,

you couldn't see the harbours for the shipping. There'd be a rush of folks to it, as there is in one of our inns, to the dinner table, when they sometimes get jammed together in the door-way, and a man has to take a running leap over their heads, afore he can get in ... Do you know the reason monkeys are no good? because they chatter all day long ... and so do the blue-noses of Nova Scotia – it's all talk and no work; now, with us it's all work and no talk ...

The lessons Haliburton wanted to impart to his fellow Nova Scotians were directed at the authorities. They were sugar-coated, but carried a punch:

You've seen a flock of partridges of a frosty mornin in the fall, a crowdin out of the shade to a sunny spot, and huddlin up there in the warmth – well the blue-noses have nothin else to do half the time but sun themselves. Whose fault is that? Why it's the fault of the legislature; *they don't encourage internal improvement, nor the investment of capital in the country, and the result is apathy, inaction, and poverty.*

And it was good sport to make a pass at the snobs from Halifax:

I met a man this mornin, said the Clockmaker, from Halifax, a rael conceited lookin critter as you een amost ever seed, all shines and didos. He looked as if he had picked up his airs, arter some officer of the rigilars had worn 'em out and cast 'em off ... He marched up and down afore the street-door like a peacock, as large as life and twice as nateral; he had a ridin-whip in his hand, and every now and then struck it agin his thigh, as much as to say, Aint that a splendid leg for a boot, now? Won't I astonish the Amherst folks, that's all? ...

Twenty-two installments of *The Clockmaker* appeared in *The Novascotian*, beginning 24 September 1835. The series was published in book form the next year in Halifax; in 1838 a second series was published in London; a third series appeared in 1840.

The following year brought tragedy to Thomas Haliburton. His wife, Louisa, died on 29 November 1841. She had lived at Clifton for less than five years. Life in Clifton changed dramatically for Haliburton after Louisa's death. Six of his eight surviving children were still at home, and his son Thomas was suffering from an illness which ended in his death in 1847.

In 1841, when the Inferior Court of Common Pleas was abolished, Haliburton was appointed to the Supreme Court of Nova Scotia, a position he held until 1856, when he retired, sold Clifton, and moved to England. That same year he married a widow, Sarah Harriet Williams. Three years later Haliburton was elected to the British House of Commons and stayed in office until his death in Middlesex, England, in 1865.

Clifton was purchased by James Pellow, a Windsor man who had amassed something of a fortune in the California gold rush. The house was sold again, in 1871, to Ezra Churchill, a merchant, shipbuilder, and politician. He was appointed senator in 1871.

As the years went by, Clifton passed through the hands of several owners, most of whom tinkered with the architecture, expanding and altering, until the house that Thomas and Louisa Haliburton had built was virtually unrecognizable. For a while it operated as a hotel; then, in 1939, the government of Nova Scotia bought it and opened it to the public as a branch of the Nova Scotia Museum.

In the summer of 1890, on Ferry Hill, close to Clifton, Clifford Shand was starting construction of a wedding present for his bride, Henrie Vaughan. Shand was a great-grandson of a Scottish immigrant, Patrick

Haliburton's home,
Clifton, today

Shand, and a son of Andrew Shand, who had established the Windsor Furniture Factory in 1871. His bride was a granddaughter of a shipbuilder, Bennett Smith. The house, completed in 1891, was one of Windsor's finest, on a site overlooking the Avon River. Its plans had come from the latest style book, Shopell's *Modern Houses*, published that year by the Co-Operative Building Plan Association of New York Architects. The house was so wonderfully flamboyant and so intricately detailed that it became a landmark in Windsor. Today it forms part of the letterhead of the Canadian Heritage Information Network.

Because of the family furniture business, Shand had access to craftsmen who could create the fanciful em-

Shand house, Ferry Hill,
Windsor

bellishments that the plans called for. Joseph Taylor of nearby Falmouth was retained as builder. A respected contractor, Taylor could thank, to a degree, several local clerics (Presbyterian, Methodist, Anglican, and Baptist) for his fine reputation. These gentlemen, while disagreeing on theological concerns, were united in their opinions on matters architectural. Each used Taylor to build his church.

The exterior of the Shand house had verandahs, balconies, turrets, and a tower, all of it joyously embellished and as ornate as spindles, tracery, and treillage could make it. Topping it all was Clifford Shand's tower. One of the special effects he wanted, the tower served as a lookout from which he could watch the Avon flowing by and cast his eye over the main street of the town below.

Inside, elegant panelling was crafted by four skilled cabinetmakers from his father's furniture factory. No visitor could help but be impressed, for the panelling dominated the interior. The central hall gleamed with rich wood, and the glow from a handsome fireplace, framed by a cherrywood mantelpiece nine feet high, added to its warmth. Mantels of similar height adorned the drawing- and sitting-rooms. Even the bathroom was a thing of beauty with its oak-panelled walls and a bathtub, zinc with a copper inset, also encased in oak. The house is now a branch of the Nova Scotia Museum and is open to the public. The original finish of the fine wood still enhances the house today.

Six years after their house was completed, Clifford and Henrie Shand may have watched from their tower as flames engulfed the whole main section of Windsor, destroying many of its fine shops, businesses, and homes. The houses on Ferry Hill were spared. Once again Joseph Taylor was called in from Falmouth. He began the work of rebuilding, which was carried on by many other master builders.

When Thomas Chandler Haliburton graduated from King's College School in 1815 the institution was already twenty-seven years old. It had opened its doors to the 'salubrious' air of Windsor on 1 November 1788, but the quality of the air was not the only advantage the school enjoyed. Its founder, the esteemed Bishop Charles Inglis, also rejoiced in the school's location – a safe twenty-five miles from the temptations of Halifax, a town he considered to be full of sensual high living, a consequence of the corrupting influence of 'society,' including the blatant example being set by the lieutenant-governor and his lady, John and Fanny Wentworth.

The Academy, as it was initially called, was a grammar school. A university, King's College, opened in 1789. The Academy was then renamed King's College School.

Charles Inglis, created Anglican Bishop of Nova Scotia in 1787, was a staunch Loyalist who had received his landmark appointment – first overseas Anglican bishop – as a reward for service to the Crown during the American Revolution. His diocese encompassed Nova Scotia, New Brunswick, Prince Edward Island, Newfoundland, Upper and Lower Canada, and Bermuda. The staggering extent of this territory made it difficult for him to visit his parishes and clergy frequently, but his journals show that he made valiant attempts to do so. He spent much of his time in Nova Scotia, however, and, latterly, in his beloved Annapolis Valley.

The slender, aristocratic Inglis wanted to establish a school that offered an education in Latin and English. In this he succeeded, just as he had prevailed in the matter of its location. Windsor had been a popular retreat for the 'codfish gentry of Halifax' since about 1759, and home to gentlemen of the Church and the Bar – a rarefied atmosphere in which, presumably, it was assumed that the boys would be hard pressed to find distractions. By the time the school was founded, the town was well established, at least as a village of some pretensions.

The first principal of the Academy was the Rev. Ar-

Rev. Charles Inglis, Bishop of Nova Scotia

The original Francklin house built in 1762 and the Georgian addition built late in the nineteenth century, King Street at College Road

hibald Payne Inglis, a nephew of the bishop. The first boy to be registered, one of seventeen students, was the bishop's only son, John, the youngest of his four children. (Inglis had lost his wife, Peggy, and his eldest son, Charles, five years earlier, leaving him with two daughters, Margaret and Ann, as well as John.) John's connections did nothing, however, to save him from the rod when discipline was deemed necessary. He later became the third Bishop of Nova Scotia.

King's College School educated the sons of gentlemen, the military, and the clergy – as long as the offspring could meet entrance requirements. This meant that, by age eight, they had to be able to read and write. The tuition fee was reasonable, but the school's location in Windsor meant that most boys had to live in residence, a requirement that added considerably to the cost of education, but perhaps not too unreasonably. Richard Uniacke, as solicitor general and Speaker of the House, once raised the matter in his inimitable forthright fashion. The Legislative Assembly was discussing funding for the poorhouse. That institution was then costing £1,600 per year – one-quarter of the province's revenue. 'A child could be boarded and educated at Windsor for £20 per annum,' Uniacke stated indignantly. It was a sum eight or nine pounds less than it cost the province to keep a child in the poorhouse.

Initially, accommodation was found for King's students in the Israel Andrews house in Windsor. Classes were held for the first year in the home of Susannah Francklin, widow of Lieutenant-Governor Michael Francklin. The house, built in 1762, stood on property Francklin had acquired in 1759.

Coach house and stables
behind Francklin house

Susannah and her son, James Boutineau Francklin, rented facilities to King's College School for five years. The connection with the school became a permanent one when, in 1808, Elizabeth Francklin, Susannah and Michael's daughter, married the Rev. William Colsel King, who later became principal. (Another daughter, Susanna Boutineau Francklin, married William Haliburton after the death of his first wife and raised young Thomas, creator of Sam Slick.)

The Francklin house remained in the family but was remodelled by the daughter of Elizabeth and William King, Mary Grace, and her husband, George Wiggins. They added an imposing coach house and stables. Their daughter, Alice Wiggins, great-granddaughter of Susannah and Michael Francklin, married Hadley B. Tremain. That couple wanted to add space but deferred to her father's wish that the old house not be torn down. Instead they added to it a Georgian home, built late in the century. The two buildings, still joined today, are on King Street at the end of College Road.

The second president of King's College, and also principal of King's College School, was the Rev. William Cochran, a scholarly and idealistic Irishman who had arrived in Nova Scotia in 1788 after five disillusioning years in the United States. Inglis ordained Cochran even though he lacked theological training. He became president and principal in 1790. He was a man of formidable appearance and 'an inspired and natural teacher,' according to Brian Cuthbertson in *The First Bishop*. Cuthbertson added that Cochran was also a stern disciplinarian. 'When, for example, young John Inglis and Thomas Rowland, without leave, drank tea at the home of the English master, Cochran was so angry at their disobedience that he made them fast for 23 hours.' He also appears to have been liberal with the cane. On one occasion when a student, possibly John Inglis, was to be severely caned, Prince Edward tried to intervene and stop the punishment; Cochran, however, would not tolerate any outside interference in matters of discipline. It should be remembered, however, that such discipline was not unusual, but was in fact the norm for the times, and it was never suggested by school authorities that Cochran was doing more than his duty in such matters.

At this time the school's students were examined before an intimidating panel of gentlemen. The examinations were, as *The Royal Gazette and the Nova Scotia Ad-*

vertiser reported on 3 June 1794, 'severe, strict and minute.'

Newport Landing   *225*
and Windsor

On Thursday, the 15th ult. was held the Quarterly Examination of the Students of the Academy at Windsor. The Bishop of Nova Scotia, Judge Brenton, and several gentlemen of the place attended. The business of the day, which lasted five hours, commenced with an Examination of the higher Classes in Grotius *De Veritate Christianae Religionis* – a Book well calculated to lay a solid and extensive foundation for religious knowledge. The first class was then examined in Longinus on the Sublime, and Horace's *Art of Poetry*; the second Class in Homer and Livy; the third Class in Xenophon and Cicero; and the other Classes successively in the Greek Testament, Ovid, and Caesar. The Students were next examined in Geography, use of the Globes, and Mathematics; and then gave in their Latin and English Themes and Verses ... The examination in each branch, was severe, strict, and minute. The Students, both in it, and in the delivery of their several pieces acquitted themselves in a manner that did very great credit to them. Their improvement and progress were evident, and struck those who were present.

Plans for expanded facilities moved slowly. The boys shared teaching facilities with King's College, whose building, started in 1794, took many years to complete. There still were no facilities for boarding, however. By 1807 Cochran was patiently explaining to the board that it would be hard to see the school expand until it had a building to be both home and school to the students. Finally, in 1815, architect John Plaw designed a stone building at a cost of £7,200 'of which,' according to the school's honorary historian, L.S. Loomer, '£3,000 came from the Arms Duty Fund collected during the British occupation of Castine, Maine, in the War of 1812.' Opened in 1822, it stood above the lower playing field. After it was destroyed by fire in 1871, a wooden building was constructed in 1877 on the same site, then moved up the hill in 1905 and later named Willets House, after an outstanding headmaster. It was torn down in 1979.

Cochran was succeeded as head of King's College and King's College School in 1808 – at the college by the Rev. Charles Porter, and at the school, which now had twenty-seven students enrolled, by the Rev. William King.

A disastrous fire destroyed the old King's College building in 1920 in spite of boasts by the school fathers that their buildings had electricity, hot air, and hot water and that 'every precaution has been taken to minimize the danger from fire. Fire escapes have recently been attached to both buildings, and extinguishers are placed ready to hand, while a fire hose is ready to be connected with the hydrant in front of the building.'

King's College moved to Halifax in 1923, leaving the school sole occupant of the 69-acre site, on a hilltop with a vista that stretches from Windsor out over the Avon Valley. Two outstanding original stone buildings still stand on this the oldest university campus in the Commonwealth, outside of England. They are Convocation Hall and the Hensley Memorial Chapel.

Convocation Hall served as the focus for all gatherings at King's College. In addition, it housed the college library. Opened in June 1863, it was an imposing structure. Even before it was finished, *The Halifax Reporter* of 21 February 1863 noted approvingly:

This building is now approaching completion. It is a long, beautiful edifice in the Norman style ... it is built of the native freestone – a stone well adapted for such a work ... the spectator's attention is at once attracted by a beautiful circular window over the semi-circular apsis at the west end ... the roof is timber of open work, stained dark oak ... the gallery rail is of wood of massive form and good characteristic design;.the alcoves for the reception of the various specimens in the museum are placed between the bays of the windows behind the pillars supporting the gallery; the shelving for the books in the gallery is fitted in similar manner.

Convocation Hall, King's-Edgehill School, Windsor

The report did not exaggerate the building's beauty. The interior, with its gently curving alcoves and finely arched windows, was open to a vaulted ceiling. Above, a gallery extended around three sides. From this platform students reached bookshelves which lined the whole upper walls of the building, making what was already an imposing interior quite breathtaking.

When King's College moved to Halifax in 1920, Convocation Hall became part of King's College School. After decades of neglect, the building fell into disrepair. Now, thanks to a remarkable and meticulous restoration, during which the plaster and wood of many years were removed, the full beauty of the original interior has emerged, as gracious in style and rich in fine woods as it was in 1863. The school's inviting library facilities are housed here again, in a historic atmosphere. Convocation Hall is a gem of Nova Scotia architecture.

The second of the two old buildings that still grace the campus is the Hensley Memorial Chapel, a small

Convocation Hall now houses the King's-Edgehill School library

stone building named to honour the school's devoted librarian and professor of divinity. It was built in 1877, a year after his death. In the academy's early years the boys attended Charles Inglis's parish church, Christ Church, until the wardens decided to charge pew rent. Then, until the Hensley Chapel was built, they attended services in other local parishes, in a small college chapel, or in Convocation Hall.

The history of the school can be seen on the chapel's walls, in commemorative plaques and stained-glass windows. At the rear of the chapel, new windows depict the major event in the school's recent history. The school crest and that of Edgehill Church School for Girls (established in 1890) symbolize the union of these two distinguished institutions in 1976.

An institution as old as King's must naturally harbour a ghost. The spirit of 'Pa Buckle' is said to appear from time to time. Buckle was headmaster of Brighton School, near Blenheim, when Winston Churchill was a student there, and is said to have predicted that young Winston would one day become prime minister. Hired by headmaster E.T. Handsomebody, Buckle taught at King's College School from 1904 to 1935. When it came time to retire, he had nowhere to go, and so stayed in the headmaster's house, cared for by the headmaster's wife. He died in 1940, two months before his prediction about Churchill became a reality. His ghost is said to haunt the house, making an occasional appearance in black robes and a straw skimmer, and with his ever-present cigar.

More notable than any ghosts are the graduates. Today King's-Edgehill recalls with pride that in its long illustrious history it has graduated numerous Rhodes Scholars, members of provincial and federal governments, judges, ambassadors, admirals, bishops, university presidents, authors, a prime minister (Sir Charles Tupper), Major Sir John Inglis KCB (the hero of Lucknow), the Rev. Canon Reginald Helser Bullock (Chaplain to Queen Victoria), two sons of Benedict Arnold, and three Fathers of Confederation.

CHAPTER TWENTY-ONE

Mount Uniacke

For sheer magnificence few buildings in nineteenth-century Nova Scotia could equal the elegance of Richard John Uniacke's wilderness mansion. Travellers encountered it unexpectedly just southeast of Windsor as they bumped along the old Post Road that led to Halifax. There it stood in lonely splendour, its soaring portico in startling contrast to the dark forest that surrounded it.

Built between 1813 and 1815, Mount Uniacke became, in spite of its isolation, a centre for the political and social life of Nova Scotia. Uniacke was the province's powerful attorney general. He called his estate Mount Uniacke after his ancestral home in Ireland. From there, on more than one occasion, family influence and prestige had reached across the Atlantic to advance Uniacke's career and, later, those of his six talented and handsome sons.

Oral tradition, recorded in the late nineteenth century, relates that young Uniacke first saw the 11,000-acre site on which he would build his country home when, as a youth, he was being taken to Halifax to be tried for treason. Certainly the career of the man who has been called the most influential Nova Scotian of his time began inauspiciously. Cut off financially by his father because of his involvement with Irish nationalists, Uniacke left home and found his way to Philadelphia in 1774. There he met Moses Delesdernier, a Nova Scotian trader on the lookout for settlers and financing for his own faltering affairs. Uniacke tried to draw on his father's funds in Ireland to finance a partnership with Delesdernier, a move that so incensed his father that the young adventurer was promptly disinherited. Uniacke and his new partner took up lands in Cumberland County at the head of the Bay of Fundy.

At the time of the American Revolution there was much unrest in Cumberland County. It broke into open rebellion in 1776, and Uniacke became involved with the rebels. He was captured and marched off to Halifax to be tried for treason. During the trek along the Windsor-to-Halifax road, the guards with their prisoners stopped by a lake to rest. Uniacke, then penniless and in disgrace, is said to have been captivated by the beauty of the place, vowing that he would return one day to build a home. In Halifax, the charges against him were dropped, owing, in all probability, to his family connections.

In 1775 Uniacke, then twenty-two, had married Moses Delesdernier's twelve-year-old daughter, Martha Maria. Even in an age of youthful marriages, Martha was still very much a child. She stayed at home with her parents for two years. At the end of that time her husband left for Ireland to finish his legal training. Because he was in debt, he sold Martha's inherited property in Halifax to finance his journey and left Martha, then fourteen and pregnant, with her relatives.

When Uniacke returned from Ireland in 1781, his career quickly took an upward turn, thanks partly to his talent and partly to a reconciliation with his family, who had connections they could bring to bear on his behalf. That year, at age twenty-eight, he was appointed solicitor general for Nova Scotia. Two years later he was elected to the Legislative Assembly, just at the time that the Loyalist migration was beginning. It was to double the population of the province, from 20,000 to 40,000, fill Halifax with a new élite, and set into motion constant feuding between the two groups. Uniacke became the champion of the pre-Loyalists, or 'old comers,' in opposition to the 'new comers,' Loyalists who, fiercely devoted to the Crown, sought rewards for their loyalty in the form of patronage appointments.

Uniacke vied for, but lost, the plum appointment of attorney general when it became available in 1784. It went to Sampson Salter Blowers, a Loyalist. Uniacke had to be satisfied with an appointment as advocate general of the Court of Vice Admiralty. It, however, became the basis of his fortune. A mutual dislike developed between Uniacke and Blowers and quickly burgeoned into full-blown enmity. When, in 1791, Blowers challenged Uniacke to a duel, Chief Justice Thomas Strange had to intervene to prevent the confrontation. In 1797 Blowers was appointed chief justice, and Uniacke attorney general. The next year, Blowers again issued a challenge. The cause: Blowers claimed that Uniacke had engaged in a street fight with the Loyalist candidate (a protégé of Blowers), for the attorney-generalship, and had beaten him so badly that he might have caused that unfortunate man's death shortly afterwards. Duels were then illegal, but that did not bother these two bastions of the law. For a second time, the two were forcibly prevented from duelling.

Although he had been elected Speaker of the House of Assembly in 1789, Uniacke had not run in the 1792 election because of the animosity directed at him by the Loyalists. In 1798 he returned to the assembly and once more became its speaker, a position he would hold until 1805 when he resigned his seat. In 1808 he was appointed a member of His Majesty's Council for Nova Scotia. He had a seat at the council table and retained his appointment as attorney general until his death in 1830.

Uniacke became a figure of great influence in Nova Scotia. While in the assembly he fought for its right to have the sole constitutional authority to frame and amend bills for the raising and spending of taxes. He made presentations to the British government for a federation of the British North American colonies, while striving to have Nova Scotia's trade freed from the constraints of imperial regulation. His greatest fear was of the triple 'heresies' – atheism, republicanism, and democracy – which he saw spreading through the new United States. They might well, he thought, infect the remaining British North American colonies. He was a giant of his time. His fiery temper, charm, incisive mind, wealth, ambition, fierce determination, and intense devotion to the Church of England as the established church led to a life of fractious confrontations.

Although by the late 1790s Uniacke had the largest law practice in the province, his fortune (reputed to have been £50,000) came from the immense fees he earned as advocate general of the Court of Vice Admiralty. This was the court which adjudicated the prizes captured by Nova Scotian privateers and the British navy during the long war with revolutionary France and the War of 1812 with the United States.

By 1813 Uniacke had the wealth to turn his dream of a country estate into reality. Construction of Mount Uniacke began that year. The energetic Uniacke was by then sixty years of age. His adored wife, Martha Maria, had died in 1803, when she was forty, having borne

Richard John Uniacke, painted as attorney general of Nova Scotia by R. Field in 1811

him six daughters and six sons, one of whom had died at birth. He had been devoted to her and always kept the day of her death exclusively to her memory. A few years before his own death, he recalled for his children that 'it is more than 20 years since I saw her leave this world with the smile of an Angel, free from every care and anxiety except for those she left behind her.' He would name the lake at Mount Uniacke after her. Five years after her death, he married Eliza Newton. Their only child, a son, was four years old when the construction of Mount Uniacke began.

The 11,000 acres where Mount Uniacke stood were anything but fertile, yet Uniacke persisted in trying to turn the rocky Nova Scotia bush into the lush green hills of Ireland. His success with this was, at best, limited. Earl Dalhousie, then lieutenant-governor, described the site in 1817:

Mount Uniacke, situated on the margin of a fine Lake and surrounded by the woody wilderness mixed up with great granite rock, is very gentlemanlike, and may in time be a pretty place, but at present has little to recommend it, except the new comfortable house and the cordial hospitality of its Proprietor ... he was planting potatoes in hills (like the molehills) or sowing oats with grass seed ... the ground is left for 10 years to what little grass may grow, and while the stems and trunks of the large wood rot and become more easy to take out. As no manure is given, nor a ploughing practicable, I shall be hereafter much astonished if either Potatoes or oats come to maturity upon it.

But the house was comfortable, and its proprietor

Mount Uniacke

indeed cordial. Dalhousie later referred to The Mount as 'the only Gentleman's seat on the road.' Mount Uniacke is a grand, two-storey, porticoed manor. Its width accommodates a wide, warm, and welcoming hall, one of its outstanding features. A row of small Adam chairs against one of the walls recalls the days when children used to sit, politely, in its grandeur. The spacious rooms, each heated by a wood stove, are still filled with the original mahogany furniture that Uniacke bought from the London cabinetmaker George Adam. In the dining-room and drawing-room Uniacke, his family, and guests enjoyed spirited conversational jousting. In the library, a haven for his enquiring mind, are his own chair, desk, and books. The cats, like the family, were well treated but expected to perform. Three of the closet doors had holes at floor level so that the cats could enter readily on mouse-proofing duties.

Many tales persist of dinners at The Mount at which countless toasts honoured any or all occasions. Uniacke also loved to sit by the fire with friends and a plentiful supply of whisky and rum. On one occasion his famed wit was directed against Justice Brenton Halliburton, then president of the North British Society. Halliburton had boasted that there were no beggars in Scotland. Uniacke retorted that everyone knew that it was useless to ask for charity from a Scot.

On the side of the house that overlooks Lake Martha, Uniacke erected a large balcony. In front was a 'ha-ha,' a shallow trench, used commonly in Uniacke's day to prevent grazing sheep from coming too close to a country house, without interrupting the view with a fence.

The dining-room in Mount Uniacke

Since 1949 The Mount has been the property of the provincial government and open to the public.

Uniacke's abundant energy was largely directed to his family and his province. He was intensely proud of his six sons and six daughters. They motivated his later years as he helped them position themselves for success, using all his own influence and that of his family. He never forgot the problems of his own early years. Knowing all the shoals, he pointed them out to Norman, the eldest, when he left to get the English legal training so necessary at the time. Norman was advised that:

– If he misbehaved, his 'mother would soon sink under the burden.'
– He should be a faithful church attendant and shun those who scoff at religion. 'Their very breath carries with it the seed of contagion ... '
– Family honour must be upheld. 'Through the wrecks of ages and the ruins of fortune [Uniacke] honour has been sacred ... '
– He had a duty to his parents, his 'life and actions ... so nicely regulated as never to cause them for a moment to think that [he was] either ungrateful or unmindfull of the care and attention they [had paid him] in all stages of ... life.'
– He should write often. 'I shall now waite for arrivals,' said the father, and 'should I not receive by each a letter from you, you cannot well conceive what my sensation will be and how ill I shall be able to bear the disappointment ... '
– He should be frugal, 'and remember at the expenditure of every farthing that the farthing is furnished to you at the very dear rate of a family being deprived of a certain portion of the comforts and necessaries of life.'

Further admonitions dealt with the value of chaste language and chaste women. Norman carried the load of all these expectations but nevertheless managed to complete his law studies at Lincoln's Inn and be the second native Nova Scotian to be admitted to the English bar. He became attorney general of Lower Canada, a member of the House of Assembly there, and a judge of the King's Bench in the district of Montreal. After he retired from the Bench he returned to Nova Scotia, where he was appointed to the Legislative Council.

Uniacke's other sons were also achievers. Crofton, a lawyer, was judge of the Court of Vice Admiralty for a time and, after moving to England, practised at the English bar with considerable success. Richard John, Jr, was early appointed attorney general for Cape Breton, then became the first native Nova Scotian to be promoted to the province's Supreme Court. James Boyle also trained at the Inns of Court in London. He became, in 1848, the first premier of Nova Scotia under responsible government. The Rev. Robert Fitzgerald Uniacke was rector of St George's Church, Halifax, for forty-three years. Andrew Mitchell was president of the Bank of Nova Scotia and a member of the legislature. Of Uniacke's daughters, Mary married Vice-Admiral Sir Andrew Mitchell; Martha Maria married Thomas Nickleson Jeffery, the provincial collector of customs; Alicia married William Scott of Scotland; Anne Margaret married Kevin Leslie of Ireland; and Eleanor Rebecca married William Hackett, inspector general of military hospitals. One daughter, Elizabeth, died young.

The old attorney general, so proud of his offspring, had to endure one unforgettable day in court when his son, Richard John, Jr, was tried for murder. 'Dick' had killed a local merchant, William Bowie, in a duel – the result of Bowie's challenge to Uniacke's truth, honour, and character.

The Acadian Recorder, 31 July 1819, described the trial in words that invoke a picture of the elderly Uniacke:

About 20 minutes past 11 o'clock, the Hon. Richard J. Uniacke entered the Court, supporting his Son on his right arm ... He advanced to the Bench, and stated to the Court, under feelings which evidently almost overpowered him, that he had an imperious and melancholy duty to perform; but whatever his feelings might be upon the present occasion, they must be subservient to the laws of the land, which he did not doubt would be administered with justice and mercy; and he requested that if their Lordships thought the demand was not improper that he might be permitted to remain in the Court during the trial of his Son.

Brian Cuthbertson, a Uniacke descendant, writes in *The Old Attorney General*:

Uniacke, with his fine white locks falling over his herculean shoulders, carrying a big ivory-headed cane and wearing an eye glass remained in court during the trial. Norman, his eldest son, sat at the court table with S.G.W. Archibald, the King's Counsel. Crofton remained at Richard John's side throughout the trial ... Uniacke, as attorney general, should have prosecuted the case, but could not ... The onus fell on

S.G.W. Archibald, and Uniacke had always a great regard for him because of his role in 'Dick's unfortunate affair,' as he called it.

The young Uniacke was found not guilty.

In his will Richard John Uniacke showed his sentimental side, not always evident to the world at large: 'I wish all my children and grandchildren should each have some little article given to them to keep in remembrance one to whom they were all very dear.'

CHAPTER TWENTY-TWO

Maitland and Truro

Along the shores of Cobequid Bay, where the Bay of Fundy narrows to a point near Truro, the highest tides in the world ebb and flow twice each day. Settlers here have known the lows and highs of history as well. Along the Shubenacadie River have lived Mi'kmaq, Acadians, Irish, Scottish, and New England Planters. Among these, two names stand out, separated by nearly 150 years – Abbé Jean-Louis Le Loutre, priest and missionary, and William Dawson Lawrence, shipbuilder. One was French, the other Irish. They exemplified two extremes – the agonies of the French/English conflict and the Golden Age of Sail.

Le Loutre, who had the ear of the French court, became, in effect, a spy. (It was not unusual for the Church at that time to act in the service of the French court.) His plan, as recommended to the royal court, was to repel the British from half of Nova Scotia, along a line drawn from Truro to Chedabucto Bay. The southwest half would be British. French control would extend from the Strait of Canso, through New Brunswick, to Quebec. Part of this plan involved removing the French Catholic Acadians from British influence, ostensibly to protect them from Protestant domination. Territorial aspirations were a barely hidden agenda.

Le Loutre was the terror of the Acadians as well as the British. He became vicar general of Acadia and used his power to incite the Mi'kmaq against the British, reportedly paying them to seek British scalps in Halifax, and threatened Acadians with a similar fate if they refused to relocate according to his plan. The British put a price of £100 on his head. He was, according to the governor, Edward Cornwallis, 'a good-for-nothing scoundrel.' A French Catholic contemporary claimed that 'nobody was more fit than [Le Loutre] to carry discord and desolation into a country.' Because Le Loutre refused to allow Acadians to take an unqualified oath of allegiance to the British Crown, he is thought by some to have influenced the British decision to expel the entire Acadian population in 1755.

After the expulsion, newcomers from Ireland, Scotland, and the New England colonies arrived to settle peacefully in the area. These families would become renowned shipbuilders, ushering the Shubenacadie into the Golden Age of Sail.

One such was William Lawrence, a man whose story was worthy of a Horatio Alger novel. Born at Gilford, Northern Ireland, in 1817, he came to Nova Scotia as an infant when his parents emigrated to settle at Five Mile River in Hants County. When he was nineteen, Lawrence left home for Dartmouth, where he apprenticed for seven years as a shipbuilder – putting in a thirteen-hour day at the shipyard, then making his way to the newly opened Dalhousie College in Halifax, where he had enrolled in classes. He later honed his skills in Boston, where he studied drafting. By 1847 he was designing his first ship, built by a Halifax firm and launched in 1849.

By 1852 Lawrence was back at Five Mile River with a shipyard of his own. For £30, using timbers he cut and hauled from the nearby woods, he and his brother James built the brigantine *St Lawrence*. He moved to the village of Maitland in 1855, and there designed and built six ships in the next twelve years. They carried cargoes to all parts of the world.

The William D. Lawrence, *largest square-rigger ever built in the Maritimes*

Lawrence's interests extended beyond shipbuilding. As the member for Hants County in the provincial assembly from 1863 to 1871, he supported free education and sided with his old friend, Joseph Howe, in the battle against Confederation. When, just one and a half years later, Howe deserted the cause and accepted a position in the federal cabinet, Lawrence felt betrayed. He never wavered in his convictions.

On 27 October 1874, at exactly 1:50 p.m., the *William D. Lawrence*, a 2,459-ton square-rigged vessel, the largest ship of its kind ever built in the Maritimes, moved slowly from her stocks in Lawrence's shipyard. She slid gradually at first, then moved with increasing speed until, to quote a contemporary reporter, 'she glided majestically into her destined element.' Her proud owner had named her after himself. He watched from a height above the shipyard, alone, apart from a crowd of 4,000 spectators, some cheering, some quietly expecting the worst. Lawrence had coped with nay-sayers from the day in 1872 when he had laid her long keel on his lawn, keeping his temper when offered gratuitous advice and criticism. 'During the time I was building her,' he said, 'I had visitors from the United States, Saint John, all parts of Nova Scotia, England and even from the Continent, who with very few exceptions, were fault-finders.' They variously concluded that the ship was too big or not strong enough, would be unwieldy, and would ruin everyone associated with her.

At her launching, the *William D. Lawrence* 'went down the ways like a rowboat,' confounding all the 'experts.' Only after she was safely launched did her owner

W.D. Lawrence house, Maitland

join the throngs to revel in his achievement. The entire population of Maitland was on hand, along with visitors from Parrsboro, Londonderry, Truro, both sides of the Shubenacadie, and as far away as Halifax. They filled every boarding-house in town. The ladies of the Anglican church, no mean entrepreneurs, seized the opportunity to hold a bazaar and tea, and a 'handsome sum was realized.'

With unbridled enthusiasm, *The Halifax Morning Chronicle* called the *William D. Lawrence* 'the largest [full-rigged ship] ever built in the Dominion ... and, with the exception of the New York ship *Three Brothers* ... the largest sailing vessel in the world.' Every magnificent foot of her construction was described – overall length 272 feet, breadth of beam 48 feet, keel and keelson 8 feet thick. Her rudder weighed 7 tons, and her two largest anchors weighed 3 tons each. She had 200 tons of bolts in her. The mainmast was 200 feet, 8 inches, the spread of canvas was 8,000 yards. William Lawrence had designed her and supervised construction with his brother Lockhart as master builder. His son John moulded the timber. She was commanded by Captain James Ellis, his son-in-law. When the keel was first laid in front of his house it stretched out 244 feet 9 inches. Seventy-five local men had worked a year and a half building her. All the iron work, done by hand in Maitland, was by Isaac Douglas; she was rigged by a Mr McDonald, also of Maitland; the figurehead, a bearded man dressed in a cape and holding a scroll with the words 'God Defend the Right,' was the work of J.S. Shaw of the same town.

While they waited for the launching, the attention of the 4,000 spectators must have also turned to a house on a rise directly across from the shipyard. Its size and design proclaimed the importance of its shipbuilder owner. William Lawrence's home was built in 1868, just four years before he began work on his stately square-rigger. Twin stairways led to two front doors, much like the steps leading to a ship's bridge. From its tall windows he could watch as ship construction progressed. Its two parlours and dining-room were likely abuzz with anticipation from the time drawings were started in Lawrence's office in the el at the back of the house.

After the great ship was launched she sailed to Saint John, where she picked up a cargo and, on 4 December 1874, left for Liverpool, England, where she was to be copper-sheathed. Her builder was aboard with his daughter, Mary Jane Ellis, wife of the captain, and the three Ellis children. Mary Lawrence presumably opted to remain at home in the Maitland house. Lawrence was about to realize his dream – to sail around the world. The following spring, on 10 April 1875, he sailed from Liverpool on the *William D. Lawrence*, with a charter to carry a cargo of guano (a natural manure from the droppings of sea birds, found mainly around Peru) from Peru to France. His first stop was Aden. *The Halifax Morning Herald*, 10 December 1886, relived the eventful voyage at Lawrence's death. The ship encountered a gale and 'lost her main and mizzen top gallant masts, with royal and sky sail yards and her main-top mast at the hounds.' The paper also noted 'an incident on this voyage is worth recording, the capture of a ten foot shark. When it was killed there were found in it 55 young sharks, whose antics created considerable amusement to the sailors.'

On 1 August the ship arrived in Aden and stayed for repairs, resuming the voyage on 13 September, bound for Callao, Peru. In eighty days she crossed the Indian Ocean and sailed past Australia and on to the South Pacific. She reached Callao, Peru, safely but had to wait a year there in order to secure her cargo of guano. The adventurous Lawrence took advantage of the delay by exploring South America. From Peru the vessel proceeded to France, where the voyage finally ended in 1877.

Lawrence was home by June of that year. According to Archibald MacMechan in *The Great Ship*, he was seen 'going about Halifax in his shirt-sleeves with a red bandanna handkerchief full of guineas paying his just debts.' After his renowned ship had served nine years in the Atlantic and Oriental trades, he sold her. He had cleared a $27,000 debt and made a handsome profit of $140,000.

When William Lawrence returned to Maitland in 1877 after sailing around the world, he had been away for two and a half years. He was then sixty, and had come home to spend what were the last nine years of his life with his wife, Mary Hayes, and their children and grandchildren. Married in 1839, the Lawrences had a family of ten. Two, possibly three, of these children died before their parents. One of them, Margaret (Maggie), had died of consumption, but not before Lawrence, in an effort to save her, had taken her to the West Indies; when her health finally failed, he built her a wooden hospital bed with a head and foot that could be adjusted for her comfort.

W.D. Lawrence

In his later years, Lawrence found time to look back on a busy life. His philosophy was liberally laced with the language of the sea. 'I had to begin the voyage of life against both wind and tide,' he recalled, and 'have come out of the conflict all right.'

There is no secret in making money in shipbuilding and ship owning, but by hard work, honesty and economy. Labor is the genius that changes the forest into ships and ugliness into beauty ... there is nothing better than a sharp opposition to make a man succeed in business. Kites rise against not with the wind. No man ever worked his passage any where in a sailing ship in a dead calm ... A man don't require to know many books, but to know his trade and men, and dart at a chance like a hawk at a hen, or a cat at a mouse. How many times have we seen the shipbuilding business swell and collapse with the same suddenness and disaster! Men who did not know the stern from the bow, halyards from shrouds, or a jib boom from a tiller, have again and again taken up their investments in stocks and mortgages, even borrowed money on accommodation paper, in their mad haste to share the fabulous profits made by navigation ... The man who knows all about a ship from the keel up will make a living profit ... If I had been led away by an army of croakers when building the *W.D. Lawrence* she would never have been built. (*The Halifax Morning Chronicle*, 10 December 1886)

At his death in December 1886, Lawrence left Mary the 'residence and farm at Maitland with all the upland and marsh, and the shipyard, the half of the double house occupied by my brother, Lockhart,' all household effects, and the interest on $40,000. There were bequests to his sons, William and Thomas, and his daughters, Martha Brown, Mary Jane Ellis, Elizabeth Allen, Abigail McCallum, and Hannah Douglas. A daughter-in-law, Caroline, the widow of his son John, was to live in the farm at Five Mile River which had been his parents' home. Lawrence remembered his grandchildren as well. In 1967 the province acquired the Lawrence house with most of its original furnishings from W.D. Lawrence's granddaughter, Abbie Lawrence, the last occupant of the old homestead. It is operated by the Nova Scotia Museum and is now open to the public during the summer months.

Between 1863 and 1903 the shipbuilders of the Shubenacadie built 230 ships. This was the height of the age of sail. At the time of the launching of the *William D. Lawrence*, in the Maitland area alone, more than 17,000 tons of sailing vessels were under construction in seven shipyards that were bursting with the vitality and skills of hundreds of men. Within a few square miles, on both sides of the Shubenacadie, at the end of Cobequid Bay, skilled hands were at work in nineteen other shipyards, building, rigging, and fitting vessels that would sail to Great Britain and the Indies with their holds full of spices, silks, tea, flour, molasses, rum, and timbers.

When William Lawrence launched his great ship, most of the population of nearby Truro came to enjoy the spectacle and the sustenance offered by the church ladies and the tavern-keepers of Maitland. Truro was benefiting from the shipbuilding boom. Its growing prosperity, however, was also tied to the railway. The town had been connected by rail to Halifax for almost fifteen years, but now Sandford Fleming was at work completing the Intercolonial Railway. It would make Truro a hub on the route west and north over the Cobequid Mountains, into New Brunswick, on to Rivière-du-Loup on the St Lawrence, and from there to Montreal and Toronto.

Times were good in Truro. It would be officially incorporated the following year. Splendid Victorian houses, bespeaking wealth and position, were being built. They would be followed by the substantial, turreted Queen Anne homes for which Truro is noted today.

There had been settlers on the site long before this period of prosperity – Acadians, then settlers from Ireland, Scotland, and New England – but with that prosperity most of the town's earliest buildings were torn

John Doggett house,
111 Willow Street, Truro

down and replaced. But one lovely old home, built in 1839, still stands at 111 Willow Street. It was financed by one man's success in an enterprise that predated both shipbuilding and railroading. John Logan Doggett owned an inn which was in operation in 1837, possibly earlier.

Doggett was born in 1805. When he was twenty-three, he married Esther Pearson, a widow with three young sons. She and Doggett had five more sons and a daughter. Their hostelry, no longer standing, was on the common, on the west side of the square. It was originally called Doggett's Hotel, but in June 1860, its owners decided that a change of name was warranted. The Prince of Wales, the future Edward VII, had come to Canada, to Nova Scotia, to Truro – and to John Doggett's inn.

His Royal Highness was driven to the leading hostelry of the village, Doggett's Hotel ... There the Prince rested and dined. Later as a result of this the name of the place was changed to Prince of Wales Hotel and the room the Prince occupied ever after, till the building disappeared, was referred to as the 'Prince's Room.' It remained furnished as it was when he occupied it that few hours in passing. (*The Halifax Herald*, 12 June 1939)

Long before the Prince of Wales stepped over the threshold, however, Doggett had sold his hotel and purchased 230 acres running from the square on the east side of Willow Street, south from the common. The first owner of this land had been Alexander Miller, one of the original grantees of Truro Township. In 1840, a year after buying the property, Doggett built a Gothic Revival cottage, embellishing its broad gable and verandah with fanciful bargeboard and treillage.

On Doggett's death the house passed to his unmarried son, Albert, and his daughter, Martha, and then to his adopted daughter, Renew Walsh, who married Colonel Oliver Heard. The Doggett house stayed in the family until 1971.

Another business associated with Truro was the textile mill founded by Charles Stanfield. It gained renown for a product that became a household word – Stanfield's Unshrinkable Underwear.

The compelling forces of love and business caused Charles Stanfield to emigrate to Tryon, Prince Edward Island, from his home in Wakefield, Yorkshire. He knew there was a place waiting for him at home, in a printing business owned by his father. A comfortable living was assured, but Charles was not interested. He apprenticed himself instead to his uncle, who ran a textile business at Bradford. In 1855, aged twenty-seven, he left England with the skills to start a business of his own – but where? The question was eventually settled by the attractions of the Island, its sheep, and one Lydia Dawson.

Charles Stanfield may have gone first to Philadelphia. A descendant suggests that he was a private, uncommunicative man, so his exact movements are unknown. Nor do we know what he looked like, for he would never allow a photograph to be taken. Presumably he left the United States because he heard rumours of civil war and, as a textile man and a Britisher, he would have sided with the South, the source of the cotton supply. Stanfield decided to accompany a friend north to the British colonies. On his journey he stopped at Tryon and met Lydia Dawson, then sixteen, the daughter of Samuel Edward Dawson and Jane Lord. He decided to marry her, but Lydia's father disapproved of the match. Charles left for England, but within a year he was back to marry Lydia and make plans for the Tryon Woollen Mills. The business was a partnership with a Mr Lord, a relative of his new mother-in-law. An advertisement in *The Islander*, 2 March 1858, stated that the mill was in operation: 'Stanfield and Lord inform farmers that after this date their new mill at Tryon will be ready for dyeing, fulling, and dressing cloth.'

By 1867 the farther fields of Nova Scotia looked greener, particularly near Truro, since the railway promised speedy delivery to the western market. Stanfield sold the mill, of which he was then sole owner, to his brother-in-law, Samuel E. Dawson, realizing a profit of $11,000.

With a new partner, William Craig of Newfoundland, Stanfield next founded a soft-felt-hat manufacturing business in Truro. In 1868, when bowler hats became a rage, they opened a hard-hat plant as well. These were the first factories in Canada to produce hats. Later Stanfield added a cloth-manufacturing section, but it failed to prosper.

In 1872 he moved to Windsor, selling his Truro interests to Craig and purchasing a carding mill on the swiftly flowing Ste-Croix River. For ten years, while living in Windsor, Stanfield pursued a variety of interests between Truro and Ste-Croix: the Union Woollen Manufacturing Company near Bible Hill, on the outskirts of Truro; his carding mill; and his hat-manufacturing business. The last named enjoyed considerable success, according to *The Halifax Morning Herald* of 27 November 1880. The paper lauded Stanfield's ability to show up the so-called superior business enterprise of Montreal, Toronto, and Quebec by taking advantage of the Intercolonial Railway, shipping $14,000 worth of hats to Montreal and Toronto in 1879 and $8,000 worth of hats to Saint John, with a standing order, just in from Montreal, for all the goods that he could produce.

When a reporter asked Stanfield why the merchants of Halifax did not order many of his hats, he replied, 'They are so in the habit of importing and there is little enthusiasm among Halifax men for "home made" goods ... I am afraid we shall not command the Halifax market for some time.'

There was another move to come – the final one. In 1879 he and Lydia returned to Truro. Three years later he built his two-storey frame mill on the Salmon River, which would provide the necessary power for a carding machine, a spinning jenny, and, later, weaving equipment.

In Truro, Charles and Lydia bought a three-gabled house at 44 Dominion Street. It had been built in 1868 by Peter MacGregor Archibald, the great-great-

44 Dominion Street, Truro, built by Peter MacGregor Archibald, later home to Charles and Lydia Stanfield

grandson of Samuel Archibald, who, with his three brothers, David, James, and Thomas, had arrived in Truro in 1762 on a vessel filled with thirty-eight other passengers – their wives, children, and in-laws. Peter Archibald's trim frame house was similar to many in Truro, with a traditional fan-transomed door. But the new owner, Charles Stanfield, added something untraditional. He installed radiators, an innovation that conducted heat to the house through a hook-up with the local steam laundry.

Behind the house stood a barn with a workshop where he pursued other creative endeavours. Here he designed the product that would make his name a household word: ribbed underwear. Next – a milestone in the underwear business – came the drop seat, or 'trapdoor.' These two success stories eclipsed the more ordinary aspects of his fine-cloth business.

In 1896 Stanfield sold to his sons, Frank and John. They, at their Truro Knitting Mills, replaced old machinery, adopted new production methods, took out patents, created trademarks, and embarked on the firm's first advertising campaign. They speculated that women, who in those days sewed their own 'underwear suits' from knitted cloth, would prefer to buy them ready-made, and began producing 'packaged undergarments.' Just in time for the Klondike Gold Rush of 1897, they developed heavy 'shrink-proof' underwear. It brought gold to the Stanfields as well. Their warm, ribbed, underwear was shipped to the Yukon as fast as it could

Frank Stanfield's house, 38 Dominion Street

Frank Stanfield

be manufactured, and the business expanded to meet the demand.

Stanfield's Limited was incorporated in 1906. In 1907 John Stanfield was elected a member of Parliament, and later became a senator. Frank took over the firm as managing director. Over the years his business interests grew to include the insurance industry and the trust company business. Charles Stanfield's Dominion Street house passed to daughter Eleanor, who lived in it until 1942.

The success of the Truro mills could be seen in Frank Stanfield's house, built in 1903 at 38 Dominion Street, next to his parents' home. It followed the popular Queen Anne style, with bays, gables, and a columned verandah. A Palladian window was tucked in its central gable. A respected politician, as well as an astute businessman, Stanfield was first elected to the provincial legislature for Colchester County in 1911, then re-elected three times. He resigned in 1930 to become lieutenant-governor, but died suddenly less than a year later. 'His death,' said one account, 'has removed from this province one of her most brilliant sons, who loved her well.' Frank Stanfield was the father of Robert L. Stanfield, premier of Nova Scotia from 1956 to 1967 and leader of the Progressive Conservative Party of Canada from 1967 to 1976.

Over the years, merchandising methods changed dramatically from those used by Charles Stanfield. The quiet man who founded the family firm believed in marketing, but not in advertising. One wonders what he would have thought of a 1978 billboard in Saint John. There, a man and woman were shown in bed, barely covered by a sheet. The man, his head inclined towards the woman, was urging her to 'hand me my Stanfields.' Eyes left the road; cars swerved; tires screeched. The provincial safety officer said that he considered the sign a potential hazard to the motoring public, adding thoughtfully, 'I've never seen one around Fredericton.'

NORTHERN NOVA SCOTIA
AND THE EASTERN SHORE

CHAPTER TWENTY-THREE

Amherst, Parrsboro, and Pugwash

There were thirty-six Fathers of Confederation. Four came from one pretty town on the Isthmus of Chignecto. Amherst was home to Edward Barron Chandler, Jonathan McCully, Robert Barry Dickey, and Charles Tupper. (Fathers of Confederation are defined as those delegates who attended the Charlottetown, Quebec, and London conferences which led to the creation of Canada – the first two conferences in 1864, the last in 1866.)

To varying degrees these four men contributed to the founding of their country, and to varying degrees they were admired, disliked, honoured, or reviled by their constituents. On occasion, too, they were the subject of rumoured peccadilloes which did nothing to tarnish their reputation with the voters.

Chandler, born in Amherst in 1800, grandson of a Loyalist, son of the sheriff of Cumberland County, was educated in Nova Scotia but lived most of his life in New Brunswick, ending his illustrious career there as lieutenant-governor. He and Tupper, who became prime minister of Canada, were the subject of most of the rumours and speculation concerning alleged indiscretions.

A son, Sir Charles Hibbert Tupper, tackled the subject of his charismatic father's reputation in *The Life and Letters of the Right Hon. Sir Charles Tupper, Bart., G.C.M.G.*, which he edited. In it, he quoted a conversation between two constituents:

One said, though a strong Liberal he did not believe that Tupper was as bad as painted; the other in great surprise asked why; whereupon his friend told him he had been making enquiries about the family and understood that the sons were all respected and that the daughter was an exceptionally fine woman. He did not therefore believe that Tupper could be so bad a man with such children nearly all of whom were of age! The other said that it was a fact that his children were in good standing and nothing could be said against them, but Tupper was as bad as he was said to be. The reason he gave for the children being so good was that Tupper married a remarkably fine woman!

For a few years after their marriage in 1846, Tupper and that 'remarkably fine woman,' Frances Morse, shared a house with her parents until it was destroyed by fire. Then, tragically, the young couple, parents of a daughter (Emma) and a son (James Stewart), lost an infant daughter, Elizabeth (Lillie).

By the early 1850s the Tuppers were settled into their newly completed home at 186 Victoria Street. The house had its entrance on the gable end, while, on the façade, two trim bay windows overlooked the street. Directly above the bays were five-sided Scottish dormers, a feature appearing infrequently in the Amherst region. An addition, built some years later, had a bay window similar to the other two, adding a unifying element to the whole.

With the move to a new home the Tuppers' fortunes improved. Tupper was practising medicine (his office was in the house) and taking his first tentative steps into the tantalizing world of politics, a world for which he was eminently well suited.

Sir Charles Tupper and one of his children

Tupper house, 186 Victoria Street, Amherst

Tupper was by this time in his early thirties. He was a man of medium build, wiry and muscular, gifted with good looks, an active mind, and an abundance of nervous energy. After six years of medical training, first in Wolfville, Nova Scotia, then in Scotland, he returned to Amherst. In short order he became the trusted and revered physician for a host of grateful patients scattered throughout Cumberland County. 'If Tupper gives up on you,' it was said, 'you might as well turn your face to the wall.'

A letter from Dr Tupper to the House of Assembly in 1853 requested payment of £13 for professional services to the 'Sick and poor Indians in the County of Cumberland,' indicating that Native people also came under his care. Many grateful patients never forgot his kindness and devotion, nor his exhaustion when he finally reached their homes in remote regions of the county. In 1867 he became the first president of the Canadian Medical Association.

Tupper's political career took off in a flurry of flag-waving and fiery speeches. It was 1855 when the ambitious and eloquent young physician sought a seat in the assembly as a Conservative. He promptly took on and defeated the popular Joseph Howe – an upset victory which ensured that, by the time he arrived in Halifax to take his seat, he was already known as a man to be reckoned with. Two years later he was named provincial secretary. In May 1864, only nine years after his dramatic entry on the political scene, he became premier of Nova Scotia.

Tupper's colleague, Senator Robert Barry Dickey, was another Amherst politician who brought honour

Robert Barry Dickey

Grove Cottage, the R.B. Dickey house at 150 Church Street, Amherst, now the Cumberland County Museum

to the town as a Father of Confederation. A grandson of Irish immigrants who settled in Cumberland County in the mid-eighteenth century, Dickey was raised on a farm near Amherst and studied for three years at King's College School. Because of his family's straitened financial situation he left school at age fifteen and, for six years, articled with an Amherst lawyer, walking the six miles between farm and town each day until he was called to the bar in 1834.

At about this time, Dickey's father, Robert McGowan Dickey, and his mother, Eleanor Chapman, moved from their farm into Amherst, where they had recently built a new home, a small frame house that they called Grove Cottage. Within a few years, the senior Dickey was elected to the legislature from Cumberland County, a position he held for fifteen years until his retirement in 1851. He died three years later.

Grove Cottage was inherited by Robert. His legal practice, after twenty years, was thriving. He built an addition to the house, moved his office there, and added new fireplaces and dormers to provide light for the second floor. Simple bargeboard added a decorative touch. Grove Cottage thus appeared to be more house than cottage, although it retained its original name. (The terms 'house' and 'cottage' had little to do with size. Andrew Jackson Downing, in his *The Architecture of Country Houses*, explained that the designation house or cottage depended upon the number of servants employed – anything with fewer than three servants was, by definition, a cottage.)

Tall, erect, and fair-skinned, Robert Dickey enjoyed

James Dickey house, 182 Victoria Street, Amherst

cultural pursuits, along with his legal and political interests. He loved to travel. By the mid-1880s he had crossed the Atlantic thirty times. In 1844 he married Mary Blair Stewart. Their three sons and two daughters grew up in Grove Cottage.

One of the Dickey sons, Arthur Rupert, followed in his father's political footsteps, but at the federal level, as a member of Parliament. He lived at 169 Victoria Street, a house built about 1870. Another son, James A. Dickey, became a mayor of Amherst. His home, at 182 Victoria Street, purchased in 1895, was originally a three-storey building, but a fire in the 1930s destroyed the top floor.

Robert Dickey lived a long and productive life. He died in 1904, aged ninety-three, after a career in which he had been a respected businessman, a legislator, and a judge of probate. As a member of Nova Scotia's Council, he had been a delegate to the Charlottetown and Quebec conferences, had fought to bring a reluctant Nova Scotia into Confederation, and, as a reward, once that goal was achieved, was appointed to the Senate.

Today Grove Cottage serves as the Cumberland County Museum at 150 Church Street. The house has undergone many changes and renovations over the years, not all of them to its advantage. Inside little or nothing of the original detailing survives. At one time Mayor James Dickey added a verandah to the front of the house, but it, as so often happened, failed to survive the rigours of wind and weather. The portico which now shelters the front door is a relatively recent addition.

The fourth Father of Confederation from Amherst was Jonathan McCully, two years older than Robert Dickey and also born on a Cumberland County farm. He too was a lawyer and a judge, but there the similarity ended. Bristly and difficult, McCully succeeded, according to one biographer, 'by grit more than brains.' And he knew the right people. McCully was a Liberal and a friend of Joseph Howe, but he split with Howe and converted to the Confederation cause at the Charlottetown Conference. For this he was rewarded by an appointment to the Senate in 1867. He died ten years later in Halifax, a wealthy man.

McCully's mother, Esther Pipes, was descended from an English family who came to the Amherst area as part of an immigration from Yorkshire during 1772/4. Lawyer William Thomas Pipes, another offshoot of this distinguished family tree, lived for a time at 183 Victoria

Jonathan McCully

Street. This impressive house, built in the Gothic style about 1870, housed more than its share of notables: two provincial premiers and a chief justice of the Supreme Court of Nova Scotia.

The first owner of the house was Sir Charles James Townshend, who represented Cumberland County provincially and federally and then, in 1907, became Chief Justice of the Supreme Court of Nova Scotia. The second owner was Pipes, who became premier of the province in 1882. From 1877 to 1942 the house was owned by Edgar Nelson Rhodes, Pipes's partner and son-in-law. An eminent politician, Rhodes was a member of Parliament and Speaker of the House of Commons before moving to provincial politics, where he became premier and provincial secretary. Later Rhodes returned to the federal scene and was minister of fisheries under R.B. Bennett, and then minister of finance. He was appointed to the Senate in 1935. The Rhodes connection brings the story of the Victoria Street house full circle, for it seems likely that the man who had built the house was Nelson Rhodes, Edgar Rhodes's father.

Nelson Rhodes was a founder of Rhodes, Curry Company, a firm that grew to become the largest building contractor in the Maritime provinces between 1880 and 1920. Nathaniel Curry, the other founder, was his uncle. It seems likely that Rhodes, Curry built the house during the firm's early years, since Townshend and Dickey were the firm's solicitors. Rhodes, Curry built massive public buildings; they also built houses by the hundreds, using only two or three floor plans, in growing industrial towns such as Glace Bay, Sydney, and Springhill. They revolutionized the building trades through mechanization, prefabrication, and the use of newer, inexpensive materials.

By the 1880s Amherst was a bustling industrial town, thanks to the energy and inventiveness of its citizens, the arrival of the Intercolonial Railway in 1876, and the development of the coal industry. There were and are, however, still links to the quiet village known to the Tuppers, Dickeys, Chandlers, and McCullys. Two early homes date back to the founding, when the town (built on the site of an Acadian settlement, Les Planches) received its British name in memory of Lord Jeffery Amherst, who, with Admiral Boscawen, had captured Louisburg in 1758.

Two brothers, Jesse and John Bent, Jr, arrived in Nova Scotia from Massachusetts in 1760. Three years

John Bent house, 171 Victoria Street, boyhood home of artist Alex Colville

later their names appeared on a list of grantees for Cumberland Township. Jesse settled at Fort Lawrence. John Bent, Jr, became one of the founders of Amherst, along with Alpheu Morse and Elisha Freeman. It was either John Bent, Jr, or his son, also John Bent, who built the modest house, now 171 Victoria Street. The building retains only the general outline of the original but is of interest today as the boyhood home of the distinguished Canadian artist Alex Colville.

Charles Donkin, a justice of the peace, built his small, attractive house (2 Charles Street) about 1833. The land had been owned by his father, William, and his grandfather, Robert, before him. The house has Venetian windows and simple, classic detailing. A dormer above the door is likely a later addition. Robert Donkin was known as a 'zealous member of the Methodist church,' so it is not surprising that Charles Donkin's son Joseph, to whom he sold the house in 1886, was a Methodist minister. Joseph and his wife, a woman with the memorable name of Ervina Donkin, lived in the house until 1906 when they sold it to Sterling Hatfield.

Amherst was never again home to its most famous son, Charles Tupper, after his election victory in 1855 made a move to Halifax imperative. But Tupper still owned land in Cumberland County and had an interest in Ottawa House, a hotel at Partridge Island, near Parrsboro, on the Minas Basin.

It is unclear whether Ottawa House was built in the 1770s or 1780s; certainly many buildings, including two inns, were located there by 1774. In the next decade, the hostelry was being run by one of Parrsboro's

The home of Charles Donkin, 2 Charles Street

first settlers, the energetic and far-seeing James Ratchford. Born in Cornwallis, near Starr's Point, in 1763, Ratchford settled on Partridge Island in the 1780s. He married Mary Crane and began as an apprentice to his uncle, James Noble Shannon, who had recently built a home and store at Partridge Island following the American Revolution. When Shannon died in 1822, Ratchford became sole owner of a thriving import and shipping business. The location could hardly have been better, since Parrsboro (named after John Parr, governor of Nova Scotia from 1782 to 1791) and Partridge Island were at the junction of the main route between Amherst and Halifax. Amherst and the Tantramar Marshes provided much of Halifax's food supply, and the route from there led through Parrsboro, by ferry to Windsor, then on to Halifax by road.

There were few positions in that early community that were not filled by the industrious and important Mr Ratchford. He operated the ferry to Windsor, carried on a shipbuilding and lumbering business, and, at one time or another, served as justice of the peace, postmaster, town clerk, magistrate, clerk of the market, and colonel of the militia. When he died in 1836 at seventy-two he had become unquestionably the most influential man in that part of Nova Scotia.

The year before Ratchford died, his son, James, Jr, advertised the building:

To let ... The hotel at Partridge Island, Parrsborough, at present occupied by Robert Boston – the house is large and commodious (having been built expressly for the purpose) with convenient stables, etc. and is pleasantly situated near the public landing, from whence the post road leads to Cumberland; there are about 100 acres of cultivated land attached ... (*The Novascotian*, 16 April 1835)

Ottawa House has three very distinct sections, with the oldest section, that dating from the eighteenth century, in the centre. Over the years various owners made a multitude of architectural changes, including bow windows, doors, and an inviting two-storey verandah that stretched across the front of the building. Windows were cut whenever and wherever the spirit moved. Doors were added by whim. Surprisingly, the result is a building which, in spite of a complete disregard for symmetry and balance, became eccentric, playful – and completely appealing.

Perhaps, as one report has it, the verandah was added by Sir Charles Tupper during the time that he had a vested interest in the property. Certainly Tupper owned land at Partridge Island. In 1881 he purchased a site from Caroline Sophia Coster, widow of the Rev. Nathanial Coster. Tupper also bought land from Peter Blake of Parrsboro in 1881. Some of his land, as indicated on deeds, was originally James Ratchford's property. After the Conservative party's defeat in 1874, Tupper went to Parrsboro for nearly a month, although only three years earlier the Tuppers had purchased a summer home, Highland Hill, in St Andrew's, New Brunswick. It takes little imagination to picture a robust, middle-aged Tupper, sitting on the verandah at Ottawa House, talking politics and drinking in the spectacular view that lay before him.

Ottawa House was bought in 1895 by the Cumberland Rail and Coal Company and served as a summer house for the manager of the Springhill Mines. It is now owned by the province and maintained by the local historical society.

During Parrsboro's heyday, according to Melville DeWolfe of Kentville, it was 'not unusual to see 100–200 boats off the Island from Horton, Windsor and all along the shore to trade.' Captains and crews from these vessels made their home in Parrsboro. Perhaps the most notable of them was Captain James Merriam, a feisty and determined seafaring man who ran into labour troubles on a voyage to Saint John. For reasons unknown, the seven or eight crew members refused to sign on for the return voyage. The captain, according to local legend,

Ottawa House, on
Partridge Island, near
Parrsboro

undeterred, sailed his three-masted schooner back to Parrsboro by himself, a feat that ensured him an honoured place in the annals of Parrsboro history.

Captain Merriam and his wife, Hannah, lived in a cottage at 29 Whitehall Road. Built in the early 1850s, it is one of the most attractive houses in town – a simple one-and-a-half-storey building, still with its original windows, looking much as it always has. Three generations of Merriams owned the house for almost a century, happily resisting any misguided thoughts of 'modernizing' the exterior. It stands today, typical of the many small mariners' cottages that dotted the Nova Scotia landscape throughout the nineteenth century. The Merriam name is linked to Ottawa House as well. Carl B. Merriam, master mariner, owned the hotel in the 1900s.

Not far away, in the village of Pugwash, a simple white frame house stands amid spacious lawns, overlooking the Cumberland Strait. Its exact age is unknown, but not so its history. During many of the years that it stood silently by the sea it was the property of first one, and then another, of Pugwash's best-known sons.

The first owner was a man who might have become, had fate not intervened, an honoured name in the political annals of Nova Scotia. He was the local boy who 'made good,' and did it without leaving home in search of greener pastures. The second was a local boy who found such pastures – pastures that were to become far greener than either he or anyone else in Pugwash could have imagined.

The first of these Pugwash sons, Henry Gesner Pineo,

*Captain Merriam's home,
29 Whitehall Road,
Parrsboro*

Jr, is remembered (when at all) for his pro-Confederation stance in the political storms that divided Nova Scotia in the years leading up to 1867 and afterwards. At thirty-seven, he was the only pro-Confederation candidate to be elected to the provincial legislature in the general elections that year. (His leader, Hiram Blanchard, was also elected, but his election was later voided.)

Pineo's interest in politics came as no surprise. His father, Henry Gesner Pineo, Sr, of Huguenot descent, had been an associate of Alexander Stewart, an Amherst lawyer who was one of the province's most influential Tories. Through that association the father eventually became a member of the Council. From there his political associations blossomed, as did the appointments he was able to make for family and friends. The younger Henry became the U.S. consular agent in Halifax, a son-in-law became presiding officer for elections in Pugwash, and other relatives were given similar minor posts.

At one point Pineo, Sr, locked horns with Charles Tupper for control of the party in Cumberland County. Then, in 1866, he switched loyalties and climbed on the pro-Confederation bandwagon. His son climbed on with him.

The younger Pineo had been managing his father's business affairs in Pugwash, and acting as justice of the peace and an officer in the militia. After his election in 1867 he steadfastly supported the Confederation cause. In the election of 1871 he was swept back into office. His political future seemed bright.

But if ever a family was star-crossed, it was the Pineos. Back in 1840 Henry Pineo, Sr's, daughter, Amelia, had

Pineo/Eaton house,
Pugwash

Cyrus Eaton

died. In the 1860s, two sons, Edward and Alexander, died, the latter leaving four young children. A son-in-law, Alexander Black, also died, leaving a widow, Emeline, and three small sons. These deaths did not seem out of the ordinary for the times – early death was an almost expected part of life. But in 1874 the Pineos once again became victims of fate.

That April, two of the senior Pineo's sisters, Lavinia and Sarah, died of tuberculosis within three days of each other. The press then announced that their nephew, the promising politician Henry Pineo, Jr, was also ill, 'with slight hopes ... entertained for his recovery.' He died at age forty-four on 12 May 1874. A little more than three weeks later, his wife, Charlotte, died. Then, on 14 September, Henry Pineo, Sr, died, leaving his wife, Harriet, to mourn his loss and that of their three sons, a son-in-law, two sisters-in-law, a daughter-in-law, and the daughter who had died in childhood. Harriet died eleven years later, survived by three daughters, one of whom, Emeline, had, two years previously, lost an eleven-year-old son when he was thrown from his pony. Emeline and her only daughter died two years later.

Thus the Pineo name disappeared from Pugwash. But Henry Gesner Pineo's home by the sea remained. Years later it became the summer home of Cyrus Eaton, one of the most renowned Canadians of his day – a man who promoted peace when, at the height of the Cold War, the very idea of peace with East Bloc countries was anathema to American politicians. When, in 1961, Eaton (by then an American citizen) was awarded the Lenin Peace Prize, it was presented to him in Canada, because the government of the United States would not allow one of its citizens to accept such a prize from an unfriendly nation.

Cyrus Eaton was born at Pugwash Junction in 1883, a sixth-generation Canadian and the great-great-great-grandson of David Eaton, who had arrived in Cornwallis Township with the New England Planters in 1761. Cyrus was the son of Joseph Howe Eaton (could there be any question of where his parents' loyalties lay?) and Mary MacPherson. The fifth of nine children, he grew up in Pugwash and was educated at Amherst Academy, Woodstock College, and McMaster University. He married Margaret House in 1907.

With the support of John D. Rockefeller, Eaton founded the Continental Gas and Electric Company in 1912. By the time he was forty-two, he had acquired control of the Goodyear Rubber Company and the Trumball Steel Company in Warren, Ohio, and had formed Republic Steel Corporation, third-largest in the United States. Then came 1929. When the Great Depression arrived, Eaton, it was said, lost close to $100 million. Undeterred, he was soon president of the Chesapeake and Ohio Railroad and director of a multitude of companies. His ambition was boundless.

Eaton was a complex and brilliant man. He enjoyed poetry and philosophy and always found creative solutions to any problem. He refused to recognize the impossible. Thus this white-haired, pink-cheeked financier became a self-appointed goodwill ambassador, working endlessly to promote a dialogue between the United States and the USSR. His work was, to say the least, controversial. Unmindful of relentless criticism, he continued to work quietly and persistently in pursuit of peace. In 1954 he inaugurated the Pugwash Thinkers Conference, a yearly meeting of some of the world's most original thinkers. Eaton already owned the Pineo house (it was operating as an inn and restaurant called Pineo Lodge), and there, each year, 'men of learning' relaxed and exchanged ideas.

At the first conference, Eaton's distinguished guests were Julian Huxley, English biologist, author, and philosopher; John A. Wilson, University of Chicago archaeologist; F. Cyril James, vice-chancellor of McGill University; Julian Boyd, professor of history at Princeton University; James Wiggins, executive editor of *The Washington Post*; Patrick McGinnis, president of the New Haven and Hartford Railroad; and Henry S. Commager, professor of history at Columbia University, New York.

Eaton's first marriage ended in divorce in 1934. Twenty-three years later, on 20 December 1957, he married again. This time his bride was Anne Kinder Jones, at age thirty-four, forty years his junior. She was confined to a wheelchair but took an active part in the Pugwash conferences.

Cyrus Eaton never lost his love for the land of his birth and, for the rest of his life, he vacationed at his cattle ranch near Deep Cove, Nova Scotia. His untiring efforts to achieve world peace were eventually recognized in Canada and abroad. By the time he died in 1979, he had been the recipient of a host of honorary doctorates and awards – a prophet heralded, at last, in his own country.

CHAPTER TWENTY-FOUR

Pictou and Lyons Brook

It was 1765 – only sixteen years after Edward Cornwallis founded Halifax. The government, eager to lure loyal Protestant settlers to the province, had for some years been offering large grants of free land, offers eagerly taken up for the cleared areas of the lush Annapolis Valley and the South Shore. On the Northumberland Strait, around what became Pictou County, it was another matter. There, dense forest still blanketed the land.

By 1765 the fever for claiming and granting land was at its peak. Officials in Halifax were ready to talk to anyone who promised settlers, and so adventurers, ordinary speculators, noblemen, and those forming companies swarmed in upon authorities there. One such company was made up of men from Pennsylvania, New York, and New Jersey. It was known as the Philadelphia Company. One of its members, Edmund Crawley, along with thirteen associates in a group called Crawley and Company, received 200,000 acres of free land in Pictou and Colchester counties. Their land became known as the Philadelphia Grant. The company's obligation was to find 1,000 Protestant settlers – one for every 200 acres. This was to be accomplished within four years, the whole grant to be planted and enclosed in thirty years. Another developer, an Irishman, Alexander McNutt, also from Philadelphia, got 100,000 acres there, some of which was in his own interest. His was called the Irish Grant.

Thanks to an advertisement in a Philadelphia newspaper, six families boarded the *Betsey* on 5 May 1767. Leading the little band was John Harris, a doctor and the son of one of the Crawley Company's associates. His wife, Eliza, eight months pregnant, was with him. Also aboard was Robert Patterson and his wife and five children. He was the expedition's surveyor, an educated and influential Scot who later became the leading man in the little settlement of Pictou. Captain John Hull sailed his ship up the rocky coast without benefit of the lighthouses which, in later years, warned ships away from treacherous shoals. He landed briefly at Halifax, continued on along the Eastern Shore, overshot the Strait of Canso, was directed back, and, at last, reached Pictou harbour after a month's voyage. On the night of their arrival Eliza Harris gave birth to a son, Thomas.

The first arrivals were followed within two years by four more families. By 1769 there were 120 settlers. The exclusivity of the grants was reflected in the statistics: 119 of the settlers were Protestant, and the lone Catholic was married to a Protestant.

Six years after the first small group landed, the Philadelphia Company brought almost 200 impoverished Scots Highlanders to the harbour aboard the *Hector*, a vessel so decrepit that she was later condemned. To these desperate people the promise of free land seemed a dream. The voyage over, however, was more like a nightmare. The 200 settlers, almost a third of them children, spent ten weeks in the ship's hold with smallpox and dysentery rampant. Many small bodies were buried at sea.

They landed on 15 September 1773 and found the few settlers from the *Betsey* who had remained, including Dr Harris, some Mi'kmaq, and endless, unbroken forest. Encouraged only by their piper and the knowledge that their long ordeal seemed over, the company rallied its spirits, men donned their kilts, and the passengers straggled off the ship, following piper John MacKay.

That first winter was one of starvation. The ill and weary men, women, and children who had survived the miserable voyage had scant provisions and no 'King's Bounty' (government rations), as did the Loyalists who came ten years later. But the *Hector* Scots were survivors, and thanks to their spirit the settlement of Pictou grew. Pictou's *Colonial Patriot* of 4 January 1828 described them as 'the hardy race of Scotch mountaineers, whose strength and iron constitution, is evidenced by the length of their lives ... It is from this stock that many of the present inhabitants sprung, and they are not the children of effeminacy.'

That same paper carried a prime example of this on 7 March of that year when it announced the death of one member of the *Hector* group, the oldest inhabitant of the district: 'Died. On Sunday night last at the East

River, William McKay esq. aged 97. He went to bed in perfect health at his usual time and was found dead about half an hour after. He had had 19 children, 98 grandchildren and 14 great-grandchildren.'

The 1817 census for Pictou and vicinity described the inhabitants as 'Scotch almost to a man or their descendants.' The census included five men named William McKay. One would have been the Highlander who died at ninety-seven. One of the others owned a farm on the East River, near Stellarton. That William McKay had more than produce on his farm. He had a coal mine and had received permission from the governor, Sir John Wentworth, to work it. William leased seams of coal to his sons, John and Alexander McKay. (There were then in Pictou eleven John McKays and six Alexander McKays.) The brothers took lighters (flat-bottomed boats) up the East River to collect the coal, then back to supply the townspeople with fuel for their homes. John also had fuel to fire his blacksmith operations, one of the first in Pictou.

John McKay house, Coleraine Street

In 1819 John McKay built a house on Coleraine Street, a modest storey-and-a-half building of coarse stone, similar to a crofter's cottage, to which a clapboard extension was later added at the north end. Eight years later the house was for sale. *The Colonial Patriot* of 28 December 1827 listed: 'That valuable Property, where the subscriber formerly resided, consisting of a House, store and shop. The property is so well known, that it needs no further descriptions. John McKay.' McKay was not one to waste words.

In 1776, three years after the *Hector* unloaded its suffering passengers in Pictou, Thomas McCulloch was born near Paisley, Scotland. He was to become one of Pictou's most famous citizens, and to alter the course of education in the province – although he had never intended to settle in Nova Scotia at all. McCulloch grew up in a centre of intellectual enlightenment, receiving a broad education at the University of Glasgow, where he studied logic, languages, medicine, science, history, and theology. He was ordained, chose to become a missionary in the British colonies, and was posted to Prince Edward Island. He never arrived there.

McCulloch and his young family reached Pictou in November 1803 on their way to the Island, but they were advised not to try crossing the Northumberland Strait at that time of year. By winter's end, the people of Pictou had come to know him, and they pleaded with him to stay and accept a parish with them. They had been captivated by this dynamic Presbyterian cleric with his broad knowledge of theology and his devotion to liberal education. McCulloch pursued his ministry in Pictou, and his reputation spread, thanks to his writings and preaching.

In 1824 McCulloch decided to devote his considerable energies almost exclusively to Pictou Academy, which had its beginnings in an institution he had founded in 1806. He was determined to make available an interdenominational liberal education with emphasis on the sciences and mathematics. This represented a challenge to the classicism and Anglicanism represented by King's College in Windsor. Thus Thomas McCulloch took on a number of formidable opponents. The battle was joined when he and his pen encountered the Anglican Church and the Halifax establishment in general, and Bishop John Inglis, Richard Uniacke, Enos Collins, and Charles Ramage Prescott in particular (although the latter two were mainly concerned with the competition represented by Pictou's growing economic strength). In addition McCulloch had already parted ways with the Established Church of Scotland – the Kirk. He had been ordained in the Secession Church, a body which, although still considering itself Presbyterian, held more liberal views than the Established Church, and stood for increased autonomy for the congregation and against patronage in the church. In 1817 McCulloch and other Seceders united as the Presbyterian Church of Nova Scotia.

McCulloch's first students were boarded in his home.

*The entrance to Pictou
harbour, 1839;
watercolour by Edward
Cavalié Mercer*

The sturdy brick house, sited on a knoll, was originally a simple single-storey building, similar to those he had known in Scotland. Its steeply sloped roof covered a sleeping loft above the main floor. Sometime after 1890 a gambrel roof and dormers were added, providing more headroom on the second floor. McCulloch later named his home Sherbrooke Cottage after Lieutenant-Governor John Sherbrooke, a supporter of the Academy. (Having taken on the Anglican establishment, McCulloch needed to know where his support lay and reward it.) The house, set back on the north side of Haliburton Road, is owned by the province and operated by the Nova Scotia Museum.

When the school opened, McCulloch's wife, Isabella Walker, fed and boarded his students in addition to caring for her own brood of four – Michael, Helen, and Elizabeth (all born in Scotland), and David (born in Pictou), aged, respectively, six, five, four, and one. During the next eleven years the couple had five more children: Isabella, Thomas (later a professor), William (later a minister), James, and Robert. Two of the nine died in childhood.

A log building near the property soon served as a schoolhouse for the growing numbers of students, but it fell victim to arson, a visible testimony to the fact that McCulloch's stand on education had made him enemies. A new building was built on Church Street, and the academy was incorporated in 1816. (The building is no longer standing, but its original location is now identified by a historical marker.) Here McCulloch taught Greek, Hebrew, logic, moral and natural philos-

Sherbrooke Cottage, Thomas McCulloch house, Haliburton Road

ophy, chemistry, and political economy. The struggle for financial support never ended. The assembly eventually gave the Pictou Academy an annual grant, but would not make it permanent, as it did with the Anglican King's College in Windsor. This exacerbated the battle between Pictou and Halifax, angry Pictonians contending that the Legislative Council in Halifax was composed of men who had never been more than twenty miles outside the city. The struggle culminated in accusations that McCulloch wanted power, religious and political.

At the same time McCulloch's reputation was broadening. He had started to write for *The Acadian Recorder*, creating a character, Mephibosheth Stepsure, who satirized acquisitive society, as epitomized by Halifax. (Stepsure attracted a devoted following, as would Thomas Haliburton's Sam Slick a few years later.) McCulloch was also becoming known as a scientist and naturalist. The Academy housed his collection of birds, animals, insects, and shells. It was of such high calibre that it drew the world-renowned naturalist James Audubon to Pictou and Sherbrooke Cottage in September 1833. Audubon, on his way back to Boston from Labrador, accepted specimens that he greatly admired. Pictou's *Colonial Patriot* of 3 September 1833, claimed ecstatically that Audubon was 'one of the wonders of the world.' He could 'inoculate half a country with his own mania ... we know not a man better worth seeing.'

The long battle with the powerful Anglican Church affected the Pictou Academy adversely, and it looked as if it could not survive. Then, in 1838, McCulloch was offered the post of first president of Dalhousie University, the non-sectarian college founded by the lieutenant-governor, the Earl of Dalhousie. The offer included a professorship in logic, moral philosophy, and rhetoric. It was an opportunity to be the leading educational light in the province. McCulloch, an inspired and versatile teacher, was tiring of the battle for the academy. He accepted the post, a position he held until his death in 1843.

In its obituary *The Novascotian* was barely able to set aside the antipathy which had led to years of verbal jousting with Pictou's *Colonial Patriot*:

As he was, perhaps contrary to his own wishes, drawn frequently into polemical contests it is to be deplored that he occupied much time that might have been more usefully employed. As he possessed an original and powerful intellect ... he might under more auspicious circumstances have left something that would imperishably have connected his name with literature and science ... During life he had inveterate enemies and numerous friends in every section of Nova Scotia.

Pictou Academy was fortunate in having not only a dynamic founder but, equally important, worthy local support. One ally was the wealthy merchant Edward Mortimer. Judge and politician, Mortimer was a power in the eastern part of the province – a forceful and witty man known by some as the 'King of Pictou' or the 'Oat Meal Emperor from the East.' Most important to Thomas McCulloch, he supported the Presbyterian Secessionists.

Mortimer, of Banffshire, Scotland, had arrived in Pictou in 1788 on a trading venture, and remained, opening a store and becoming involved in the lumber and shipping trade, the source of his considerable fortune. He married Sarah Patterson, a daughter of Squire Robert Patterson, who, after two decades in Pictou, was known as the 'venerable settler [who] presided over the others.' Construction of the Mortimers' home, Stone House, began in 1810. Stonemasons and carpenters from Scotland worked for four years on the building. The reported cost was £10,000. By 1813 Mortimer had established a firm of which he was the principal, with William Liddell of Glasgow and George Smith of Pictou.

Mortimer died in Pictou in 1819. His widow, Sarah, lived there until 1835, then several owners later, in 1894, this fine Georgian dwelling came into the hands of Lord Strathcona, Donald Smith, Chief Factor of the Hudson's Bay Company, who named it Norway House, after the Hudson's Bay Company post in the Northwest Territories. Located at the end of Haliburton Road, it is now a home for the elderly.

According to his biographer Susan Buggey, Mortimer's death at age fifty-one 'left the issue of Pictou Academy in the hands of his inexperienced successor in the assembly, George Smith, and the obdurate Thomas McCulloch, [and] contributed to the political and religious conflict of the 1820s.'

George Smith was also a Scot, and a successful timber merchant and shipbuilder. A Reformer, he spent twenty-six years in the Assembly, including the Council, first representing Halifax County and then the county and

Edward Mortimer

township of Pictou. Whatever else he and Edward Mortimer accomplished, braving politics in Pictou may have been one of their most perilous activities. Week-long elections were frequently volatile: opposing sides battled in the streets, to the accompaniment of the pipes.

In 1810, while his associate, Mortimer, was building his splendid house, George Smith was also keeping the stonemasons busy. His house (now 115 Water Street), spare and well-crafted, featured Scottish five-sided dormers. It blended comfortably into the Pictou streetscape, where even a casual observer could tell at a glance that this was a town built by Scots. In 1837 George Smith sold the house to his brother Edward, of the Hudson's Bay Company, who lived there until 1851, when financial reversals forced him to sell.

Brother George had moved next door into a frame house he built at 117 Water Street. Within a year he too suffered reversals and mortgaged his home for £5000 to the Hon. Samuel Cunard. George Smith died in 1850. By the next year the house was in the hands of his son-in-law, Dr George Johnston, a renowned surgeon and a founder of the Medical Society of Nova Scotia in 1854. In 1862 it was owned by Alex McDonald, Speaker of the Assembly.

Elsewhere along Water Street other stone houses of the Scots still stand, as sturdy and tenacious as were their builders.

Another stone building houses a favourite drinking spot – Lorrain's Inn (on Church Street), a two-and-a-

Sarah Patterson Mortimer

George Smith house,
115 Water Street

half-storey stone-block Georgian building with three five-sided Scottish dormers. The stonework was done by its owner and builder, John Lorrain, a Scottish mason who purchased the property in 1820. The Pictou Masons met in his inn, and it also served as the stage stop for the Halifax line. Lorrain advertised in *The Colonial Advocate* of 3 June 1829: 'TOMB AND HEAD STONES, cut and carved ... for sale on reasonable terms, and payment made easy.'

He was doing well enough to need help. The same newspaper carried an advertisement for 'a smart active lad as an apprentice to the Stone Cutting and Mason trade.'

Perhaps he needed help because he had encountered problems related to the previous lad he had apprenticed. A notice directly below the advertisement announced: 'Runaway. An indented apprentice named William Edmond, about 16 years of age – reward for his apprehension. John Lorrain.'

But if the apprentices were not happy, the customers of Lorrain's Inn certainly were, particularly on 30 November, St Andrew's Day. *The Colonial Patriot* printed for posterity a record of the prodigious feats of drinking that had taken place that day in 1827:

On Friday, the 30th ult. according to ancient custom, most scrupulously observed and revered by all Scotchmen abroad from the land of their birth, a party to the number of 35 gentlemen assembled at Mr Lorrain's Inn, to celebrate the memorable Festival of St Andrew, the titular Saint of Scotland. A meeting on such an occasion, at all times tends to call forth

Lorrain's Inn, Church Street

an association of ideas highly agreeable to the minds of Scotia's sons, when met together ...

And, as Scotia's sons everywhere celebrated St Andrew's
Day, those in Pictou did themselves proud with the following toasts:

1   The pious memory of St. Andrew, the tutelar [*sic*] Saint of
Scotland.

2   Our most gracious Sovereign, George IV. Long may he
live to reign over a free, loyal and happy people – 9 times 9 –
God save the King.

3   The tutelar Saints of England, Wales and Ireland, St.
George, St. David, and St. Patrick.

4   His Royal Highness the Lord High Admiral and the British Navy – 3 times 3 – *Rule Britannia*.

5   The other branches of the Royal Family – 3 times 3 –
Honest Men and Bonny Lasses.

6   To the immortal memory of Wallace and Bruce, whose patriotic deeds will never be forgotten – *Scots wha hae wi' Wallace*
bled.

7   His Grace the Duke of Wellington and the British Army –
3 times 3 – *Duke of York's March*.

8   His Excellency the Governor General Earl Dalhousie,
May the colonies over which he presides duly appreciate his
valuable services – 3 times 3, with repeated cheering – *Reel of*
Tulluchgorum.

9   His Excellency Sir James Kempt, our gallant Governor,
the warm promoter of the true interests of Nova Scotia – 3
times 3, with repeated cheering.

10   The Honourable Michael Wallace, and the other
members of his Majesty's Council – 3 times 3, with repeated
cheering – A *Man's a Man for a' that*.

11   'The Land o' Cakes,' and all that is nearest and dearest to
Scotchmen – 3 times 3 – *Auld Lang Syne*.

12   The Clergy of Scotland – 3 times 3.

13   The Kirk of Scotland, and free toleration in religious
matters.

14   The Lord Bishop of Nova-Scotia, and the Clergy of the
Established Church.

15   His Honour the Chief Justice, and the Bench of Nova-
Scotia – 3 times 3.

16   The Agriculture, Fisheries and Commerce of Nova-
Scotia. May they prosper under the benign influence of the
British Government – 3 times 3 – *Speed the Plough*.

17   The Town and Trade of Pictou. May success attend the
enterprize of her merchants. 3 times 3.

18 The Albion Mining Company. May their exertions be crowned with success. 3 times 3.

19 The memory of the Right Honourable George Canning; an able statesman, an accomplished scholar and an honest man.

20 The fair daughters of Acadia – 3 times 3. *Green grow the Rushes O.*

21 To the memory of Robert Burns, Scotia's sweetest Bard.

22 The Wizard of the North, Sir Walter Scott.

23 The British Constitution. 3 times 3.

24 May Scotia's sons be as free as the wind that blows over the heath and over the mountains. 3 times 3.

25 The immortal memory of Nelson. May old England never want such heroes to lead our tars to victory. 3 times 3. *Hearts of Oak.*

26 May harmony and conviviality always prevail in the celebration of this annual festival. 3 times 3.

27 To all Scotchmen who are celebrating St Andrews throughout the world. 3 times 3.

28 The internal improvement of this Province, good roads and bridges. 3 times 3.

29 Hugh Denoon, Esq. our worthy Chief Magistrate. 3 times 3.

Joseph Gordon, a Mason, would have known that Lorrain's Inn did not always ring to the sound of twenty-nine consecutive toasts but had its more serious moments when the Masons were in attendance. During Gordon's time in office 'the Annual Communication of Grand Lodge was held in Pictou for the first time.' A Pictou native, Gordon was a partner in the hardware business of Dawson and Gordon. Married to May Bennet, he had six children. He was, according to his obituary in 1902, 'a man of urbane disposition and pleasing address rendering him a general favorite.'

Whatever else may be said to add to this sketchy picture of Joseph Gordon, his house, on Denoon Street, has character and individuality enough to suggest that its builder did as well. The attractive vernacular Gothic building, built about 1866, featured a projecting, three-sided central bay, its door flanked by tall windows. A Nun's Coif gable above gave the house particular distinction, and a sense of playful grace.

In 1817 the Rev. Thomas McCulloch briefly put aside his concerns for Pictou Academy and the state of higher education in the province to look into a matter that was the only topic of conversation in town.

Eliza Glennie Dawson, thirty-one, widow of a wealthy

Scottish merchant, John Dawson, had left Pictou in spectacular fashion. She had run off to Boston with a prominent local man, deserting nine of her children, but taking her five-year-old daughter, Margaret, with her. Abraham Patterson, son of John 'Deacon' Patterson, the founder of Pictou, took one of the Dawson children, Charlotte, into his home. Thomas McCulloch took another, Elizabeth, and raised her with his family. Eliza's other offspring, Catherine, John, and George, remained in the care of her brother George Glennie in Pictou. (Her four stepchildren, by John Dawson's first wife, were, at the time of her departure, in their late teens and early twenties.) The abandoned wife, 'a most worthy woman,' was forced to take in boarders and do laundry for Pictou Academy in order to support her ten children.

The tale of the lovers' sojourn in Boston ended in tragedy – a story that may well have served the parents of Pictou when searching for an object lesson for their young. It would have required little embellishment.

The Dawson saga only recently came to light through letters acquired by the Provincial Archives of Nova Scotia. They were found, 'sooty and musty' in a local attic. The letters tell how Eliza Dawson's life ended in the slums of Boston, and of the battle that she waged by mail to manage what was left of her estate in Pictou.

Joseph Gordon house, Denoon Street

It had been mishandled, first by her lover's brother, then by her own. The matter would probably have ended in hopelessness had it not been for one of Pictou's leading merchants, Abraham Patterson.

John Dawson had died intestate in January 1815. Two years later, when his widow left for Boston, the estimable Edward Mortimer was named guardian of the Dawson children. Mortimer died in 1819, and Abraham Patterson agreed to serve as guardian and also to manage the Dawson estate, which was by this time in disastrous shape. By 1828 Eliza was penning pleading letters to Patterson, describing herself as a 'destroyed woman.' Then, in February 1831, her lover, the man for whom she had left her home and family, died in Boston.

The following year, Abraham Patterson was so concerned about Eliza and Margaret that he retained a Boston lawyer, James Fullerton, to investigate. Fullerton found them living in slums near the Boston harbour. Eliza had become an alcoholic, Margaret a prostitute. The lawyer wrote to Patterson, describing with horror the state of 'these truly wretched and degraded people':

I had much trouble in finding them, and at last after wading thro a place where a sty appeared to have stood, the wood work having been used for fireing and the usual contents strewed about the ground, dreadfully offensive to more senses than one, I arrived at the entrance of a wretched shed with the floor broken in and door off the hinges, the window mended with rags and old hats. In a bed in one corner was Mrs Dawson sick from want and intemperance, haggard and the picture of human calamity at its lowest point of depression. In the middle of the room sat the daughter Margaret drawn up into the smallest possible compass to enable her to find a shelter under a scanty and ragged plaid cloak – a healthy looking girl but from the testimony of the neighbors, is no better than she should be, intemperate also and exposed to the evils which always follow in its train, etc., too indolent and vicious to do any honest labour for the maintenance of her miserable parent or herself.

Fullerton made arrangements for their care and reported to Abraham Patterson: 'I gave them my obligation to furnish them with necessaries of life in small parcels from time to time that they might have nothing to exchange for rum – I gave them an order on a store where they will be furnished with groceries, clothing, bread etc., but not a drop of rum which is a sad disappointment to them.'

Ten months after the death of her lover, Eliza, too, was dead. The story then took another turn. Fullerton, clearly touched by Margaret's situation, placed her in a home in Boston called the Refuge for Penitent Females. It was well equipped by the wealthy of Boston and under the supervision of a woman 'having much of the milk of human kindness in her disposition.' Fullerton anticipated the 'complete restoration to society of this long lost member of an amiable and worthy family' and assumed that her family would 'welcome her back to their virtue and their society.' He explained to Patterson his devotion to Margaret's welfare: 'I have two daughters just entering life with fair prospects. Should either be led astray which sometimes happens in spite of our best endeavor to prevent it, I can imagine with what feelings of gratitude I should acknowledge the disinterested efforts of strangers in doing for them what I hope to do for Margaret.'

Abraham Patterson advanced Margaret the money for stage fare from Boston to Pictou. In 1834 her claims against the estate were settled for £205. Forty-eight hours later she was married. Patterson had continued to help her, even though the prevailing sentiment among the pious of Pictou was that the town could happily do without her. Although Fullerton assumed that her errors would 'have been brushed from mortal recollection by the wings of time,' Patterson, more practically, feared that she would be viewed as a walking morality lesson, so he made a pragmatic arrangement for Margaret – he found her a husband. Thus, on 19 April 1834, she collected her £205 inheritance and, two days later, married Thomas Harvey Patterson, thirty-six, of the Town Gut, Pictou. The couple moved to far-off Guysborough, out of sight and, everyone hoped, out of mind. Thomas died in 1862. Margaret outlived him by thirty-five years. *The Pictou Advocate* of 12 March 1897 announced her death: 'At Pictou on March 4, Margaret, relict of the late Thomas Patterson, in the 85th year of her age, leaving an only daughter to mourn her loss.'

No one knows how much the young Dawsons in Pictou knew of their mother's life in Boston. But, as Abraham Patterson wrote: 'In a small community like this every thing put in circulation goes through the settlement, and, as in most communities there are some ill disposed, vicious and degraded characters. This had added much to the embarrassments of the sisters and makes the cause extremely awkward.'

These two sisters survived the difficulties of their

childhood. Charlotte, seven years old when her mother departed, was raised by Abraham Patterson and his wife. She eventually married Dr Joseph I. Chipman, and, after his death, J.H. Geldert, a partner in the founding of *The Eastern Chronicle*. Elizabeth, nine years old when her mother left, was raised with the McCullochs, and eventually married their son, David. He became Collector of Customs for the busy port.

By the time that Elizabeth Dawson McCulloch reached middle age, she and David were living comfortably in a house on West Cottage Street, which was, at the time, the largest brick house in town. Built about 1863, the two-and-a-half-storey building had a projecting central bay with double lancet windows above the door and elaborate bargeboard on the gable to provide a decorative touch. Inside, eight fireplaces provided heat. The McCullochs' home dominated its immediate area as the story of Elizabeth's mother had once dominated much of the talk in the town.

Scots settled throughout Nova Scotia, but in Lyons Brook and Pictou it is clear to the eye that, in this part of the province, they predominated. The work of Scottish stonemasons is seen everywhere. Much of the finest work was produced by the mason Robert Hogg and his son John, who had emigrated from Canonbie, Dumfriesshire, in 1831. They were responsible for a handsome house built for John MacKenzie at Lyons Brook.

The home of David and Elisabeth Dawson McCulloch, facing West Cottage Street

MacKenzie's home may have been the Hogg family's first project. It was a quietly elegant stone structure, quite obviously the home of a gentleman. The craftsmanship is of top quality. The house was built on land left to John MacKenzie in 1815 by his father, Daniel, who had come to Lyons Brook from Invernessshire and established a saw mill and a farm, Mill Brook. Construction of the house began in 1831. The Hoggs were able to use stone from the owners' own quarry, for by this time John and his brother, Charles, had a well-established quarry on the bank of Saw-Mill Brook. Within a few years, MacKenzie stone would be shipped across the Northumberland Strait to Charlottetown to be used between 1834 and 1837 in the construction of Province House.

The MacKenzie house became a family affair. John Hogg married Catherine Fraser, a sister of John MacKenzie's wife, Mary. When John MacKenzie died in 1861, Catherine and John Hogg and their four children moved in with Mary MacKenzie. She and John had been childless.

When Mary MacKenzie died in 1888, she left the house to her niece Mary, the wife of Captain Thomas O'Brien. Mary O'Brien in turn left the house to her daughter, also called Mary, the wife of Robert Taylor. Mary Taylor had a brick extension built at the rear of the house. Not to break with tradition, she passed the house on to her daughter, Betty. And so, until 1982, for 150 years, the old stone house was owned by four generations of the same family. It stands today, its elegance and sturdy simplicity a tangible reminder of the Scottish presence in Nova Scotia.

*John MacKenzie house,
Lyons Brook*

CHAPTER TWENTY-FIVE

Antigonish

Oran
Do dh Ameriga
air fonn
Coire cheithich

Gu bheil mi m onrachd sa choill ghruamich
Mo smaointinn luaineach cha tog mi fonn
Fhuair mi n t aite s n aoghaid nadair
On threig gach talanta bh an am cheann
Cha deun mi oran a chuir air doigh ann
Nuair ni mi toisheachadh biodh mi trom
Chaill mi ghaelic seach mur a abhist domh
Nuair a bha mi s an duthaich thall.

Song to America (The Gloomy Forest)

I am all alone in the gloomy forest
My spirit restless and I don't raise a song.
I found this place contrary to nature
Since each talent which was in my head has deserted me.
I cannot put a song together in it.
When I begin I become downcast.
I lost my Gaelic compared to what I used to have
When I was in the country over the sea.

This Gaelic ballad was called *The Gloomy Forest*. The bard was John MacLean. He was among the best-known Gaelic poets in Scotland and, when he emigrated, his fame spread through North America. *The Gloomy Forest* (all eighteen verses) created a furore in Antigonish, Cape Breton, and in Scotland. On this side of the Atlantic, MacLean was applauded for his accurate interpretation of pioneer life. In his homeland, those who heard his ballad bemoaned his fate. Some in Scotland even offered to pay his expenses so that he and his ballads could return home.

John MacLean, like most of his countrymen who came to Nova Scotia, was seeking a better life for himself and his family and a better future for his descendants. The choice of destination was easy. And there were reasons enough for leaving.

By the 1790s Scotland's clan chieftains were finding that leasing their land to sheep farmers was far more profitable than renting patches to tenant farmers. Some chieftains sold out to English landlords or married into wealthy English families. The population was increasing and the economy was slow. Over time, evictions, common in the Highlands and Western Islands, became known as the Highland Clearances. Dissatisfied Scots were vulnerable to the enticements offered by a new life in a new land. The lure of property of their own, coupled with freedom from economic pressures and overbearing landlords, was irresistible.

Enter the emigrant agent and his tall stories. He might be employed by a landlord trying to clear unwanted tenants from his farm, or perhaps he was working for a shipping company looking for paying passengers. Sometimes he worked on his own, charging a price per head to transport eager emigrés across the Atlantic. For any and all reasons, the emigrant agent told tales of free and fertile land and an easy road to wealth. An unprincipled agent with a honeyed tongue could persuade thousands. Thus, their hopes high, Scottish emigrants clambered on board small, crowded vessels for voyages that lasted weeks. When they disembarked, tired and often ill, mourning those who had died at sea, they faced the gloomy forest, rugged, uncleared, and lonely.

John MacLean, his wife, and three children landed in Pictou in 1819. He was one of approximately 40,000 Scots who came to Nova Scotia between 1770 and 1850. MacLean was one, and perhaps the best, of those few Scots who could turn emotion into verse, expressing their deepest feelings through the symbolism and lilting cadence of Gaelic poetry. MacLean was able to articulate what most immigrants only felt. And so his first ballad spoke of anger at the lying agent, the sorrow of lost dreams, of the loneliness of life in the wilderness and the fear of a loss of cultural identity. He wrote of aching limbs, of winter's penetrating cold and the summer's searing heat. He wrote of a diet of potatoes. He wrote of the curse of his new life. His ballad achieved fantastic popularity in Scotland and served as a powerful deterrent to many Scots who were considering a move to North America.

MacLean continued to voice the emotions of Scots in Nova Scotia because he remained there, struggling to build a new life. He lived to see some of his hopes realized, thanks to his own hard work. Initially, his poetry reflected bitterness about his fate, perhaps because he was one Scot who had not been suffering financially at home in Scotland. There, as a poet, he had been under the patronage of the Laird of Coll. He composed many more ballads in Nova Scotia. One, a lament on the death of Mrs Julia MacNiven Noble (of Whycocomagh, formerly of Tiree), is accepted as one of the most powerful Gaelic laments.

MacLean became contented over the years. He enjoyed the conviviality of rural life, frequently walking for miles to sing and read his well-loved ballads in which, by then, he was speaking cheerfully about life in Nova Scotia. He became something of a poet laureate, and his work is studied in universities today.

The bard MacLean settled first in Pictou County at a spot identified in *The Gloomy Forest* as 'behind the mountains, in the middle of the wilderness at Barney's River.' Later he moved to Marshy Hope, west of Antigonish, where he is remembered in the names of a school, post office, and cemetery – 'Glenbard.'

Two years after his death, MacLean's simple dwelling burned to the ground, but in short order friends built a house nearby for his widow and her six children. Located about seven miles west of Antigonish on Highway 4, it is a storey-and-a-half frame building with a central

MacLean house, Highway 4, about 7 miles west of Antigonish

dormer – no Highland cottage this. The house reflected the New England influence that had by now spread through Nova Scotia. It could have been on any shore along the eastern seaboard.

The MacLean house, still owned by the family, has been home to succeeding generations of scholars and poets. Son Charles, a poet, transcribed his father's ballads and songs. A grandson, the Rev. Alexander MacLean Sinclair, grew up in the house and became the Gaelic scholar of his time. He is buried with his grandfather in a nearby cemetery. A great-grandson, Dr Donald MacLean Sinclair, became a renowned authority on Gaelic matters.

Business was slow in Halifax in 1822, the result of a postwar depression following the end of the War of 1812, when a shoemaker, John Jost, decided to leave town and head east, looking for better prospects. He stopped at Guysborough, at the head of Chedabucto Bay on the eastern shore. The town had been a fishing station and major settlement in Acadia in the seventeenth century, and was named 'Chedabouctou,' from the Indian name, 'Sedabocktook,' 'the deep extending harbour.' But its name was changed in 1783 when disbanded regiments of Loyalists settled, and decided to honour Guy Carleton, commander-in-chief of British forces in North America.

It was spring when Jost arrived in Guysborough, and the village was putting on its best face, anticipating a summer visit from Lieutenant-Governor Sir James Kempt. John Jost worked for the summer there, then returned to Halifax in the fall to talk to his brothers, George and Christopher, about possible plans for a

John Jost house, Main Street, Guysborough

permanent move and a new business. Having purchased a load of goods, of a variety that would stock a small general store, he had them shipped, and, with Christopher, set out for his new home. By the fall of 1823 the Jost brothers had sold all their stock and had money in hand to pay their bills. They returned to Halifax, bought more stock, and, with John's wife, Sarah Amelia Cook, made the permanent move to Guysborough, where they formed the firm of J. and C. Jost.

There was business enough for both brothers, as records show daily income increasing from $2 to $150. A fishing business was added to the retail outlet. Soon there were two Jost firms, with John taking the name The British House and Christopher that of C. Jost, each firm expanding further over the years to take in sons and nephews. Most customers dealt with the Josts by bartering, and accounts were settled with fish, beef, pork, butter, woollens, shingles, and other commodities. The fishing business expanded, and two vessels were constructed for the firms.

In 1863 John, then sixty-three, sold the land next to his store to his son, Henry Marshall, who had joined the family firm and was about to marry a neighbour, Carrie Hart. Henry Marshall set about to build a house for his bride and gave the storey-and-a-half frame building a fashionable touch by putting a Palladian window in the central dormer and flanking it with five-sided Scottish dormers. The marriage never took place. The house was ready, but the bride presumably was not. Henry eventually sold the building to Ernest DesBarres,

Dr George E. Buckley's home, Main Street, Guysborough

a member of another old Guysborough family. The house still stands on the water side of the main street, next to the old Jost store, now restored as the Mulgrave Road Theatre co-op building.

Up the street from the Jost house stands the neo-classical home of Dr George E. Buckley. With its fine detailing, it was a fitting residence for the man who was coroner for Guysborough County in 1868. George had married Eva Campbell, the daughter of Stewart Campbell, a Halifax lawyer who had moved to Guysborough in 1842 and become coroner, judge, lieutenant-colonel of the militia, and member and Speaker of the Legislative Assembly. In 1867 Stewart Campbell was elected Guysborough County's first member of the House of Commons. Like all of Nova Scotia's members except Charles Tupper, he was an anti-confederate, but was the first of his province's members to support John A. Macdonald. This change of heart from the repeal cause resulted in an egg-pelting episode in Antigonish the next year, but it did not deter Campbell's political career, which lasted until 1874.

On 29 December 1898 George and Eva Buckley's daughter, Abbie, married John Alexander Tory, the fourth child and third son of Robert Kirk Tory and Honora Ferguson. John was the grandson of Henry and Ann Tory and great-grandson of James and Christiana Torey (the original spelling). James Torey, of Aberdeen, Scotland, a follower of Bonnie Prince Charlie, had emigrated to the American colonies in 1770, settling in North Carolina, where he later fought for the British in the Revolution, after which he came with the Loyalists to Guysborough County in 1783.

Guysborough District Court House, now a museum

John Alexander Tory's brother, James Cronswick Tory, became lieutenant-governor of Nova Scotia in 1930. His eldest brother, Henry Marshall, was the first president of the University of Alberta. Their sister, Sarah Jane, married William Henry Bruce, and that family included their son, journalist Charles Tory Bruce, and his son, author William Harry Bruce.

Soon after Abbie Buckley Tory's grandfather, Judge Campbell, arrived in Guysborough, the new Guysborough District Court House was completed. The building, which opened in 1843, was the third court-house to serve the community. The first, built in 1793, was in use for twenty years, during which time the jailer had to appear in court charged with helping prisoners to escape. No mean entrepreneur, he was presumably augmenting the pay he received for looking after the court and jail with bribes from the prisoners whose escape he assisted. One whose escape could not be arranged was a Mr Lee, a cooper, who was hanged from the upper window of that first building in 1808.

A second court-house, built in 1819, lasted until 1842, when the present building was erected. The old court-house, simple but stately, is now open to the public as a museum.

CHAPTER TWENTY-SIX

The Eastern Shore

Rocky, barren, bad land. Early settlers used these words to describe the coast east of Halifax, known as the Eastern Shore. Today the visitor is likely to be attracted by the intriguing place-names that belong to that stretch of coastline – Chezzetcook, Musquodoboit Harbour, Mushaboom, West and East Quoddy, Jeddore, Pope's Harbour, Necum Teuch, Ecum Secum. These and other villages were settled by a hardy group. Many had come from Lunenburg County. They saw something inviting in this forbidding coastline – land by the sea, in vacant harbours and bays – a precious commodity no longer available near Lunenburg, where land had been taken up as much as ten miles inland. Here they were able to eke out a living by fishing and farming, staying close by the sea rather than venturing farther inland.

The Eastern Shore was still largely uninhabited, in part because of its inhospitable geography, but mainly because the prime locations were held by absentee landlords, leaving little land available for permanent settlement.

One of these was Colonel John Hale, who owned land in Upper and Lower Canada, as well as some 10,000 acres on the Eastern Shore. Hale's father, scion of a wealthy British family, had served with Wolfe on the Plains of Abraham and, at Wolfe's request, had taken the news of the capture of Quebec to London. Among other notable absentee landlords were Jonathan Belcher, chief justice and later lieutenant-governor of Nova Scotia, and the influential Jonathan Binney, lawyer, merchant, and office-holder in Halifax.

These prominent men were obliged, like everyone else, to follow the rules – to place Protestant settlers on their land, one for every 200 acres. Hale made some efforts in this direction by encouraging British settlers to settle around Salmon River (later Port Dufferin) and Quoddy, but those men and women soon found greener fields in Cumberland County. A group of Loyalists made camp briefly in Beaver Harbour, but only because they were en route to Antigonish from Halifax when their ship took refuge there; after the winter they continued on to Antigonish. A few settlers arrived around 1800, but most of them moved on as well.

Towards the end of the eighteenth century, two families from Lunenburg County settled at Moser River and Beaver Harbour, followed later by others from the same area. In time, between 1800 and 1825, nearly twenty families – German, French, and English – arrived. They built log houses or brought with them sawn lumber with which to build their homes, just as many of the first settlers from New England had done.

But the new arrivals, struggling to survive, soon discovered that the land they were farming was owned by others. The parsimonious John Miers Greer of Sheet Harbour, for instance, would not even allow a church to be erected, at the settlers' expense, on a portion of his 10,000 acres.

Gradually most of the settlers were able to obtain land by grant or purchase. Those on the Hale Grant were an exception. Legally they were still 'squatting' on Hale's land. In 1819 they petitioned the government, asking that the land revert to the Crown and then be released for sale. They argued that land on the Hale Grant was 'very Rocky broken land and very small spots of it fit for cultivation.' By 1828 the land had been surveyed and lots granted.

Among those who petitioned for the Hale Grant were the Hartlings, descendants of Michael and Maria Hirtle (as the name was originally spelled), who had come to Lunenburg County from southern Germany in 1751. Their eldest son, Jacob, fathered twenty-six children by two wives. Three of his sons, Philip, Peter, and Frederick, and their nephew, John, moved from Lunenburg County to settle in the Beaver Harbour/Ecum Secum area. According to descendant Philip Hartling, in *Where Broad Atlantic Surges Roll*, by 1871 the Hartling family was 'the largest in the Salmon River census district (comprising sixteen percent of the population) as well as the largest family in the villages from Beaver River to Ecum Secum.'

Peter Hartling and his wife, Anna Barbara, had lived at Mahone Bay before relocating in the 1820s. Jacob, their eldest son, was the third in their family of eleven. He and his sons became noted shipbuilders. One son, Jacob Hartling, Jr, built a schooner, the *J.W. Young*, in 1870. The vessel received high praise for 'superior workmanship and excellence of finish,' and she was compared favourably with those vessels built along the Western Shore at the great shipbuilding centre of Lunenburg. This skill was also seen in the home that his brother Alexander built for his wife, Lydia.

On 1 January 1874, Lydia Hartling's parents, James and Sophia McLeod, sold their daughter a parcel of land for a mere five shillings, because of 'the natural love and affection' they bore her. James McLeod owned more than 200 acres near Port Dufferin, but he was more interested in the ocean and its opportunities. A sea captain, McLeod employed divers to retrieve whatever could be salvaged from the wrecks of the numerous vessels that had sunk along the Eastern Shore. McLeod worked in the West Indies as well, salvaging ships and harvesting sponges.

When the young Hartlings began construction of their new house, they had been married for three years and were parents of two-year-old Hector. Another child was expected that year.

Alexander Hartling wasted no time in building Stone House. Strangely, for its name, it was a frame building, but Hartling attempted to replicate the look of stone by sprinkling sand over grey paint before it dried on the building's wood siding, giving, from a distance, the impression of stone. Simple mouldings framed doors and windows, while five-sided Scottish dormers added

The Stone House, Port Dufferin. Its builder sprinkled sand over grey paint to give the impression of stone. Note also the stone-like corners.

a fashionable note – first introduced in Halifax and Pictou, they had been adopted in many areas of Nova Scotia by the time Hartling built Stone House. Scottish dormers provided ample light but, more than that, allowed for a view in three directions. Fashion aside, the practicality of these dormers undoubtedly explains their prevalence throughout the Atlantic provinces. They were particularly suited to the houses that stood by the sea, houses like that of the Hartlings.

Stone House was ready in time to welcome the Hartling's daughter, Jessie, who was born there in October 1874. She was the first of three generations of Hartlings born in Stone House. Alexander and Lydia's family grew to include two sons and five daughters, all of whom married and stayed nearby, either in Port Dufferin or in Beaver Harbour, or moved to Dartmouth. Their second son, Ansel, married Margaret Gallagher, and it was he who inherited Stone House. With the help of his brother Hector, he in turn added new touches, finishing the parlour, upstairs hall, and two bedrooms, carving a newel post and a balustrade, and adding a verandah.

Alexander, Hector, and Ansel wrested a living from the sea and from the scrubby, rocky land along the Eastern Shore. They built boats, ships, and houses; they fished and they farmed. From April to June they caught lobsters off Beaver Harbour or over by the north shore of Cumberland County. In summer, closer to home, they fished for herring, mackerel, haddock, and pollack. And they worked their four-acre farm. When winter came, the forest provided a living. The Hartlings owned several woodlots, so trees came down, providing firewood for their homes and wood for boats, a frame for which was usually found on the barn floor. Somehow, Alexander found time to serve as a local constable and a fence viewer. When needed he was a private in the Salmon River Rifle Company. The old homestead is still in the Hartling family.

Over the years Stone House has developed its own legends, as many old houses do, adding an air of mystery to the family history. Hector Hartling, it is said, returned from Beaver Harbour one December winter night and, while eating a snack in the pantry, heard three sharp knocks on the cupboard door. This was a 'forerunner,' the signal of tragedy to follow. Next day, the family learned that a young cousin had drowned in Rocky Brook – at the very time that Hector had heard the knocks. Another tale involved Alexander, who one night became lost in the woods, unbeknownst to the rest of the family, who assumed he was visiting a daughter. In the middle of the night, Hector awoke to hear his father calling from outdoors near a window. When he answered the call, no one was there. The next day Alexander safely made his way out of the woods.

The most authentic story concerns Margaret Hartling. On the morning of 6 December 1917 she was working in the house near her daughter while another daughter, seven-year-old Ethel, played on the verandah. Suddenly the house began to shake. Margaret immediately thought that young Ethel was up to some prank. What Margaret had felt were reverberations from the Halifax Explosion, eighty miles away.

CAPE BRETON ISLAND

CHAPTER TWENTY-SEVEN

Inverness and Victoria Counties

A home of their own. A decent living. A future for their children. An escape from relentless poverty. The adventure of a lifetime. The lure of an agent's tall tales. Hope. These were the magnets that drew thousands of Scots across the ocean to Nova Scotia.

The move began as the nineteenth century dawned. The old system of tenant farming, in which a man could rent land from the clan chieftain, was breaking down. This system had represented a form of security even though farmers had to augment their income by harvesting kelp from the sea, burning it, and selling the alkali ash to glass and chemical factories. But when the price of meat and wool increased around 1800, clan chieftains saw huge profits in leasing their land to sheep farmers. They raised rents, divided tenant farms into crofts too small to support a decent crop, and did all they could to squeeze tenant farmers off the land.

At first they left by the hundreds, then by the thousands. By 1850 some 40,000 had boarded vessels, having saved the £15 to £30 it cost to transport their families across the Atlantic. They were full of hope for a new life in the new world. During the 1820s and 1830s, Cape Breton was the most frequently chosen destination. While there were Mi'kmaq there, as well as Acadians, Irish, and Loyalists, the island was still underpopulated. In 1800 it had only 2,500 people, most making their living from the sea.

The first Scots to arrive, those with the funds to get started, usually found what they were seeking. They took up the one-quarter of the island's arable land that lay along the northwest coast and in the inland river valleys. Those who received these first grants – the best land – became known as 'frontlanders.' This was not because they had 'front' land by the sea (for some land on the coast was rocky and barren) but because they had land suitable for good crops, whether by the sea or in a river valley. With good land and hard work these settlers prospered in agriculture and trade. With their profits they bought more land and they clung to it. Many eventually enjoyed a 100-acre farm and conditions far better than they had known in Scotland. Houses, farms, businesses stayed in the family.

The first settlers to arrive at Middle River (first known as 'Wagamutook' – Mi'kmaq for 'little green river') in the early 1800s picked good agricultural land in the valley, raised cattle, and exported beef, sheep, and butter. They had access to St Patrick's Channel and Bras d'Or Lake to the south and, to the east, Sydney. There was also the Newfoundland market, 500 miles away.

At Middle River, Upper Middle River, and Lower Middle River, communities within ten miles of each other, are three stone houses built some time in the mid-eighteenth century by families who had well-established farms and now looked for comfort and permanence. They were frontlanders. All were Highlanders, most from the Kintail and Loch Alsh districts of Scotland.

Philip Finlayson and his wife, Mary MacKenzie, were from Invernessshire, near Inverness, the town often referred to as the capital of the Highlands. They had arrived in 1817, but it took thirty years before they were ready to build their stone house in Upper Middle River. Carved on the stone lintel above the door is the date it was finished: 1848. It is still in the family.

The house was built by Philip's brother-in-law, Kenneth MacCharles (of Middle River). Walls, two and a

The home of Philip and Mary Finlayson, Upper Middle River

half feet deep, were of fieldstone. Dressed sandstone was used for quoins and lintels, adding a more formal note. On the main floor, a parlour, bedroom, and kitchen were separated by a central staircase that led up to four small bedrooms opening off a hall lit by a dormer window. The style reflected the New England influence so significant in Nova Scotia. It was completely unlike styles they would have known in Scotland. MacCharles, a Scottish stonemason known for the high quality of his work, had readily adapted to new circumstances.

The Finlayson house passed from Philip and Mary to their son Donald, the eldest of their seven children, and his wife, Johannah MacCharles, a sister of Kenneth, the stonemason. They lived there with their ten children, one of whom, Kenneth, was the next owner. Kenneth was a bachelor, and the house passed to his nephew Dan MacQuarrie, the son of his sister Elizabeth and her husband, a stonecutter named, fittingly, Malcolm MacQuarrie. Malcolm's skills had been honed in Newfoundland, where he had cut gravestones of great beauty. Dan married Isabel Carmichael from Margaree and they left the house to their daughter, Ada, and her husband, Angus Fraser.

Two other stone houses in the immediate area are similar in construction and have similar stories to tell. Kenneth MacCharles may have been the stonemason for all three. One of the others is at Upper West Middle River. It was built by John MacRae for Curtsie, his wife,

John MacRae house, Upper West Middle River

their son, and two daughters. It was completed by 1856, the year he died, and was left to a son, Farquhar MacRae. The house stayed in the family for several generations. Like the Finlayson house, it had a foundation seven feet deep, thick stone walls, and stone lintels. The main floor consisted of a kitchen, parlour, dining-room, pantry, and hall. A small ornate porch, added later, provided a distinctive touch. The house has been altered in recent years, but Scottish tradition carries on – the present owners, while not MacRae descendants, raise long-haired Highland cattle known as 'Mucklecoo.'

The third stone house in the area was built at Lower Middle River in the 1830s by Duncan MacRae. Aside from its peaked Gothic dormer, it is similar in construction and layout to the Finlayson and John MacRae houses. Duncan MacRae was one of eight children born to Donald MacRae, who came from Applecross, Scotland, with his wife, Isabella MacLennan. He received the Crown grant to the property in 1832.

The Middle River stone houses are a rare find in Cape Breton. In fact, stone houses were generally rare in Nova Scotia, except in Pictou or in areas where the skill of Scottish stonemasons was available. Wood, on the other hand, was everywhere in abundance and was much more common as a building material.

The Finlaysons and the two MacRae families in the Middle River area had been successful. They had emigrated at the right time, when good land was available, and they may have come with funds that enabled them to establish themselves and make choices. Mary and Philip Finlayson, for example, had taken up their property in 1817, when there was a choice of good land. For the £3–5 fee for filing a grant, they could have a 200-acre farm tax-free for two years, with only a few demands for clearing and cultivating their acreage.

In 1827 this 'free land' policy suddenly ended. Lands now had to be bought at auction. Just at this time, immigration was reaching its peak. Scottish landlords were aggressively trying to clear tenants off their holdings to make way for sheep. The kelping market in Scotland had virtually disappeared. Now it was the impoverished Highlander who left, finding the cheapest passage available.

For most the transatlantic crossing was dreadful. Families lost members to smallpox and other scourges, the victims dying in the fetid holds of cramped ships.

Then the landing, perhaps in Sydney, or perhaps in a lonely cove along the shore. It seemed that the only real winners were the shipowners and the agents who got twelve shillings for every Scot they persuaded to emigrate. Many never reached shore. In 1833 alone, ten ships went down in the waters off Cape Breton, taking with them 600 lives.

Those who were impoverished when they came had to settle for what, if any, land they could get, and so became part of a relentless cycle. Their poor, rocky, and hilly land could not support a farm. These, then, were the 'backlanders' – a term that referred not only to the location of their lands but to their poverty. Those who could not afford to buy property ended up squatting on Mi'kmaq land. The farmer who could not scratch out a living on poor land had to work 'away,' some going to Sydney, some going off-island entirely, leaving the farming to the women and young boys. It was an almost unbreakable cycle. And then there was the potato rot, a series of blights between 1845 and 1851 which spread in the island's damp climate, infecting the crop, which was, for many, a staple of their diet.

An item in *The Novascotian*, 7 June 1847, described the destitution:

'News From Cape Breton'
Death by Starvation! – On Monday last, a girl having died at Mira, a Coroner's Inquest was held on the body, which returned a verdict of 'death by starvation.' More deaths will take place, it is said, unless a supply of food be shortly received. At the present moment, we understand, there is not a barrel of flour to be had, at any price, in the town of Sydney or in this neighbourhood.

Such conditions and reports prompted some settlers to leave Cape Breton for Newfoundland, mainland Nova Scotia, and beyond. Immigration slowed as word of conditions spread, and 'out-migration' began.

Those who distanced themselves farthest from the struggle to make a living in such circumstances were the followers of a charismatic preacher, the Rev. Norman MacLeod, who, he modestly admitted, was 'so full of the Holy Ghost that his coat would not button up.' Mac-Leod was a rigid moralist who exacted strict obedience. In 1820, aboard a vessel named *The Ark*, he had set out from Pictou to lead his people to a better home at some exotic destination. The group got as far as Cape Breton and were forced to put in at St Ann's. They decided to stay.

By 1850 the community had a new promised land, and a warmer one – Australia. MacLeod's son was living there and had written of the good conditions. MacLeod, inspired, urged his followers to move again. The St Ann's community was divided. Half left; half remained. Between 1850 and 1861, 300 devoted 'Normanites' (along with some Roman Catholics and settlers from Lake Ainslie and Port Hood) embarked on six ships destined for Australia and New Zealand. Among them were Mary MacRae (a sister of Duncan MacRae), her husband, Donald MacKay, and seventy other residents of Middle River.

Norman MacLeod died in New Zealand in 1866, at age eighty-six. His followers remained at Waipu, where they had made their home. (Malcolm Fraser, former prime minister of Australia, was a direct descendant of MacLeod's followers.) There have been many pilgrimages from Cape Breton to New Zealand and many return visits, during which family connections are sought out and the old traditions enjoyed.

Donald MacLeod and his wife, Jessie MacPherson, were from the Isle of Eigg, Scotland, Highlanders who, like most, were Gaelic-speaking Roman Catholics. They crossed the ocean in 1791 seeking a new home in Nova Scotia. Donald and Jessie were looking for an area where a priest lived permanently. Their first stop was Parrsboro. It was a seventeen-year stop, but, after that time, there was still no resident priest. They decided to move on. With their two sons and seven daughters, they packed what they could carry and, with six head of cattle and one horse, set out again. They were accompanied by their neighbours, the Kennedy family. Partly on foot, partly under sail, they made their way, first, to Antigonish, where some of the family remained, then, to Broad Cove, on the west side of Cape Breton, south of what is now the Cabot Trail. This was the home the MacLeods had been seeking.

In 1868 Donald MacLeod, grandson of 'pioneer Macleod' (so called by descendants to distinguish him from his many namesakes), built a house in Dunvegan for his wife, Catherine MacEachen, their three sons, and five daughters. A merchant, farmer, and practical man, MacLeod erected his frame house on a solid stone foundation. But he must have had an aesthetic sensibility.

He placed an eight-sided glass cupola on the shingled roof, surrounding it with a widow's walk, an amenity usually associated with sea-captains' homes, a viewpoint from which an anxious wife could scan the horizon for a returning ship. The cupola has since been removed, but the frame house is otherwise unchanged.

A descendant, the present owner of the house, recalls that the MacLeod home was always filled with music. In this it was typical of the dwellings of most Highland settlers, whose cultural traditions helped to keep the wilderness at arm's length. Among these traditions was the ceilidh, usually a spontaneous gathering with the light footwork of step-dancing and square-dancing, the boisterous accompaniment of fiddle-playing, rousing choruses of the old Gaelic songs, and, an essential, food. Some communities had 'ceilidh houses' in the middle of the settlement.

Spoken Gaelic, common among the Highlanders who came to Cape Breton, was the language of one of the oldest oral traditions in the Western world. Settlers from adjacent communities in the Highlands tended to cluster together in their new Cape Breton home and gather for the Sgeulachdan, the story-teller's Gaelic yarns, sometimes hours or evenings long, that could hypnotize the weary at day's end. Today these songs and tales, passed down from those first immigrants, tell of their initial struggle in the wilderness, or go back even farther to battles, religious sagas, and supranormal phenomena

Donald MacLeod house, Dunvegan

in Scotland. These traditions have never dimmed. In fact, Cape Breton's sagas are being exported to Scotland.

Some Cape Bretoners, backlanders in particular, barely survived. Some, like the Finlayson and MacRae families of Middle River and the MacLeods of Dunvegan, became secure and comfortable. And some men became positively affluent – merchants who held positions of prominence, who owned hundreds of acres of land and the stores to which so many were indebted.

William McKeen was descended from a Scots/Irish family. His grandfather had moved from Scotland to Ireland and then made plans to emigrate to New Hampshire. He died shortly before he was to leave; his widow made the trip, then moved again to Truro, Nova Scotia. William McKeen's mother was an Archibald of a well-known Truro family whose North Sydney branch was prominent in shipping. William, born in Truro in 1789, and his brother Samuel moved to Pictou, then Musquodoboit, and finally to Mabou, where Samuel became a miller and William a merchant.

William learned Gaelic so that he could speak to the Scottish settlers in their own tongue. Eventually he owned stores at Mabou, Inverness, and Whycocomagh, Broad Cove, and Lake Ainslie. He shipped cattle, butter, and cheese to Newfoundland and took part in the trade between Newfoundland, Nova Scotia, and the Caribbean. In addition he was involved in shipping and in salvaging wrecks. He was generally well respected as a merchant. Once, while unloading a cargo during the potato blight, he heard cries for food. 'Off the hatches, boys,' he shouted, 'we are not going to let people starve.' But while he was ready to distribute largesse, McKeen was acquiring property as well. Sometimes the only asset a settler had was his land, and it went to pay the merchant a debt. One who owed McKeen £11 for purchases from his store sold his 200 acres for £15.9.

McKeen married twice. His first wife was Elizabeth MacDougall of Musquodoboit, with whom he had eleven children. His second marriage, to Christiana Smith of Mabou, caused a family feud. His bride (with whom he eventually had another twelve children) was twenty-six years his junior, and had been engaged to marry his eldest son. Some said that young McKeen never spoke to his father again. There was a curse, they said, laid on the property.

The McKeen house in Mabou, built around 1845, was a gift for Christiana. It was heated by cast-iron stoves, the most efficient heating device then available. The fine furniture was imported from England. A linden tree, also from England, graced the front lawn. The house stood in the middle of 600 acres, surrounded by ornamental fruit trees, apple trees, and fields of grain. It could have been one of the most prosperous farms in England or the Lowlands of Scotland.

In spite of the curse, the McKeen house and land still remains in the family.

Another Cape Breton merchant, one who inspired fear and animosity among his customers, was Peter Smyth, a man renowned for his harsh and heartless approach to business matters. One Gaelic bard, Alasdair MacLean, whose kin had been evicted for debts to Smyth, was moved to pen an ode castigating the merchant:

> Thinking of your insignificant self and your proud nature;
> The wrongs to your neighbours, putting them at a loss,
> And your ugly face, as mottled as your shadow;
> I'd say it was too bad you were ever born.

The bard referred to the 'countless deceits that your clerks made over the drink.' This was a common charge against a man who, although rich and powerful, had an unenviable reputation. It is said that he had a hogshead of rum inside the entrance to his store into which customers were invited to dip without charge. Smyth did not discourage them from enjoying themselves and charging more than they could afford to their account. Accounts that became excessively large were converted

William McKeen house, Mabou

to mortages and, when his patience ran out, he was ruth-less in foreclosing, ably assisted by his lawyer son-in-law and the sheriff. (At some point in this period the priest stepped in and ordered Smyth to remove the rum.) Some claim, however, that many would have starved if he had not given them credit.

Yet this crafty Irish businessman had at least one re-deeming feature: he had the taste to build himself in Port Hood one of the most beautiful houses in Cape Breton.

Peter Smyth, born in Dublin in 1800, left Ireland for Nova Scotia at age seventeen. He spent his first years in Guysborough County as a peddlar, selling needles, pins, and ribbons, which he carried in a pack on his back. By 1832 he had a flourishing mercantile business and was trading with Newfoundland, buying and selling fish and cattle. He was also busy acquiring property and mortgages. Smyth soon owned five stores: two in Port Hood, where he built his home; one in Mabou, where William McKeen, his chief competitor, held sway; one in Judique; and one on Port Hood Island. Local legends claim that he owned a slice of Cape Breton coast that allowed him to walk for forty miles without leaving his own property, and that he owned a piece of land for every day in the year. But it was the means by which he acquired his property and his relentless pursuit of debtors that caused antipathy. It was claimed that many an unwary settler had been forced from his home, losing all he had to the wily Smyth.

Around a man so reviled there circled many stories. Once an old woman entered one of Smyth's stores, only to find the great man himself, by that time officially 'the Hon. Peter Smyth.' She called to him to wait on her, not bothering to address him by his full appellation. 'I have a proper handle,' the storekeeper rebuked. 'So,' the woman retorted, 'has a piss pot.'

In 1859 Smyth built a house that symbolized his sta-tus in western Cape Breton. It commanded a view of the entire harbour, and anyone sailing into Port Hood would recognize it as the home of someone of significance.

The stone house was built into a hill, a trim storey and a half at the front, a full two and a half storeys at back. It was styled after plans in a pattern book for Scottish town houses and even included stone blocks at the corners, designed for protection from carriage wheels, but redundant here since the road was nowhere near the door. The house was built of stone blocks, twelve inches wide and of varying lengths. On the front they were 'dressed,' or worked to a flat surface – the other three sides, which show the stonemason's chisel marks, are good and square but not dressed. The stone was probably quarried on nearby Port Hood Island. The house had a central Scottish dormer and a slate roof. The lintel and pillars give the front door an impressive appearance, which was certainly what was intended.

But, no matter how impressive, Smyth's house, right up to its slate roof, was a subject of scorn to the bard Alasdair MacLean:

> As great as is your wealth, its worth is passing, and
> Before you get gray you will be of little account
> The Evil One drove you from the truth and
> It's a sad case the way you went.
> You sold the people who always paid you
> And who fell into your grasp through your food and drink.
> They made you prosperous – and it's little you were worth
>   it –
> The kind people who put the slate roof over your head.

Meanwhile, Smyth was busy expanding his business, embarking on a political career, and raising a family. He married twice, both times to women from Guysborough County. His first wife was Mary O'Grady,

Peter Smyth's home, Port Hood

whom he married in 1830. They had two sons and one daughter, all of whom died without issue. With his second wife, Ellen Keating, he had five sons and two daughters.

Smyth had a successful political career. A Reformer, he represented Inverness County in the House of Assembly in 1847 and was re-elected regularly until 1863. In 1867 he was appointed to the Council. He became a justice of the peace, chief magistrate, and commissioner for the school board. How a man could be popular with the voters yet despised by so many seems puzzling. Fear of reprisals may explain it: many people were heavily indebted to Smyth and the vote (confined to male property-owners) was not secret. Also, Smyth had, like William McKeen, helped some men by extending credit in time of famine.

Smyth died in February 1879. His will suggests that he kept in mind the bard MacLean's ode:

> My worthy man, I'm often thinking
> Of all the schemes which run through your head.
> 'Twould be better that you pray for salvation
> If you intend to present a good appearance in the hereafter.

Smyth left $18,000 to be divided between the Roman Catholic diocese, St Ninian's Cathedral in Antigonish, Saint Francis Xavier University, and the Port Hood Roman Catholic Church and Convent School. The house and $60,000 went to his wife, Ellen, and the interest on $75,000 to her and the children. On Ellen's

Peter Smyth

The Orangedale Station

death the property passed to a son, John Ignatius, and then to his daughter, Eleanor. It remained in the family until 1960. John I., a merchant like his father, became the first mayor of Port Hood. Other descendants of the Hon. Peter Smyth distinguished themselves through significant contributions in the fields of religion, business, and medicine.

Yet today Smyth is remembered, not for his benevolence, but for a curse laid on him by one angry Scot. The curse, roughly translated, said: 'May he fall off the bridge – and may the lobsters devour his tender parts.'

Peter Smyth had walked the hills of Guysborough County as a young pedlar and, as a wealthy merchant, toured the coast of Inverness County on foot, admiring his acreage. Within a few years of his death, however, an event took place that provided an alternative mode of transportation. In the late 1800s the Intercolonial Railway came to Cape Breton Island and, in western and central Cape Breton, the focus of that entire system was a building constructed in Orangedale. That building, now restored, is a survivor of that transportation system, preserved and widely known in lore and in song.

James and Margaret MacFarlane had moved into the station-master's residence on the second floor of the newly built Orangedale station in the late 1880s, and soon a daughter, Margaret, was born, the first of their ten children. Over the years, as the MacFarlanes played host to passengers on the railway line, they welcomed many into their quarters, including Alexander Graham Bell, who returned each summer to his beloved summer home Beinn Bhreagh (Gaelic for 'beautiful mountain') in Baddeck. The MacFarlane family looked after the station until 1935. They were succeeded by other station-masters, but eventually use of the line dwindled and the building fell into disrepair. Recently the Orangedale Station Association purchased the building from Canadian National Railways, restored it, and opened it to the public. According to Mary MacLeod and James St Clair, in *No Place Like Home*, the building 'made a strong statement about the optimism of the era [when] Cape Breton was seen as a developing area with much hope for future growth.' The building achieved new fame when the Rankin Family singers, remembering Jimmy Rankin's great-great-grand-uncle, James MacFarlane, gave it new life in their popular song 'The Orangedale Whistle.'

CHAPTER TWENTY-EIGHT

Louisbourg and Sydney

In the summer of 1760 the walls of a French fortified town on the east coast of Cape Breton were systematically blown apart by the British. Until then, Louisbourg was the focus of French power in North America.

The town had already changed hands three times since it was built in 1713, when Cape Breton was still known as Île Royale. British troops under General William Pepperell had captured the town in 1745 with New England troops and a supporting British naval force. In 1748, much to the chagrin of the Americans who had besieged the town, Britain handed it back to the French in the Treaty of Aix-la-Chapelle. Ten years later Britain mounted a massive siege and took Louisbourg back. Two years later, their attention now focused on Halifax, the British destroyed the fortifications and abandoned Louisbourg.

The walled town represented a French presence in Cape Breton that had existed since the fifteenth century – first a seasonal one, as French fishermen circled its treacherous shores, then a permanent presence in the mid-seventeenth century when Nicolas Denys, who seemed to hold all of Acadia in his hand, established settlements on Cape Breton, one at St Peter's and another near a Jesuit mission at St Ann's.

Louisbourg, the fortress capital of Île Royale, was begun in 1717, during the reign of Louis XIV, and quickly became a key port of call for vessels from Europe, North America, and the West Indies. Some 2,000 people lived within the nearly two miles of high stone walls fortified with bastions, batteries, 150 cannon, and 5 guardhouses, with a garrison of 650 to 700 soldiers. They were French and Catholic, a society in which power lay mainly in the hands of colonial officials. The rest of this stratified community consisted of the military, merchants, and mariners, with artisans in the many trades that served the port and the town.

Louisbourg drew its life from the sea as well – from the men of the cod fishery who built the wharves, flakes (a platform built on poles and spread with boughs for drying cod), and storehouses that lined the harbour, and from the merchants who exported dried cod and traded in a multitude of exotic goods from around the world. The inns of Louisbourg offered the best rum from the Caribbean and fine wine from France.

One of the houses in town belonged to Michel de Gannes de Falaise, an ensign in the Compagnies Franches de la Marine, one of three units comprising the garrison. Born in Port Royal in 1702, raised in a house still standing there, de Gannes de Falaise had a distinguished lineage. He was one of twelve children born to Louis de Gannes de Falaise, an officer at Port-Royal, and Marguerite Leneuf de La Vallière et de Beaubassin, daughter of Michel Leneuf de La Vallière, governor of Acadia, and Marie Denys, whose father, Nicolas, was one of the leading figures in Acadia for more than half of the seventeenth century.

De Gannes had come to Louisbourg at age twenty. Within three years he was made lieutenant, and by 1730 he was a captain. Such a post in the military, coupled with an inheritance and the profits from mercantile ventures, made de Gannes exceedingly attractive to the young women in town. One of those young women found that attraction her undoing.

In 1727 de Gannes met Marie-Anne Carrerot La Salle de Sertrouville, the widow of an officer in his company. De Gannes became a frequent guest at the Carrerot home. After a year and a half of these visits it was assumed by all concerned that there would be an imminent marriage. When Marie-Anne discovered that she was pregnant, the marriage became essential. Unfortunately the expected proposal from Michel de Gannes was not forthcoming. Five months pregnant and still waiting, Marie-Anne sought the help of the governor and the parish priest, but neither could persuade de Gannes that matrimony was a good idea. Marie-Anne's father took the case to the Superior Council, the court of last resort in the colony. The court ruled that the child should carry the de Gannes name and that de Gannes should pay for its upbringing.

Meanwhile, de Gannes had met Elisabeth de Catalogne, and a wedding was announced. At the church,

Marie-Anne protested that de Gannes (now the father of Michelle Anne de Gannes) was obliged to marry her, not Élisabeth. The Superior Council once again became involved. They ruled that de Gannes could marry the woman of his choice. One week later, on 21 November 1730, Élisabeth became his wife. The couple became the parents of seven children. Their house, built in 1742, is one of fifty buildings reconstructed on its original foundations. The work of reconstruction was done by unemployed Cape Breton coal miners in 1963 when Louisbourg became a national historic site. It is one of the most carefully researched reconstructions in the world.

The de Gannes house was built in 1742 of 'piquet' construction. Posts were placed close together vertically in a trench, and the space between them was filled with a heavy plaster of earth, moss, small pebbles, and mussel shells. The exterior was covered with horizontal planks. The ground floor had a kitchen, two small rooms, and a central room which contained the couple's bed and a cradle for their youngest child. It was not a bedroom but rather an all-purpose room, since limited resources made privacy a luxury. The other children slept either in small rooms on the main floor or on the upper level, which had two rooms and a small loft.

In 1744, the year to which the reconstruction is dated, Élisabeth and Michel de Gannes had six children under fourteen years of age. The eldest, their daughter Marguerite Elisabeth, had, at thirteen, been at the legal age for marriage for a year. (Girls could marry at twelve and boys at fourteen, with consent. Surprisingly, consent was considered necessary until the age of twenty-five for women and thirty for men.) The de Ganneses' house was small, considering the size of their family

The British attack on
Louisbourg in 1745; a
contemporary etching

and Michel's position in the military, but Port-Royal's
winters had taught him that big houses, although more
imposing, are difficult to heat.

In 1744, after two years in his home, de Gannes was
ordered to attack Port-Royal, wrest it from the British,
and spend the winter there. The mission began, but expected naval support did not arrive. De Gannes with-
drew and returned to Louisbourg. He was reprimanded,
but regained his reputation the next year when he fought
bravely against the British forces at the capture of Louisbourg. For that action, he was admitted to the Order
of Saint-Louis.

With Louisbourg under British control, de Gannes,
the rest of the French forces, and their families, had
to retire to France. Britain and France signed a treaty
in 1748, however, enabling them to return to their
Louisbourg homes. De Gannes became town major. He
then was elevated to the lofty post of King's Lieutenant,
but he died in 1752 before he was able to take up the
position. Élisabeth had died two years earlier. Michel's
body lies under the chapel in Louisbourg. During the
1963 reconstruction it was found, his feet towards the
altar.

In 1763, the year that saw the end of French rule
in what now is Canada, Cape Breton was annexed to
Nova Scotia. Twenty-one years later, the decision was
reversed and the island became a separate British colony,
with Sydney (then known as Spanish Bay) as its capital.
The population at this time was made up of Loyalists,
Irish, Acadians, Mi'kmaq, and some settlers from the
Channel Islands. Joseph Frederick Wallet DesBarres was
the first lieutenant-governor, an appointment made in
recognition of his outstanding twenty-year survey of the
entire convoluted coastline of Nova Scotia and the
coasts of New England, the Gulf of St Lawrence, and
Prince Edward Island. DesBarres thought that the colony would pay its way by virtue of its fisheries and coal.
He brought English settlers with him, and they were
joined by New England Loyalists. Nothing but optimism prevailed.

In the spring of 1786 an eager young Anglican clergyman arrived in Sydney. Although of French descent,
he had studied theology in England and was an ardent
Loyalist, vocal in his support of the British Crown. His
name was Ranna Cossit.

On a preliminary visit the previous fall, Cossit had
been promised a parish church, a chaplaincy at the

garrison, a house, a schoolhouse, and a salary of £150, including supplements. What he found on his return fell far short of expectations. There was no house, no schoolhouse, and no church. Money to build the church had been promised by the British government, but that body had now decided that it would pay only after the building was erected.

Cossit, then forty-two, had seen enough setbacks in his life that these did not deter him from his plans. He decided to build the house and church himself. Then he would send for his wife, Thankful, and their children, whom he had left in Claremont, New Hampshire. It had been their home since their marriage in 1774, at which time Thankful Brooks was eighteen, Ranna almost thirty.

Those twelve years had been tumultuous. In the days leading to the American Revolution, Cossit had proclaimed his views from the pulpit. Each time he did so he was put in jail. Six months after his marriage, a mob of 300 threatened him. Thankful was pregnant at the time, a condition which was the norm during their twenty-eight years of marriage. None the less, Cossit remained in Claremont throughout the Revolution, preaching and, living somewhat dangerously, conveying information to the British. This pattern of preaching and politicking, which continued in Sydney, would be his downfall.

In 1785 Cossit was forced to move. Most of his flock had left. He was now the only Anglican priest in New Hampshire, and the Society for the Propagation of the Gospel in Foreign Parts was no longer paying its missionaries. Meanwhile, Thankful was pregnant again.

In 1787, a year after he arrived in Sydney, Cossit was able to send for Thankful and the six children. They moved into the newly completed storey-and-a-half frame

*De Gannes house,
Louisbourg*

house (now 75 Charlotte Street) that he had built on one of three town lots that had been granted to him along with 1,000 acres on the Louisbourg Road. The house was built of used government lumber. Cossit installed six fireplaces. He taught school in the main-floor parlour, which was also used for meetings as he gradually became part of the local political scene. Two years after the house was completed the government gave Cossit £200 towards its cost.

Meanwhile Thankful was pregnant again. In this new home she gave birth to six more children in the small birthing room at the back. This made a total of thirteen children in twenty-eight years of marriage; seven children had been born in the eight years in New Hampshire, and five more in the eleven years between the move to Sydney and her last, fatal, thirteenth pregnancy.

Thankful and Ranna raised their ten children (the others died at an early age) in the small frame house. William Smith, author of *A Caveat Against Emigration to America with the State of the Island of Cape Breton*, published in 1803, met Thankful not long before she died in childbirth in 1802. He recalled: 'The clergyman's wife assured me that a considerable time before our arrival she had supported herself, her husband and nine or ten children upon potatoes and mussels she gathered on the shore.'

While building his house, Cossit also had construction of the church to contend with. St George's was

Rev. Ranna Cossit

Cossit house, 75 Charlotte Street, Sydney

completed by 1789, a simple building of stone taken from the old French fortifications at Louisbourg. The building had three round windows on each side and a more elaborate window at the end. It was the garrison church, the place of worship for Loyalists and for the royal family, should any members decide to visit Cape Breton. It stood at 109 Nepean Street, just over a block from Cossit's home. A tower and cupola were built in the early nineteenth century but were twice replaced, the first time because of faulty construction, the second as a result of destructive winds. Now a stone tower attempts to defy the elements. St George's is the fourth-oldest Anglican church in Canada, and the oldest in Cape Breton.

Ranna Cossit was energetic and tenacious, even fearless it would seem. Robert Morgan, in *Eleven Exiles*, relates a story told by Cossit's great-great-grandson:

Rev. Ranna, on one occasion, was returning from a visit to Cow Bay and night fall found him at the Inn at Hines Road. He left his horse with a stablehand to be fed and watered and went into the Inn for his supper. During the course of his meal he noticed two very unsavory characters in a corner of the room. They were talking in whispers, glancing in his direction, and soon left the room. Rev. Ranna suspected they were up to no good. When he finished his meal and paid the host, he went outside where he found his horse, fed and saddled. Mounting, he kept a wary eye on the shadows and before long he saw the two outlaws jump from the bushes and seize his bridle. Whipping the sword from its sheath, he caught one of the men across the face and swinging on the other, cut the arm holding the horse. Spurring his mount, he then left the culprits who were howling in pain and rode off. Needless to say, he was not molested after this.

In G.G. Patterson's *History of Victoria County*, a story is told of Cossit's efforts on behalf of a young couple with wedding plans that were not welcome news to the groom's father, one Captain Jones:

Hoping to divert the young man's affections, he gave him ... the command of a ship laden with produce and ordered him to sail for Newfoundland. This did not have the desired effect, but it made the place and manner of the nuptials a curious one. As the little vessels sailed slowly down the tortuous waters of St Patrick's Channel, a boat shot out from the shore, containing a clergyman, the intended bride and two witnesses. The schooner dropped anchor, and the parties most interested, with their necessary attendants, landed on a bare rock, not more than thirty by forty feet in area, know as Stony Island. The officiating clergyman was the Rev. Mr. Cossit of Sydney.

It was natural that Cossit would not stand quietly in the shadows and watch the affairs of the new colony pass him by. He was appointed to the Executive Council in 1786. It was a body divided into factions that were continually at war. Cossit became enmeshed in the political confrontations, supporting the representative of the British Crown, DesBarres. The lieutenant-governor, however, was heavy-handed in his dealings and was a victim of Great Britain's lack of concern for squabbles in the small colony and its unwillingness to grant Cape Breton its own assembly. The British government

St George's Church, Charlotte Street, Sydney

removed him in 1787. (In 1804, when DesBarres was 82, he was appointed lieutenant-governor of Prince Edward Island; seven years later he was sent to Halifax, where he died at 103 in 1824.) DesBarres may have been controversial, but he was not dull. He danced on a table top at his hundredth birthday and, at his death, left unresolved land problems involving two women – Mary Cannon, his mistress and land agent in Nova Scotia, and a British woman, Martha Williams, to whom he may have been married. By each of these women he had children – seventeen in all.

Cossit seemed unable to keep out of political skirmishes and, in the centre of the foray, sided with or against six lieutenant-governors after DesBarres. The last of these, Major-General John Despard, complained to Bishop Charles Inglis that Ranna Cossit was too involved in politics.

Inglis convinced Cossit that he had to leave. He posted him to Yarmouth, a world away from Sydney, the burial place of his wife and the home of his family. By the summer of 1805 Cossit, then sixty-three, was starting life anew. Two years later he was inducted as rector of Yarmouth's new Holy Trinity Church, where he continued his pioneering ventures: this was among the first churches in Nova Scotia to contain an organ, and the first Protestant church to bear a cross atop its steeple. (The church was taken down in 1872.) Cossit died in Yarmouth at age seventy-one, having built three churches, in Claremont, Sydney, and Yarmouth; fought for the authority of the British Crown all his life; and contributed to the establishment of education in Cape Breton.

During its 188 years and thirteen owners, the Cossit house has been enlarged with dormers and a rear addition. In 1975 it was stripped to the original siding and restored. Now one of twenty-three historic sites owned by the Nova Scotia Museum, it is operated by the Old Sydney Society.

In 1787, while Ranna Cossit was putting the finishing touches on his house in anticipation of the arrival of Thankful and the children, another house was being put together on Charlotte Street (now 54 Charlotte Street, at the corner of Amelia). Samuel Sparrow had acquired the lot, originally deeded to a Mr Archer, in 1785. Local lore contends that he took two buildings already on the property, put them together, and topped them with a salt-box roof.

Sparrow had emigrated from Surrey, England, to South Carolina, where he and his wife, Sarah, made their home. A merchant and shipowner, he did a sufficient amount of business between Cape Breton and Halifax, shipping supplies to Governor DesBarres, among others, that he needed to stay in Sydney for extended periods of time. In fact he was there long enough to become a member of the Executive Council and, presumably, needed a residence for the duration of his term. DesBarres may have given him the Charlotte Street site in payment for money owing.

In the fall of 1787 Sparrow sold the property to Colin Frasier and returned to South Carolina. Frasier died the following year, and the small house passed through other hands until it was bought in 1840 by Thomas Jost and used as a store and home.

Thomas Jost was a grandson of George Jost of Wittenburg, Germany, who had emigrated to Halifax in 1750 and lived and worked in what was called Dutchtown. His wife was Eliza Sellon of Englishtown, Cape Breton, a woman, it would later become evident, with an acute business sense.

When they bought their new home in 1840, Thomas and Eliza Jost had two daughters and three sons. Three more daughters and a son were born after the move. No sooner had Thomas moved in than he opened his doors to the public, offering a tantalizing array of goods – fabrics of all types, rugs, window glass, pots and pans, carpenters' tools, food, clothing, beaver hats, 'Ladies' and Maids' stays (cheap),' wines, rum, gin, vinegar, and some 'excellent Brandy, vintage 1837.'

They worked in close quarters in their small shop,

Samuel Sparrow house, 54 Charlotte Street, Sydney

a room facing Charlotte Street, in the smaller of the two buildings that had been put together, but the one-room store had its own exterior entrance and a fireplace to give some comfort. The larger portion of the house contained the amenities, an attractive first-floor parlour and bedroom, each with a fireplace. There was a basement with servants' quarters, and a kitchen, its ceiling finished in lathe and plaster to keep dirt from falling on the food or into the large cooking fireplace and bake-oven. The type of slats used for the lathe are still used today in lobster traps, but made by machine instead of hand. As soon as he was able, Jost built a separate store at the rear of the building, 14 Amelia Street.

Thomas Jost died in 1853, three years after the birth of Charles Sidney, his tenth child. Eliza, then forty-six, was left with four other children under fourteen, as well as five older ones. If she was temporarily alarmed at having to run the family business, she more than rose to the occasion. At her death forty-two years later, at the age of eighty-eight, she held nearly $10,000 in mortgages and notes plus more than $4,000 in real estate holdings.

An upper floor added to the Jost house in the 1920s has been retained in a recent restoration. The various stages in the construction of the eighteenth-century building are also visible, showing the way in which such early buildings grew to accommodate needs and finances. The original salt-box roof line is clear. The house is open to the public.

*St Patrick's Church, by the
harbour, Sydney*

Down by the harbour, not far from the Jost house, is St Patrick's Church, the oldest Roman Catholic church on Cape Breton. Built in 1828, it had an Irish congregation as well as an Irish name. The Irish had been firmly established in Cape Breton since 1713, the year in which the Treaty of Utrecht reorganized the map of North America, and French settlements on Newfoundland became British. Many of their inhabitants went to Saint-Pierre and Miquelon. Others moved to Cape Breton and some Irish went with them, feeling a greater kinship to those with whom they shared a religion than to those who had sent their religion underground. During the eighteenth and nineteenth centuries, Irish settlers continued to seek the economic opportunities offered in Cape Breton, mainland Nova Scotia, and New Brunswick. They did not come directly from Ireland, however, but via Newfoundland, where strong links between Waterford and St John's brought many young men to work in the Newfoundland fishery. *The Spirit of the Times* of 7 June 1844 described these Cape Breton Irish:

The Hibernian imports with him into the land of his adoption, his indomitable independence, his readiness at repartee, his broad humor, and his broad shoulders. The primary object of the Irish is to secure temporary advantage. He readily becomes 'the serving man' until he find his pocket tolerably well 'lined.' He then purchases a spot, already cleared, and sets up for a farmer. Treat him well, and he is a good subject and a good fellow wherever found – in Cape Breton he is eminently so. When once rightly underway, he farms, as he does every thing, in earnest, and as if he intended to conquer.

The focal point for the Irish Catholics in the area of Spanish Bay was the little wooden chapel where Irish Gaelic was spoken. That first small building, erected in 1805, was replaced in 1828 with the present fieldstone church. By this time more Irish had settled in Sydney parish and they were more than willing to haul the stones, build the three-foot-thick walls, and hew the wooden beams. The cupola was added in 1850, as was an interior balcony to make room for a growing congregation. A new church, Sacred Heart, was built on George Street in 1883, after which St Patrick's became a parish hall. The Ancient Order of Hibernians claimed it in 1960. It is now a historical museum.

CHAPTER TWENTY-NINE

Sydney Mines

On a commanding site at Sydney Mines, opposite Sydney and overlooking the harbour, stand two houses that represent Cape Breton's leading industries. Beech Hill was the home of Richard Brown, the 'king' of coal mining, while at Gowrie House, 139 Shore Road, lived the Archibalds, prominent shipbuilders. The houses were built within five years of each other, Beech Hill in 1829, and Gowrie House in 1834.

Richard Brown was a brilliant young geologist, mining engineer, author, and artist who had been supervising the activities of the General Mining Association, as its first mine manager, since 1826. He was among the first to see the prospects of mining undersea coal.

Coal meant money. England's King George IV knew this and gave his brother, the Duke of York, a sixty-year lease on mineral rights in Nova Scotia. The duke, as an investment, then transferred this lease to the newly formed General Mining Association (GMA), a company started in England in 1825, after they agreed to pay him a share of their profits. The GMA, the mining arm of London jewellers Rundell, Bridge, and Rundell, had jurisdiction from Sydney to the Albion Mines (now Stellarton) in Pictou County. They believed that there were rich veins of copper ore and other metals to be found there in addition to coal, and so sent out a Cornish mining engineer to make an assessment. He reported that the minerals he found were of little value and that the GMA should concentrate on opening coal mines.

Richard Brown was twenty-six when he arrived in Cape Breton in 1826 to look at coal-mining potential. His experience with English coal mines had prompted Rundell, Bridge, and Rundell to select him to open collieries for the GMA. Under Brown, organized coal mining began in Cape Breton, and the Sydney coal field became the most valuable and extensive in Nova Scotia, with coal seams in the Cow Bay, Glace Bay, Sydney Harbour, and Bras d'Or basins. By 1833 more than 900 men were employed by GMA.

Brown took a great interest in the history of mining. He wrote of the early days when, in 1758, the Sydney main seam was opened. At that early date coal was obtained by means of simple appliances designed for the use of the garrisons at Louisbourg and Halifax. At that time the workers were mostly Irishmen who had previously been in the Newfoundland fisheries. Brown wrote of the wretched conditions under which these young men worked: hours from 5:00 a.m. to 7:00 p.m., with one hour for breakfast at 9:00 a.m., and one hour for dinner at 1:00 p.m. Both meals were preceded by a dash to the company store for a 'glass of raw rum.' In the early days miners were paid only twice a year, by which time their purchases at the company store pretty well equalled their pay. They lived in two barracks, in each of which forty men ate, slept, and brawled for six days of the week, and then devoutly recognized Sunday as a day of rest. Brown wrote *The Coal Fields and Coal Trade of The Island of Cape Breton*, which he illustrated with fine pencil sketches, and *A History of the Island of Cape Breton*. The second book was dedicated to the youth of the island, many of whom had worked in his mines at the age or twelve or thirteen, looking after the gates and the horses.

Richard Brown

Conditions had improved for the mining operation, if not for the men, by 1835 when Samuel Cunard wrote in *The Novascotian*:

The line of Railway at the Sydney Mines having been completed from the Pits direct to the North Bar, vessels can now load in all kinds of weather ... the wharf being situated within the bar, is effectually protected from sea swells and the depth of water alongside is sufficient for vessels of the largest class ... there are berths for three vessels to load at the same time. The Coal is brought direct from the Pit to the wharf, a distance of 4 3/4 miles by the Railway, and is discharged from the waggons directly into the Hatchways of the vessels, 500 tons can be shipped in one day.

Brown built Beech Hill in 1829, at the intersection of Richard and Brown streets. Built when Brown was still a relatively young man, the house was originally a modest, two-storey, five-bay structure, but it was later enlarged. It was built to withstand anything the challenging weather could produce, with exterior walls and interior partitions of brick. The exterior is sheathed in a fine, narrow clapboard.

Richard married Margaret Sibella Barrington, a talented artist and one of six children of Captain Charles Barrington of the 60th Rifles. Another Barrington daughter married Captain Robert Bridge, of the firm of London goldsmiths who had sponsored the Sydney Mines. He had accompanied Brown from England as accountant and secretary.

Margaret Sibella and Richard Brown had six children, Richard Henry, David, Charles Barrington, Henry, Margaret and Sibella. Each Sunday the Brown family made its way to the nearby Anglican church (later moved and dismantled), built by Richard Brown in 1841 as a place of worship for his miners. The building stood by the seashore, down from their house. There, in rain or shine, or bitter cold, the ordinary parishioners were waiting outside the church. Brown would be holding the key to the church door. He also carried the key to his own pew, which was always kept locked.

On 28 July 1860 an event occurred in Sydney Mines that caused an uproar in the town, and gave Richard and Margaret Sibella Brown's Beech Hill its place in local history. An unexpected visitor, the Prince of Wales (later Edward VII) came to call. The prince, age nineteen, was on a tour of Canada, representing his mother,

*Beech Hill, Richard and
Brown streets, North
Sydney*

Queen Victoria. The tour became the social event of the century. The prince captivated people everywhere he went, and those lucky ladies who danced with him remembered the event for the rest of their lives.

On that summer day, as the royal party was making better speed than expected en route by sea from Newfoundland to Halifax, the prince decided that he would like to see the Sydney Mines and the Native people there. As a result, a startled Richard Brown, lieutenant-colonel of the Sydney Mines Volunteers, learned that a royal visit was imminent. In his own words:

The *Hero* and the *Ariadne* were first descried rounding the Lighthouse Point at 9 a.m. on the morning of July 28 ... About 10 a.m., the ships having anchored in the mid-channel abreast of the mines, orders were immediately issued to the volunteers, most of whom were at their usual occupations a hundred fathoms below the surface and nearly a mile from the shaft, to muster as quickly as possible.

Lieutenant-Colonel Brown, his brothers-in-law, Captains York Ainslie Barrington and Robert Bridge; along with nine lieutenants and the company surgeon, went to receive their orders and alert the men. At noon the prince landed to review the volunteers. Despite the short notice, all officers and two-thirds of the men who had been able to get up from the mine were on hand. After inspecting the troops, the prince declared that he wanted to see some 'aborigines of the island.' Most of the Native people, however, were attending the annual festival of St Anne at Chapel Island. Only two or three women and a group of young children greeted the future king and sold him some of their handiwork.

The Prince of Wales, later Edward VII, in 1860, the year he visited Canada

Officers of the Sydney Mines Volunteer Rifles shortly after the company's organization in 1859. Richard Brown, as lieutenant-colonel, sits in the middle of the front row

Later, the prince visited Beech Hill for a reception and the reading of an address signed by all the officers. Afterwards the Browns ordered a gold spike, which they drove into the floor to mark the exact spot at which the Prince of Wales had stood in their home. Unfortunately, a later owner removed the spike and its whereabouts is unknown.

Richard Brown held his position as mine manager until 1864 when he returned to England and was succeeded by one of his children, Richard Henry Brown. The younger Brown had been educated in Windsor and then at the Engineering Department in the St Lawrence Scientific School of Harvard University. He went to England for a year's experience at the large collieries of Northumberland before taking over as mine manager at Sydney Mines and two other collieries. Like his father, he held that post for thirty-seven years, continuing his father's work and carrying out the unfinished plans that Richard had made.

When the senior Brown left Sydney Mines to go back to England, Beech Hill passed to Richard Henry, who, then unmarried, had a sister, Margaret, keep house for him. Richard Henry later married Barbara Davison. They had five children, of whom only one married. A descendant claimed that the rarefied atmosphere of their social position in Sydney Mines may have made it difficult for the Browns to find an acceptable mate.

When he retired in 1901 from the mines and the mayoralty of Sydney, which he held for eight years, Richard Henry was presented with a 'cabinet of silver' by grateful citizens. That year Beech Hill passed to the manager of the Dominion Iron and Steel Works. In 1961 it became a private residence.

Down the street from Beech Hill is Gowrie, built for the Archibalds, a name that became synonymous with shipbuilding in North Sydney. Over the years the firm Archibald and Company grew to include a shipyard, marine railway, a ship chandlery, and Gowrie Mines. It employed men in the fisheries and all related aspects of shipbuilding. Like Richard Brown's GMA, it too ran a company store, and company employees rarely got out of debt.

Archibald and Company was formed by Samuel George Archibald, a great-grandson of David, the eldest of the four intrepid and prolific Archibald brothers, Irishmen who settled in Truro in 1762 with their thirty-eight dependants – a combination of wives, children, aunts, and cousins.

David Archibald was a stern and principled man. A justice of the peace, he handed down decisions seemingly as harsh as the climate he encountered when he landed in Truro in midwinter. Once he sentenced a thief to be tied to a wagon and whipped as the wagon was driven around town.

David's great-grandson, Samuel, presumably a gentler man, was one of many illustrious progeny of the four Archibald brothers. With Peter Hall Clarke he founded Archibald and Clarke in 1832. Then Clarke left, other Archibalds joined the company, and it became Archibald and Company. The company acted as general and commission merchants, agents for the sale of coal mined near Sydney, proprietors of Gowrie Coal Mines, agents for the North Sydney Marine Railway, and shipbuilders.

Shipbuilding in Sydney had started when settlement started. A shallop of over fourteen tons and a sloop of thirty tons were launched in 1786. The following year a schooner of fifty-six tons slid down the ways. Seemingly a few men with confidence were building ships while many others were deciding whether they could survive Cape Breton's challenging climate. In *Cape Breton, Ships and Men*, John P. Parker notes that, in 1790, when the first seagoing vessel, the brig *Nancy*, was launched from Sydney harbour, the population totalled only 121, and 26 of them were getting ready to leave.

Samuel Archibald's home, Gowrie, 139 Shore Road

Of the eighty-one houses, a third were in ruins. None the less, during the next hundred years about eighty-six seagoing vessels of all types were built in the limits of Sydney Harbour, mostly in North Sydney.

Two years after the firm was established, Samuel built a home, Gowrie, overlooking his shipbuilding and mining concerns. Gowrie was an ample Georgian-style frame house, its simple exterior belying the elegance within. It was named after Blair-Gowrie, the ancestral home of his wife in Scotland. Their family grew to include nine children.

Although Samuel lived until 1871, Gowrie, for some reason, passed to his youngest brother, Thomas Dickson Archibald, then twenty-eight, and his wife, Susan Corbett, in 1841. That same year Thomas Dickson joined the family firm. It was also the year that the *Secret*, a brig of 198 tons, the largest yet launched in Sydney, was built for the Archibalds.

Born in Truro, Thomas was educated at the Pictou Academy, an institution that had been stoutly defended and supported by the Archibalds for two decades. He grew to be a man of vision and unbridled energy. In the thirty years after he joined the company, it built twenty-seven vessels at North Sydney. It was he who, with experience in the Albion Mines of Pictou County, steered the firm's expansion into the net of enterprises that became Archibald and Company. These included coal mining, shipbuilding, fishing, merchandising, insurance agencies, and a multitude of other interests. After 1853 Thomas Dickson Archibald and his cousin, Sampson Salter Blowers Archibald, were the firm's chief partners.

Senator Thomas D.
Archibald

Coal-shipping piers off the
Esplanade, Sydney 1870

Somehow Thomas found time to be involved in politics as well. From 1854 he held a seat on the Council and, from 1860 to 1863, was a member of Joseph Howe's Council. He supported measures for the deaf, urged education for the Mi'kmaq at Shubenacadie, and opposed a proposal to allow French fishermen, subsidized by their government, to bring fish into the province duty-free. During the stormy debates of the mid-1860s, however, he parted company with Howe on the issue of Confederation. When Nova Scotia entered the new Dominion of Canada in 1867, he was appointed to the Senate. He died, 18 October 1890, at Sydney Mines.

About ten years before his death, the *Canadian Biographical Dictionary and Portrait Gallery of Eminent and Self-Made Men* tersely described the domestic front:

Senator Archibald has had three wives, and buried all of them. The first was Susan, daughter of William Corbett, Esq. of Pictou; the second Elizabeth, daughter of George Hughes, Esq. of Boston, Mass., and the third, Maria Louisa, relict of John Burnyeat, Esq. ... He has seven children by the first wife, and none by the others.

And so, while Loyalists like Ranna Cossit raised their families and raised the heat in local politics, while well-known merchants raised the bills and the ire of their customers, the island's miners and mine managers, ship's crews and shipbuilders, spread abroad the reputation of the island, making it attractive both to Britain and to mainland Nova Scotia.

While settlement progressed, a tug-of-war took place over the years which resulted in union and disunion between the island and the mainland. Annexed to Nova Scotia in 1763, Cape Breton was granted separate status in 1784, then reannexed in 1820. Cape Bretoners knew that their value to the politicians in Halifax lay in their mines, their fisheries, their lumber and gypsum. They were nothing if not independant, and fervently disputed the renewed political link with Halifax. The separatist movement was celebrated in doggerel:

We are the Cape Bretonians, who look for separation,
From Nova Scotia proper, we'll dissolve the annexation,
Indeed forsooth Cape Breton with such a population,
Must all submit to Halifax, and the cursed annexation,
But these worthies all well know, tis now in contemplation
In the metropolis of England to dissolve the annexation

Then Nova Scotia will cry out, must I suffer amputation,
For I'll surely lose a limb if they break up the annexation,
Then hurrah for the great surgeons who'll perform the
   operation ...
So who's the Cape Bretonian now, whatever be his station,
That will not agitate incessantly, to cause this separation.
(*Spirit of the Times*, 30 August 1844)

The spirited politics of union and disunion within Nova Scotia was only settled when, in 1846, Britain's Privy Council decided that annexation to the mainland would be permanent. And, as the nineteenth century progressed, this question of union within Nova Scotia was echoed by the spirited politics of union or disunion with the Canadas.

But throughout the years, as political questions were being resolved with rhetoric and rapprochement, Nova Scotia enjoyed its status as an international community. Its links with the diverse countries of origin of its settlers were strong, and its name and its ships were known in ports around the world. Its reputation as a safe haven had attracted the mosaic of settlement which formed the diverse 'community of communities' the province is today.

This international community had the Atlantic as its workplace, and the hearth was warm at home.

Acknowledgments

From the beginning it was clear that this book was going to be a joint project. It all began in the spring of 1988 when Allan Dunlop, Associate Provincial Archivist at the Public Archives of Nova Scotia, responded to our request for assistance by meeting with us in the Archives and introducing us to Marie Elwood, Chief Curator of History at the Nova Scotia Museum Complex, and Philip Hartling, archivist at the Public Archives of Nova Scotia. We explained that, on the basis of our four published books about early homes and families in Ontario, we had been urged to turn our research to Atlantic Canada, where an 'old' home means one built in the eighteenth and not the nineteenth century, where the struggle for the first representative and responsible governments in Canada took place, and where the vibrant days of the Golden Age of Sail were part of the lives of the province's early settlers. Together they continued to help us and directed us to other knowledgable men and women who were overwhelmingly welcoming and generous both with their time and with their personal research. They are all justifiably proud of what Nova Scotia has done to preserve its built heritage and ready to share their treasures. They saved us from gaffes of pronunciation, understood the devotion which grew for these homes by the sea, and, in some cases, read parts of the manuscript.

Our thanks go to 'Mr Halifax,' author and the city's honorary civic historian Louis Collins, who spoke with us in his book-lined study on several occasions and led us through the history of his city over nearly 250 years. He brought to life the men and women who had walked its streets, from wealthy and powerful merchants, to vivacious Fanny Wentworth, and reformer Joseph Howe, who paced through the night with his wife before answering the challenge to a duel issued by the son of Chief Justice Brenton Halliburton. Dr Collins continued to answer our many questions by phone and read the Halifax chapters.

Brian Cuthbertson, Head of Heritage for the Nova Scotia Department of Tourism and Culture, author, and a descendant of Attorney General Richard John Uniacke, assisted us with information about many of the province's heritage homes and read sections of our manuscript. Also in the Department of Tourism and Culture, Wayde Brown, Heritage Officer, provided us with information on the historic buildings in which we were interested, explained aspects of settlement, and read the section on northern Nova Scotia, his home. Daniel Norris, Heritage Planner with the City of Halifax, spent a day touring Halifax with us, showing us early buildings from a Halifax town house to The Music Room, the romantic retreat of Prince Edward, Duke of Kent, and his mistress, Julie. Scott Robson, Curator, History Collection, The Nova Scotia Museum, gave us information about some of the twenty-three heritage buildings the province administers and helped us obtain archival photographs of others.

Our thanks go to the staff of the Public Archives of Nova Scotia (PANS) who were unfailingly helpful and, in particular, to Margaret Campbell, Head, Photographs and Documentary Art; and Gail Judge, both of whom spent time helping us make our way through the photographic collection at PANS so we might assemble the collection of archival material we were so anxious to include. We would like to thank Irene Fennell, researcher/genealogist, who has searched the files of PANS for us over the last few years, responding to many and varied requests for information. We are also grateful to Margaret Martin, bibliographer at the Halifax City Library, for her assistance with items in that collection, and to Elizabeth Ross, with the Federal Survey of Historic Buildings in Halifax.

Richard Henning Field, Director of the Dartmouth Heritage Museum, helped us locate some of Dartmouth's historic buildings, read the Dartmouth section of the manuscript, showed us through his beautiful and authentically restored home in Lunenburg, and kept in touch with our progress.

As we attempted to record the long and troubled history of Nova Scotia's blacks, we were helped by Henry

Bishop, Curator of the Black Cultural Centre for Nova Scotia, who read part of the manuscript; by historian Dr. Pearleen Oliver; and by Dr Bridglal Pachai, author and former curator of the Black Cultural Centre, now chairman of Nova Scotia's Human Rights Commission. We also received help on the subject of black history from Professor Mary Sparling, Curator, St Mary's College Museum, Mount St Vincent University.

There are many experts dealing with special aspects of Nova Scotia's settlement. Professor Neil Boucher of Université Sainte-Anne, Pointe-de-l'Eglise, drove with us along the French Shore and gave us invaluable assistance by reading the sections of our work that dealt with Acadian history.

Planter history has received specialized attention in the recent past through the efforts of a group of dedicated scholars who are working in a field that had largely been ignored in past years by Canadian historians. The work is centred at Acadia University in Wolfville, and there author, historian, and professor Margaret Conrad met with us, encouraged us, and read the sections of the manuscript that pertained to Planter history. Barry Moody, also author and professor at Acadia, met with us in his home in Granville Ferry, near Annapolis Royal, helped us select homes to feature there, and read the sections which dealt with Port-Royal (Annapolis Royal) and Planter history. Also at Acadia we are grateful to Gwen Davies, associate professor, and to Heather Davidson, researcher, who shared with us her work on the Atwell/DeWolf and Calkin houses.

The Loyalists doubled the population of Nova Scotia in 1783 and we are indebted to Marion Robertson, author of *King's Bounty*, for reading our material on that subject and offering us advice regarding Shelburne's Loyalist history. Also in Shelburne we want to thank Nancy Hart, Gail Burland, and Mary Lee Gonzaga, who helped us determine which buildings would adequately reflect that community's fascinating history. Susie Sweeney showed us around Yarmouth and environs, bringing to life her colourful community. Janet Muise helped with her research into the history of local houses in Yarmouth, and Peter Crowell, curator of the nearby Tusket Courthouse Museum, read the Yarmouth chapter and offered much helpful advice.

In Windsor we saw L.S. Loomer, honorary historian of King's-Edgehill School, surrounded by a collection of rare antiquarian books. He talked of the history of Windsor, of the Acadians in the area, and of King's College School and read the relevant sections of the manuscript. We were fortunate to see Convocation Hall at King's-Edgehill School 'before' and 'after.' The old building is unique in Canada, and the school the oldest in the overseas British Empire. John Messenger showed us his school with understandable pride and welcomed us, as did Louise MacQuarrie, Alumni Chairman. In the Windsor area Father Edward Dowling, Jesuit Archivist in Toronto, was also exploring the mystery of Sherman Hines's house and shared his research with us. It was a pleasure to meet Sherman Hines in his home and to keep in touch during our research.

We acknowledge gratefully the help of F. Thomas Stanfield in Truro, who read our account of the career of his ancestor Charles Stanfield.

At Parrsboro, historian Conrad Byers drove with us to Ottawa House to show us that old hotel where one can imagine the ebullient Sir Charles Tupper sitting on the spacious verandah, swapping yarns and admiring the spectacular view.

Caroline Fraser is administrator of the Hector National Exhibit Centre in Pictou, and a descendant of a Scot who crossed the Atlantic on the *Hector*. She is also an energetic woman with a full schedule, but she took time to show us around town, to share the centre's research, and to read the Pictou section.

Cape Breton has its own distinct history, and we found three mentors to guide us through its complexities. Ken Donovan, author and historian of Fortress Louisbourg, gave countless hours of his time introducing us to the historic old homes in Sydney and Sydney Mines; guiding our research; responding to calls for help; and reading the section on Cape Breton's history. James St Clair, professor, Bachelor of Community Studies Program, University College of Cape Breton, and president of the Nova Scotia Highland Village Society, talked of Cape Breton's people and read the Cape Breton section, interpreting for us the many factors that brought about the Scottish immigration to the island. Dr Robert Morgan, Director of the Beaton Institute, was welcoming, and generous with his own research. Hilda Day, of Sydney, was full of tales of the Brown family and the history of mining in Cape Breton. In Baddeck, Joan MacInnes, historic inventory convenor for Victoria County, took us through the Middle River

area where the Finlayson house was being restored and
where Highland cattle were grazing.

The experts we met were welcoming and full of the hospitality for which their province is known. They shared their work with us and were more than generous with their time. Their pride in Nova Scotia's built history led them to share their treasures with others. This has been very much a joint project.

Our sincere thanks go to all the owners of the houses we have included, for their kindness in allowing us to see their beautiful homes. Many shared their personal research. Whether sitting in front of the fire in a 1710 house in Annapolis Royal, chatting with the well-informed owners of two of our houses – a fascinating Halifax house and an old stone house in Cape Breton – or admiring Mahone Bay from a gracious home in Chester, enjoying the hospitality of the couple who restored the old Planter's Barracks, the warmth of the old buildings was matched by the warmth of their owners. It was an honour to meet the late Dr Isabel MacNeil in her home in Mill Village.

The staff of the National Archives of Canada were extremely interested and supportive, including in particular Marina Royo of the Cartographic and Architectural Archives Division.

We are very grateful to Chris Reardon, who did the current photography for *Atlantic Hearth*. He had recently completed a fine photographic study of Louisbourg in *Louisbourg, The Phoenix Fortress*, and we were delighted that he agreed to work with us on this book.

One last word of thanks. We are grateful to a well-known Canadian institution and a resident of River Bourgeois for the title of this book. It was Farley Mowat, who has created countless titles of his own, who gave us our title: *Atlantic Hearth*.

We acknowledge with gratitude the grant we received from the Canada Council which enabled us to begin research on the built heritage in the four Atlantic provinces. We are also grateful to the Ontario Heritage Foundation and the Ontario Arts Council for their support. And to The Honourable Henry N.R. Jackman, Lieutenant-Governor of Ontario, we wish to express our heartfelt thanks for his support of our research when this project was beginning. His ongoing interest in our work over the last five years has indeed been encouraging.

Select Bibliography

BOOKS

Allison, David. *History of Nova Scotia*. Halifax 1916

Bannerman, Jean. *Leading Ladies, Canada 1639-1967.* Dundas 1967

Bauchman, Rosemary. *The Best of Helen Creighton*. Hantsport, Nova Scotia, 1988

Beck, J. Murray. *The Government of Nova Scotia*. Toronto 1957

Beer, Henry R. *The Pictou Plantation, 1767.* N.p. 1967

Bell, Winthrop P. *The "Foreign Protestants" and The Settlement of Nova Scotia*. Toronto 1961

Blakeley, Phyllis R., and John N. Grant. *Eleven Exiles*. Toronto and Charlottetown 1982

Bourneuf, François Lambert. *Diary of a Frenchman* edited and translated by J. Alphonse Deveau. Halifax 1990

Brebner, John B. *The Neutral Yankees of Nova Scotia: A Marginal Colony During the Revolutionary Years*. New York 1937

Brown, Richard. *A History of the Island of Cape Breton*. London 1869

Brown, Thomas J. *Place Names of the Province of Nova Scotia*. North Sydney 1922

Byrne, Cyril, and Margaret Harry, eds. *Talamh An Eisc: Canadian and Irish Essays*. Halifax 1986

Calneck, W.A. *History of the County of Annapolis*. Belleville 1972

Campbell, D. (Dugal), and Raymond A. MacLean. *Beyond the Atlantic Roar: A Study of the Nova Scotia Scots*. Toronto 1974

Campbell, Rev. J.R. *A History of the County of Yarmouth, Nova Scotia*. Belleville 1972

Cameron, James M. *Pictou County History*. Pictou 1972

The Canadian Biographical Dictionary and Portrait Gallery of Eminent and Self-Made Men. Toronto 1880

Centennial Book Committee, Parrsboro. *Heritage Homes and History of Parrsboro*. Parrsboro, Nova Scotia, 1988

Collins, Louis W. *In Halifax Town*. Halifax 1975

Conrad, Margaret, Toni Laidlaw, and Donna Smyth. *No Place Like Home: Diaries and Letters of Nova Scotia Women 1771–1938*. Halifax 1988

Conrad, Margaret, ed. *Making Adjustments: Change and Continuity in Planter Nova Scotia 1759–1800*. Fredericton 1991

– *They Planted Well: New England Planters in Maritime Canada*. Fredericton 1988

Creighton, Helen. *Bluenose Ghosts*. Toronto 1957

– *A Life in Folklore*. Toronto 1975

Crossman, Evelyn de Blois. *Millidge Ancestors*. Winnipeg 1980

Crowell, Edwin. *History of Barrington Township*. Belleville 1974

Cuthbertson, Brian. *The First Bishop: A Biography of Charles Inglis*. Halifax 1987

– *The Old Attorney General Richard John Uniacke*. Halifax 1980

– *The Loyalist Governor: A Biography of Sir John Wentworth*. Halifax 1983

Daigle, Jean, ed. *The Acadians of the Maritimes*. Moncton 1982

Dalhousie, George Ramsay, Earl of. *The Dalhousie Journals*, edited by Marjory Whitelaw. Ottawa 1978

Davies, Richard A., ed. *The Letters of Thomas Chandler Haliburton*. Toronto 1988

Davison, James Doyle, ed. *Mud Creek: The Story of The Town of Wolfville, Nova Scotia*. Yarmouth 1985

Dent, J.C. *The Canadian Portrait Gallery and Biographical Review*. Boston 1900

DesBrisay, Mather Byles. *History of the County of Lunenburg*. Toronto 1895.

Deveau, J. Alphonse. *Along the Shores of Saint Mary's Bay: The Story of a Unique Community: Volume I, The First Hundred Years*. Church Point, Nova Scotia, 1977

Dictionary of Canadian Biography, Volumes 1 to 12. Toronto 1966–90

Donovan, Kenneth. *The Island: New Perspectives on Cape Breton's History 1713–1990*. Fredericton and Sydney 1990

Donovan, Kenneth, ed. *Cape Breton at 200: Historical Essays in Honour of the Island's Bicentennial 1785–1985*. Sydney 1985

Duncanson, John Victor. *Newport Nova Scotia: A Rhode Island Township*. Belleville 1985

Dunn, Charles W. *Highland Settler: A Portrait of the Scottish Gael in Nova Scotia*. Toronto 1953

Eaton, Arthur Wentworth Hamilton. *The History of King's County*. Belleville 1972

Field, Richard Henning. *Spirit of Nova Scotia: Traditional Decorative Folk Art 1780–1930*. Halifax 1985

Fitch, Catherine, David Hyslop, James R. MacFarlane, and Tanya Rafuse. *Chester: A Pictorial History of a Nova Scotia Village*. Chester 1983

Fitzgerald, Owen. *Cape Breton: A Changing Scene*. Sydney 1986

Gowans, Alan. *Building Canada: An Architectural History of Canadian Life*. Toronto 1966

Grant, Rev. George M. *Ocean to Ocean: Sandford Fleming's Expedition Through Canada in 1872, Being a Diary Kept During a Journey from the Atlantic to the Pacific*. Toronto 1970

Green, Lorne Edmond. *Sandford Fleming*. Don Mills 1980

Haliburton, Thomas Chandler. *The Clockmaker; or The Sayings and Doings of Samuel Slick of Slickville*. Halifax 1836

– *An Historical and Statistical Account of Nova-Scotia*. Halifax 1829

Halifax Landmarks Commission. *Landmarks of the City of Halifax*. Halifax 1971

Hardy, William George. *From Sea Unto Sea, Canada 1850 to 1910, The Road to Nationhood*. New York 1960

Harris, R. Cole, ed., and Geoffrey J. Matthews, cartographer/designer. *Historical Atlas of Canada*, Volume 1. Toronto 1987

Hart, Harriet Cunningham. *History of the County of Guysborough*. Belleville 1975

Hartling, Philip. *Where Broad Atlantic Surges Roll*. Antigonish 1979

Hichens, Walter W. *Island Trek*. Hantsport, Nova Scotia, 1984

Howe, Joseph. *My Dear Susan Ann: Letters of Joseph Howe to His Wife, 1829–1836*, ed. M.G. Parks. St John's 1985

– *Western and Eastern Rambles: Travel Sketches of Nova Scotia*, edited by M.G. Parks, Toronto 1973

Jackson, Elva E. *Cape Breton and the Jackson Kith and Kin*. Windsor, Nova Scotia, 1971

Jenson, L.B. *Nova Scotia Sketchbook*. Halifax 1969

– *Vanishing Halifax*. Halifax 1968

Kealey, Linda. *A Not Unreasonable Claim: Women and*

Reform in Canada 1880s–1920s. Toronto 1979

Kirkconnell, Watson. *The Streets of Wolfville, 1650–1970.* Wolfville 1970

Kirkconnell, Watson, and B.C. Silver. *Wolfville's Historic Homes.* Wolfville 1967

Langille, Jacqueline. *Thomas Chandler Haliburton.* Tantallon 1990

Latremouille, Joann. *Pride of Home: The Working Class Housing Tradition in Nova Scotia 1749–1949.* Hantsport, Nova Scotia, 1986

Leefe, John G. *The Atlantic Privateers: Their Story 1749–1815.* Halifax 1978

Loomer, L.S. *King's-Edgehill School, 1788–1988.* Windsor, Nova Scotia, 1988

MacDonald, A.D. *Mabou Pioneers.* Antigonish n.d.

MacDougall, J.L. *History of Inverness County Nova Scotia.* Truro 1922

Macgillivary, Don, and Brian Tennyson. *Cape Breton Historical Essays.* Sydney 1980

MacKay, Donald. *Scotland Farewell: The People of* The Hector. Toronto 1980

MacKinnon, J.G. *Old Sydney: Sketches of the Town and Its People in Days Gone By.* Sydney 1918

MacLean, Hugh. *Man of Steel: The Story of Sir Sandford Fleming.* Toronto 1969

MacLeod, Jack. *The Oxford Book of Canadian Political Anecdotes.* Toronto 1988

MacLeod, Mary K., and James St. Clair. *No Place Like Home: The Life and Times of Cape Breton Heritage Houses.* Sydney 1992

McNabb, Debra, and Lewis Parker. *Old Sydney Town: Historical Buildings of the North End.* Sydney 1986

MacNutt, W.S. *The Atlantic Provinces: The Emergence of Colonial Society, 1712–1857.* Toronto 1965

Marble, Allan E. *Nova Scotians at Home and Abroad: Biographical Sketches of over Six Hundred Native Nova Scotians.* Windsor, Nova Scotia, 1977

Martin, John Patrick. *The Story of Dartmouth.* Dartmouth 1957

Miller, Thomas. *Historical and Genealogical Record of the First Settlers of Colchester County.* Halifax 1873

Moody, Barry M. *Maria Madeleine Maisonnat.* Toronto 1990

More, James F. *The History of Queen's County Nova Scotia.* Belleville 1972

Morgan, Henry J. *Types of Canadian Women, Past and Present.* Toronto 1903

Murdoch, Beamish. *A History of Nova Scotia, or Acadie.*
Halifax 1865

Nicholson, John A., Charlotte MacIver, Mabel Mac-
Kenzie, Catherine MacLean, Peggy MacLeod, Edith
MacPherson, Alena MacRae, Eva MacRae, Georgie
MacRae, and Wallace MacRae. *Middle River Past and
Present: History of a Cape Breton Community.* Sydney 1985

Pacey, Elizabeth, George Rogers, and Allan Duffus.
*More Stately Mansions: Churches of Nova Scotia
1830–1910.* Hantsport, Nova Scotia, 1983

Pacey, Elizabeth *Georgian Halifax.* Hantsport, Nova
Scotia, 1987

- *Historic Halifax.* Willowdale 1988

Pachai, Bridglal. *Beneath the Clouds … of the Promised
Land: The Survival of Nova Scotia's Blacks.* Halifax
1987

- *Blacks of the Maritimes.* Halifax 1987

Parker, John P. *Cape Breton, Ships and Men.* Bucking-
hamshire 1967

Patterson, Frank H. *John Patterson: The Founder of Pictou Town.* Truro 1955

Patterson, George G. *History of Victoria County, Cape
Breton.* Cape Breton 1978

Patterson, Rev. George. *A History of the County of Pictou, Nova Scotia.* Montreal 1877

Penney, Allen. *Houses of Nova Scotia.* Halifax 1989

- *The Simeon Perkins House: An Architectural Interpretation 1767–1987.* Halifax 1987

Percy, H.R. *Thomas Chandler Haliburton.* Don Mills 1980

Perkins, Simeon. *The Diary of Simeon Perkins.* Toronto
1948–77

Perry, Hattie A. *Mary Hichens and Her Namesake.* Barrington, Nova Scotia, 1985

Poole, Edmund Duval. *Annals of Yarmouth and Barrington, Nova Scotia in the Revolutionary War.* Yarmouth 1899

Poteet, Lewis J. *South Shore Phrase Book.* Hantsport,
Nova Scotia, 1988

Raddall, Thomas. *Halifax: Warden of the North.* Garden
City, New York, 1965

Regan John W. *Sketches and Traditions of the Northwest
Arm.* Halifax 1908

Robertson, Marion. *King's Bounty: A History of Early
Shelburne, Nova Scotia.* Halifax 1983

Rybczynski, Witold. *Home: A Short History of an Idea.*
New York 1986

Saunders, Kathleen. *Robert Borden.* Don Mills 1978

Schull, Joseph. *Laurier: The First Canadian.* Toronto 1965

Schull, Joseph, and J. Douglas Gibson. *The Scotiabank Story: A History of the Bank of Nova Scotia, 1832–1982.* Toronto 1982

Sherwood, Roland Harold. *Pictou's Past.* Hantsport, Nova Scotia, 1988

Stephenson, Marylee, ed. *Women in Canada.* Toronto 1973

St. Clair, James. *No Place Like Home: The Life and Times of Cape Breton Heritage Houses.* Sydney 1992

Stewart, Gordon, and George Rawlyk. *A People Highly Favoured of God: The Nova Scotia Yankees and the American Revolution.* Toronto 1972

Tennyson, Brian. *Impressions of Cape Breton.* Cape Breton 1986

The Heritage Trust of Nova Scotia. *Founded Upon A Rock.* Halifax 1967

– *Seasoned Timbers*, Volumes 1 and 2. Halifax 1972–4

The Lunenburg Heritage Society. *A Walk Through Lunenburg.* Lunenburg 1979

The Port Williams Women's Institute. *The Port Remembers.* Kentville 1976

The Truro Inventory Committee of The Cobequid Arts Council. *Truro: Our Enduring Past*, Volumes 1 and 2. Truro 1986

Tierney, Frank M., ed. *The Thomas Chandler Haliburton Symposium.* Ottawa 1985

Tour of H.R.H. the Prince of Wales through British America and the United States. Montreal 1860.

Tupper, Charles. *The Life and Letters of the Rt Hon Sir Charles Tupper*, edited by Sir Charles Hibbert Tupper. Toronto 1926

Unitt, Doris J. *Sir Sandford Fleming.* Peterborough 1968

Wallace, Arthur W. *An Album of Drawings of Early Buildings in Nova Scotia.* Halifax 1976

Watts, Heather. *On the Road From Freshwater Bridge.* Halifax 1978

Whitelaw, Marjory. *Thomas McCulloch: His Life and Times.* Halifax 1985

Wickens, Sonia. *Seal Island: An Echo from the Past.* Yarmouth 1988

ARTICLES, PAMPHLETS, AND SCHOLARLY PAPERS

Bitterman, Rusty. 'The Hierarchy of the Soil: Land and Labour in a 19th Century Cape Breton Community.' *Acadiensis* 18/1 (Autumn 1988)

Buckner, P.A. and David Frank. 'Atlantic Canada Before Confederation.' *The Acadiensis Reader*, volume 1. Fredericton 1975

Candow, James. *The New England Planters in Nova Scotia*. Environment Canada 1986

Candow, James, and Marie-Claire Pitre. *The Deportation of the Acadians*. Environment Canada 1986

Christianson, David J. *Excavations at a Pre-Expulsion Acadian Site*. Belleisle 1983

Donovan, Kenneth. 'Communities and Families: Family Life and Living Conditions in Eighteenth Century Louisbourg.' *National Museum of Man Material History Bulletin*, no. 15, 1982

Elwood, Marie. 'The Shand House.' *Canadian Collector 12/4*. (July/August 1977)

Erickson, Paul. Archival Report. *A study of the site of the Sellon property in the old Halifax North Suburbs*. Halifax n.d.

Field, Richard Henning. 'Proxemic Patterns: Eighteenth-Century Lunenburg-German Domestic Furnishings and Interiors.' *National Museum of Man Material History Bulletin*. Fall 1985

Fulton, Gordon. '"Old Town" Lunenburg, Nova Scotia,' Historic Sites and Monuments Board of Canada Agenda Paper 1991–92. Ottawa 1992

– Research notes. *Lunenburg National Historic District*. Ottawa 1991

Fortier, L. (Honorary Superintendent of Fort Anne). 'The Old Fort at Annapolis Royal.' Paper prepared for the United Services Institute of Nova Scotia. Halifax 1950.

Hamilton, Jean. 'A Broadaxe and a Fiddle.' *The Atlantic Advocate*. January 1975

Lawrence, Abbie B. *History of Maitland*. Maitland n.d.

Macdonald, Elizabeth. *The Three Brothers*. Mahone Bay n.d.

MacMechan, Archibald. *The Great Ship*. Halifax 1967

Morgan, Robert J. *Poverty, Wretchedness, and Misery: The Great Famine in Cape Breton, 1845–1851*. Sydney 1983

Oliver, Pearleen. *From Generation to Generation: A Bicentennial of the Black Church in Nova Scotia 1785–1985*. Dartmouth 1985

– *A Root and a Name*. Dartmouth 1977

Plaskett, William. *Lunenburg: An Inventory of Historic Buildings with Photographs and Historical and Architectural Notes*. 1984

Public Archives of Nova Scotia. Report: 1968 *Robert
Hales' Journal of an Expedition to Nova Scotia*, 1731
Skinner, Helen. 'Horticulturalist's Haven.' *Century
Home*. Winter 1988
The Heritage Trust of Nova Scotia. *The Prince and
Hollis Buildings*. Halifax 1976
Thomas, C.E. 'St. Paul's Church, Halifax.' *Nova Scotia
Historical Society* Volume 7. 1960
Williams, Maureen. *A Study on the Cultural Significance
of John MacLean*. n.p. 1985
Willis, N.P., and W.H. Bartlett. *Canadian Scenery:* Vol-
ume 2. London 1842

Index

The names of all married women have been cross-indexed under both married and maiden names.

Photo Credits

With the following exceptions, all photographs are by Chris Reardon.

Chapter One

Edward Cornwallis (p. 4): PANS N-650
A View of Halifax circa 1750. Artist: Mosesafter Harris (p. 5): NAC C-10888
The Church of St. Paul and the Parade at Halifax, 1 March 1764. Artist: Richard Short (p. 6): NAC C-004293

Chapter Two

HRH Prince Edward, Duke of Kent (p. 10): PANS N-5418
Madame de Saint-Laurent (p. 11): PANS N-5419
Governor Sir John Wentworth (p. 14): PANS-1292
Lady Frances Wentworth (p. 15): PANS-7227
The Governor's House and St Mather's Meeting House, Hollis Street, Halifax. Artist: Richard Short (p. 15): NAC C-2482
Government House from the North East July 1819. Artist: John Elliott Woolford (p. 16): NAC C-3559

Chapter Three

The Careening Yard, Halifax, 1786. Artist: J.S. Meres (p. 19): NAC C-2557
Thomas B. Akins (p. 22): PANS N-1170

Chapter Four

Enos Collins as a young man (p. 26): PANS, with the permission of Joan Pitt, London, England
The *Shannon* and the *Chesapeake* entering Halifax harbour in 1813. Artist: Alfred Sandham (p. 27): NAC C-971

Gorsebrook, the home of Enos Collins, destroyed in 1959 (p. 28): PANS N-1933
Bishop Hibbert Binney (p. 32): PANS Acc. No. 1987-26S Anonymous coll. no. 46

Chapter Five

Joseph Howe, the real folk hero of his province (p. 40): PANS N-6381
Susan McNab Howe (p. 41): PANS N-2216

Chapter Six

Artillery Park, 1842. Artist, Alexander Cavalié Mercer (p. 44): NAC C-3420
James Forman, Jr (p. 52): PANS N-7488
Mrs James Forman (p. 53): PANS N-7489

Chapter Seven

Captain John Taylor Wood (p. 57): PANS N-1168
Adams Archibald (p. 59): PANS N-5489
Mrs. Adams Archibald (p. 61): PANS. Notman proof 44390

Chapter Eight

Samuel Cunard (p. 63): PANS Bollinger neg. 49127-12
William Cunard (p. 64): PANS Notman no. 50699 N-4320
The Tupper house, Armdale (p. 67): PANS N-5337
The young Sandford Fleming, 1845 (p. 74): NAC C-8692
The Hon. D.A. Smith driving the last spike for the Canadian Pacific Railway, 7 November 1885 (p. 76): NAC C-003693

Chapter Nine

Richard Preston (p. 81): With the permission of Henry Bishop, Curator, the Black Cultural Centre for Nova Scotia

Chapter Ten

Seccombe house (p. 93): Photograph by the authors
Eisenhauer house (p. 99): Photograph by the authors
The Earl of Dalhousie (p. 101): PANS Acc. No. 7819
Zwicker's Inn, Mahone Bay, from *Sketches in Nova Scotia for 1818*. Artist: John E. Woolford (p. 102): Courtesy, William Inglis Morse Collection, Special Collections, Dalhousie University Libraries

Chapter Twelve

Simeon Perkins (p. 115): PANS N-627
Liverpool docks in the 1890s (p. 119): PANS 1987-265.39

Chapter Thirteen

The Seal Island Light (p. 135): PANS Acc. No. 1989-468. Photos by Bob Brooks circa 1957

Chapter Fourteen

The Argyle District Court-House (p. 139): With the permission of the Argyle District Court House Archives, Tusket. Film 12 print 21 A
Job Lyons Hatfield (p. 142): PANS 1985:13
Abraham Lent (p. 143): PANS 1992
Ebenezer Corning house (p. 144): Photo by P. Crowell
Herbert Huntington (p. 150): PANS N-7544
The Hon. John Lovitt, Senator, June 1897 (p. 153): NAC PA 25892

Chapter Fifteen

View of Digby, 1835. Artist: Mary Hall (p. 171): NAC C-4259

Chapter Sixteen

Senator John W. Ritchie (p. 180): NAC C-011352
The Hon. Sir William Johnstone Ritchie, Chief Justice of Canada, 1891 (p. 181): NAC PA-27237
The Rt. Hon. Sir John Sparrow David Thompson (p. 186): PANS N-30

Chapter Seventeen

Maison Acadienne, circa 1740. Artist: Azor Vienneau (p. 194): Nova Scotia Museum collection 87.120.5

Chapter Eighteen

Hannah Prescott (p. 203): PANS Acc.No. 6404

Chapter Nineteen

Exile of the Acadians from Grand Pré (p. 207): NAC C-024549

Chapter Twenty

The Hon. Mr Justice Haliburton (p. 215): PANS N-2112
The residence of Judge Haliburton. Artist: William Henry Bartlett (p. 217): NAC C-2416
Bishop Charles Inglis (p. 222): PANS N-875

Chapter Twenty-One

Richard John Uniacke (p. 231): Nova Scotia Museum Collection 49.6.31

Chapter Twenty-Two

The Great Ship, the *William D. Lawrence* (p. 238): PANS N-5303
William D. Lawrence. From Anti-Confederation Members of the Legislature 1866 (p. 241): PANS N-7496
The Hon. Frank Stanfield (p. 248): Courtesy of the Colchester County Museum, Truro

Chapter Twenty-Three

Charles Tupper and young child (p. 252): NAC PA-25368
Robert Barry Dickey (p. 253): PANS N-7545
Jonathan McCully (p. 255):
Cyrus Eaton (p. 262): PANS photo collection

Chapter Twenty-Four

The entrance to Pictou harbour, July 1939. Artist: Edward Cavalié Mercer (p. 267): PAC C-13769
Edward Mortimer (p. 270) and Sarah Patterson Mortimer (p. 271): Courtesy of the Hector National Exhibit Centre, Pictou

Chapter Twenty-Five

The Buckley house (p. 284): Photograph by the authors

Chapter Twenty-Six

The Stone House, Port Dufferin (p. 289): Photograph by Philip Hartling

Chapter Twenty-Seven

The merchant, Peter Smyth (p. 306): Courtesy of Lieutenant Commander Paul McCulloch and Mrs McCulloch

Chapter Twenty-Eight

The expedition against Cape Breton, 1754 (p. 310): NAC C-1090
Ranna Cossit (p. 313): PANS photo collection

Chapter Twenty-Nine

Richard Brown (p. 321): PANS N-1142
The Prince of Wales (later Edward VII) in 1860 (p. 323): NAC C-023174
Officers of the Sydney Mines Volunteer Rifles, 2nd Company, 4th Regiment, July 1859 (p. 323): PANS N-2020
Senator Thomas Dickson Archibald (p. 326): The Beaton Institute, University College of Cape Breton
Coal-shipping piers off the Esplanade, Sydney 1870 (p. 326): The Beaton Institute, University College of Cape Breton

Illustrations on endpapers are from *An Album of Early Buildings in Nova Scotia*, by Arthur W. Wallace (Halifax 1976), courtesy Nova Scotia Museum.